D0886463

Cutting Code

Steve Jones
General Editor

Vol. 30

PETER LANG
New York • Washington, D.C./Baltimore • Bern
Frankfurt am Main • Berlin • Brussels • Vienna • Oxford

Adrian Mackenzie

Cutting Code

Software and Sociality

PETER LANG
New York • Washington, D.C./Baltimore • Bern
Frankfurt am Main • Berlin • Brussels • Vienna • Oxford

Library of Congress Cataloging-in-Publication Data

Mackenzie, Adrian.
Cutting code: software and sociality / Adrian Mackenzie.
p. cm. — (Digital formations; v. 30)
Includes bibliographical references and index.
1. Computer software—Social aspects. 2. Coding theory.
I. Title. II. Series.
QA76.754.M33   303.48'33—dc22   2005022537
ISBN 0-8204-7823-7
ISSN 1526-3169

Bibliographic information published by **Die Deutsche Bibliothek**.
Die Deutsche Bibliothek lists this publication in the "Deutsche
Nationalbibliografie"; detailed bibliographic data is available
on the Internet at http://dnb.ddb.de/.

Covert art: image generated by software available at Russel, R. Linux Kernel
Graphing Project, available at http://fcgp.sourceforge.net/lgp/ (26 January 2006)
Cover design by Sophie Boorsch Appel

The paper in this book meets the guidelines for permanence and durability
of the Committee on Production Guidelines for Book Longevity
of the Council of Library Resources.

Acknowledgments

This book came out of the years between the mid 1990s and 2002. Code and software grabbed hold of me as a philosopher-turned-programmer. Working in academic and commercial settings, the properties of code as a material-form became very palpable. In Sydney, Dave Sutton, Chris Chesher and John Sutton offered various reasons to play with code. Ian Johnson (Archeology Computing Laboratory, University of Sydney), Jon Patrick (Information Systems, University of Sydney), and Ian Somerville (Computing Department, Lancaster University) were important in helping me to self-displace from coding amidst the entropic drifts of the dot-com era to thinking about code and software. Pete Rossiter at Forge Research, Redfern, Sydney and Simon Monk at former KMS, Manchester, generously offered access to their offices and work-lives. Penny O´Hara steered me through an apprenticeship in ethnography. Colleagues in the Faculty of Social Sciences, Lancaster University, especially in the Institute for Cultural Research, the Sociology Department, the Centre for Science Studies and the Institute for Women's Studies have for several years and in various ways made work on this book more gregarious. In revising the book, Ann Cronin, Mathew Fuller, Charlie Gere, John Law and Lucy Suchman were directly helpful. They kindly commented on chapter drafts. Steve Jones supplied prompt and solicitous advice. Celia Roberts, more than anyone else, enduringly encourages me not to overcode everything and to look for life off-screen. Finally, time itself should be acknowledged. It kept going even when I stopped.

Earlier versions of several chapters of this book appeared as "Bringing sequences to life: how bioinformatics corporealizes sequence data." *New Genetics and Society*, 22(3), 315–332; "These things called systems: collective imaginings and infrastructural software." *Social Studies of Science*, 33(3), 385–387; "The performativity of code: software and cultures of circulation." *Theory, Culture & Society*, 22(1), 71–92.

Contents

Chapter 1

Introduction: Softwarily

Softwarily: "in a way pertaining to software"

> Raymond, *The New Hacker's Dictionary,* 1996, 417.

Software. A generic term for those components of a computer system that are intangible rather than physical. It is most commonly used to refer to the programs executed by a computer system as distinct from the physical hardware of that computer system, and to encompass both symbolic and executable forms for such programs.[1]

This book explores software as a social object and process. It examines some of the social relations that obtain in the neighborhood of software. Why software? There are many reasons to try to understand what software is, and what it does. These might include significant software-related events, economic importance, relevance to scientific knowledges and contemporary technologies, indispensability to military, government, education, health and commercial institutions, the intricate and often striking transformations of audiovisual entertainment, industrial production and art. The main reason, however, is that software embodies a mixture of mutability, contingency and necessity symptomatic of recent time.

In the Hollywood film *Swordfish* (Sena 2001), the central character is a brilliant down-and-out hacker, Stan Jobson. Divorced, having lost custody of his daughter, and paroled from an American federal prison on condition that he touchs no computer for five years, Stan is brought face to face with the enigmatic and charismatic Gabriel Shear in a Los Angeles nightclub. At gunpoint, he is given a laptop computer and sixty seconds to crack a computer security system. As the countdown nears zero, Stan, working furiously, achieves the practically impossible and accesses the system. Impressed, Gabriel offers Stan the money he needs to reopen a custody battle for his daughter. This scene from early in the film shows software as hard, obdurate and unyielding for some people, but plastic and malleable for others.

Borrowing a concept from physics, we could say that software undergoes phase transitions, or changes of state. It solidifies at some points, but vaporizes at others. This mutability perhaps explains why software remains surprisingly peripheral in many academic and nonacademic accounts of new media, digital cultures, virtual community, network identities and communicative mobilities that have emerged in the 1990s. Software's fringe existence seems to corroborate the commonsense notion that it is "intangible" rather than physical, that it is something more like a social convention or rule than machine-thing. The characteristics of software as a material object, as a means of production, as a human-technical hybrid, as medium of communication, as terrain of political-economic contestation—in short as sociality—seem hard to represent. Software as a material with specificities, singularities, traits and modes of existence has been displaced by software as mundane application, as infrastructural element in a wider social or technological change (the information revolution, "digital culture," "new media," "network society" or "convergence").

Code: Transforming symbolic forms

The term "software" designates a multidimensional and mutating object of analysis. It encompasses different practices of production, consumption, use, circulation and identity. Through analyses of software, I argue in this book that what software does and how it performs, circulates, changes and solidifies cannot be understood apart from its constitution through and through as code. Code, even defined in the minimalist technical sense as a "rule for transforming a message from one symbolic form (the source alphabet) into another (the target alphabet),"[2] cuts across every aspect of what software is and what software does. One way to resist an abstracting turn away from software is to attend to its code-like character. Attending to code as practice and material might show how software becomes invisible, how its occlusion from analysis occurs and how it nonetheless becomes at times very visible and significant.

In the period between 1995–2005, software occasionally became a highly visible and invested object; certain software viruses and pathological forms, open-source software projects such as the Apache webserver or GNU/Linux operating systems (see chapter 4), the Y2K bug, blogging, deCSS (chapter 2), the browser wars (chapter 5), the Human Genome Project (chapter 3), and the web made software visible as a public object of rampant financial speculation and widespread concern. The almost mystical authority associated with software and people who work with software (hackers, geeks, programmers, inventors, engineers) in these situations merits analysis. Such analysis cannot assume that we know what software is. Following the movements of code shows that many objects, practices, environments and behaviors are becoming more software-like. Software itself, however, looks increasingly like a neighborhood rather than an intangible, abstract formalism. In one of the few wide-ranging accounts of programming and software development written by a programmer, Ellen Ullman (1997) says, "Some part of me mourns, but I know there is no other way: human needs must cross the line into code. They must pass through this semipermeable membrane where urgency, fear, and hope are filtered out, and only reason travels across. There is no other way" (15). "Crossing-over" into code is not easy. The code present in operating systems, web-browsers, email servers, mobile phones, computer games, audio players, can be analyzed under the "rule" of technical definitions of code, but the rule has become astonishingly convoluted. The symbolic forms representing "human needs" that the rule brings into relation are themselves very complicated. The technical, minimalist definition of code has been decompressing itself in various ways for decades.

Much of what is taken for granted about new media, the Internet, the web and mobile devices relies on the mundane acquisition and exercise of technical skills in programming and configuring code. While cinema, newspapers, magazines, science fiction novels, artworks, television, the web, government reports, policies and legislation figure new media in many different ways, the production of new media largely depends on the creation of software that remains largely invisible or somewhat infrastructural (Bowker and Star 1999). People work with specific hardware platforms, chosen computer languages, protocols, standards and a relatively narrow range of software applications. These practices are highly context-specific and localized in various ways. Despite appearing "merely" technical, technical knowledge-practices overlap and enmesh with imaginings of sociality, individual identity, community, collectivity, organization and enterprise. Technical practices of programming interlace with cultural practices.

Software as relation, operation or ontology

Academic work on new media (see Manovich 2001 and Lessig 1999) attributes profound formal significance to code. But how to handle code as a material remains problematic. It can be analyzed formally (for instance, by using the principles of variability, modularity and transcoding described in Manovich 2001), but that approach may raise more problems than it solves, since its terms are themselves derived from software design. Also, any such formal analysis tends to abstract software from the practices and contexts attached to coding. In response to the liveliness of those practices and contexts, Neff and Stark (2004) note, "Code is not set in stone, as buildings literally are, but is it as mutable as we would like to think?" (10).

Code does supply a remarkably "context-free grammar"[3] for software in certain senses. That is, code seems to work, act or operate regardless of what the software is meant for and where it is. One explanation of this would point to the abstract nature of code. Like Ellen Ullman, computer scientists do model software as a symbolic form using mathematical concepts. As Lew (1985) describes it, "Almost all the entities arising in the study of computer software systems including computer programs, languages, data structures, and operating systems, can be abstractly (mathematically) defined as 'algebraic systems': i.e., as sets of objects together with certain 'relations' and 'operations' associated with the sets" (51). From this perspective, the operation of software ultimately reduces to relations and operations (such as sorting, comparing, copying, removing) on items of data. There is something at once appealing and mystifying about this formalism. It isolates code from particular contexts and distills it down to relations and operations. The actual code that programmers read and write expresses abstract relations and formal operations between entities grouped in sets. The concrete domain in which these entities, relations and operations encounter lives, institutions and events seems detached from their code-formed relation.

However, no computer code, not even textbook demonstrations of principle, can maintain this level of abstraction. While theoretical computer science sometimes treats software as a quasi-mathematical-logical entity susceptible to complete formalization, code itself inevitably slips into tangles of competing idioms, practices, techniques and patterns of circulation. It is tempting to say that there is no "program" as such, only programmings or codings. One look at the source code (the program text that programmers read and write) for the Linux kernel strongly hints at that (see chapter 4). Code can be read as permeated by all the forms of contestation, feeling, identification, intensity, contextualizations and decontextualizations, signification, power relations, imaginings and embodiments that comprise any cultural object.

But perhaps, it could be argued, the formality of software resides at another level. Computer scientists develop ontologies to formalize how computation can be carried out in a given domain. In this technical sense, an ontology does not say what something is or how it exists, but rather sets out concepts and relations useful in building a model: "an ontology is a description (like a formal specification of a program) of the concepts and relationships that can exist for an agent or a community of agents" (Gruber 1993, 199).[4] With somewhat less formal ambition, this book too develops an ontology of software in order to handle code as material and practice (this chapter will provide the most high-level account of the relations and operations that later chapters will develop). The difference between a computational ontology and my software ontology lies in the purpose of the abstraction and formality. Whereas a computational ontology is meant to provide a way of designing and organizing the operations and processes a computation will perform, my ontology of software has other, more contested ends in mind. Instead of introducing a consistent model of a complicated set of relations, it seeks to make inconsistency and lability conceivable.

Ontology as resistance to abstraction

The purpose of this new ontology might be, as the anthropologist Paul Rabinow recently suggested, to provide ways of responding to "a world experienced as contingent, malleable, and open" (Rabinow 2003, 67); that is, an ontology is a conceptual ensemble designed to make sense of empirically felt variations in experience. The appearance of new entities and the ever-present possibility of new concepts, techniques, sensibilities, practices and representation are very much part of the contemporary terrain of software. An ontology of software would conceptually register malleability, fragility, circulation and backgrounding without reducing it to something else. In this respect, an ontology of software could be practical, useful equipment.

Why account for software ontologically? The formalisms of code have their attractions. Picking up on this formalism, Manovich (2001) argues that studies of new media should turn to computer science: "To understand the logic of new media, we need to turn to computer science. It is there that we may expect to find the new terms, categories, and operations that characterize media that became programmable. From media studies, we move to something that can be called 'software studies'—from media theory to *software theory*" (48, italics in original). The terms, categories and operations to which Manovich refers stem from code and different styles of code. Data structures and algorithms that might allow the programmability of new media to be understood are found in code, even if theoretical computer science textbooks abstract from code and express algorithms in pseudocode (chapter 3), a way of describing operations without using any specific programming languages.

But software studies need not directly transfer terms, categories and operations from computer science. Despite its formality as rule-governed expression, code, as we will see, is an unstable volatile material. Rather than treating data structures (lists, tuples, queues, sequences, dictionaries, hashtables, etc) as the fixed categories and components found in new media objects, or treating algorithms (sorting, searching, addressing, swapping, optimizing, encoding, decoding, etc) as the abstract essence of computational processes, I use code to understand the mixture of mutability and stasis associated with software. Using code reduces the risk of freezing and formalizing software. Software in its specificity is not a given. What software does is very intimately linked with how code is read and by whom or what, that is, by person or machine. Sociologists and anthropologists of technology have established that any formalization needs to be understood "in-use:" "analyses of situated practice … point to the contingencies of practical action on which logic-in-use, including the production and use of scenarios and formalisms, inevitably and in every instance relies. In this way such analyses provide an alternative to idealized formulations of reasoning as disembodied mental operation" (Suchman and Trigg 1992, 173).

Rather than treating formalisms as natural or fixed, taking code seriously means understanding how they become ordinary or obvious in code-like situations. If "any trace, sign, inscription, representation, graphism, and citation is originally, and always, an expression, indication, icon, or moment of articulation in some practice" (Lynch 1993, 291), then the written formalism of code contains expressions, indications or moments of articulation in some practice.

Defamiliarizing software-like situations

Two motivations steer this ontology of software. First, the ontology should register some of the mutability and contingencies associated with software rather than reducing them to stable forms. Second, the attraction of formality has to be accounted for through the specificities of code as a material articulated, felt, shaped and changed in practices, whether located in communication, entertainment, commerce, government, production or science.

An analogous situation has been tackled by the anthropology of art. The anthropologist Alfred Gell (1998) has argued that the problem for an anthropological theory of art is that what counts as art changes in different contexts. To attribute the status of art to something and then analyze it as an art object is to forget about how it becomes an art object. For instance, what a Western visitor perceives as indigenous art objects while visiting village art studios in Bali largely depends on an institutional context by which the objects have been framed (Gell 1998, 12). Gell's radical but generative solution is to consider all "art objects as persons" (9) in order to then analyze "art-like situations" (13). The anthropological-theoretical move of reducing art objects to persons allows Gell's analysis to move between subjects, objects, practices, materials, institutions and cognitions, actions and feelings with great facility. (In "reducing" art-objects to persons, Gell continues previous defamiliarizing moves found in anthropology in relation to persons.) In art-like situations, a visible, physical, material thing triggers a "cognitive operation" that attributes agency to something. Art-like situations are differentiated by social relations obtaining in their neighborhood. Concretely, these relations exist as actions they authorize and perform. With respect to software, the analogous question would be: What makes something a "code-like" situation?[5]

By analogy to art, what code does can be more generally framed as a problem of agency, as a problem of who or what does what to whom or what. As Gell (1998, 17) suggests, it is not necessary to possess a philosophically rigorous understanding of agency. There are as many philosophical accounts of agency as there are genera of action. Across all of them, agency refers to events that are not merely physical; agency makes a difference between something that just happens (a leaf falls, the sun sets) and something that is an action to which a cognitive dimension is attached. When a door slams, when there is laughter in the street or when mail arrives, these are not just physical events, they are action-events. Wherever agents are, patients, people or things undergo action.

Many of the main results of social, cultural and political studies of cultural processes over since the mid-1990s can be framed as attempts to conceptualize distributions of agency. For instance, anthropologies and cultural studies of the consumption of popular media have repeatedly argued that consumption is not a passive activity but a highly complex and variable process. Similarly, analyses of social norms and gender identities based on speech acts and performativity have suggested that everyday determinations of agency related to gender, class and race result from a complicated interplay of acts, institutions and events. Law, as a body of rules attached to sophisticated processes of articulation, administration and elaboration, is another distribution of agency. Art, as Gell argues, is an involution of agency that forms part of any cultural environment. If software matters, and if power, law and art are associated with software, then code as a material has become a significant way of distributing agency. Code is certainly not a unique involution of agency, but the patterns and permutations of agency that attach to it are particularly powerful and symptomatic.

Attributing actions

Software is not usually treated as a physical event. Cognitive operations— searching, recording, writing, creating, recalling, ordering—or events are associated with it. The possibility of attaching agency to software is essential. Attribution of agency is a precondition of any social relation whatsoever, whether attributed to friends, colleagues, strangers, guests, family, even to things (for instance, a child playing with a doll treats it as a real agent). Software is sometimes explicitly envisaged as possessing full-blown agency (as in artificial intelligence), but more often it is regarded as possessing secondary agency, that is, as supporting or extending the agency of some primary agent: the programmer, the corporation, the hacker, the artist, the government or the user.

Because the same thing or person can be both agent and patient—and can switch roles quickly—attributions of agency sometimes encounter interesting instabilities, and different varieties of agency proliferate. Much of Gell's (1998) fascinating account presents different permutations of agency found in art-like situations. The transactions and pathways along which agency migrates through software are truly legion. They range from "software agents," pieces of code to which people delegate specific actions, to the architectural models of software systems based heavily on social relations such as server, client, manager, worker, producer, consumer, and so on. Contrary to the idea that software obscures these agential transactions, code renders some of them very vividly. We will analyze some examples in later chapters; the important thing here is that code is agency-saturated. Even when code is relatively invisible or hidden in the interstices of other technical devices (such as an elevator, a remote control, or a traffic light system; see Thrift 2004b), agency behaviors are becoming the norm in contemporary expectations of things.

The general point that agency is distributed between humans and nonhumans has been well established in many different fields: in cognitive anthropology (Hutchins 1995), cognitive science (Clark 1997), social anthropology (Gell 1998) and in social studies of technology (Callon 1987). In more supple engagements with technology in which technical objects are no longer considered as objects but as mediations, hybrids or even quasi subjects (Latour 1996, 213). "Computer" or "information" technologies (terms starting to sound quaint, if not stale) have migrated out of the "centres of calculation" (Latour 1987) in which they first materialized during the cold war (Edwards 1996). These "centres of calculation," organized around mainframe computers, were enclosed, removed and insulated from the domains of art, commerce, home and politics. Today, the distribution of software throughout the interstices of urban life and its growth in new forms of media and communication such as the web cannot be understood in terms of older "big-iron" (Raymond 1996, 64) models of technology.

Software has hybridized itself wildly with other media and practices and is likely to continue doing so as sensor networks and distributed computation become more ubiquitous. Analysis based on hybridization or network, such as the actor-network theory (Law and Hassard 1999), has trouble accounting for some asymmetries in this growth. As the anthropologist Marilyn Strathern (1999) writes,

> [There is] no refuge for the social anthropologist in the idea of hybrids, networks and invented cultures either. These do not, of themselves, indicate a symmetrical, sharing morality.... For neither a mixed nature nor an impure character guarantees immunity from appropriation. On the contrary, the new modernities have invented new projects that forestall such imaginings. We can now all too easily imagine

monopolies on hybrids, and claims of ownership over segments of network. (135)

Even viewed as hybrid human-nonhuman network, it remains to be explained how software is variably appropriated, owned and imagined.

For present purposes, the question is how to account for the specific types, dynamics and distributions of agency associated with software. Amid the attribution, delegation and extension of agency through code, what problems are implicit in saying what software does? Is not code a direct expression of human agency in relation to things ("start," "move," "stop")? Deciding where code locates agency in software, how code distributes agency and who or what else possesses agency becomes complicated at certain moments. The critical agent in a situation becomes hard to identify, ambivalent, even threatening. A virus might be slowing the computer down, a browser might be opening popup windows all over the screen (see chapter 2) or the system may be "thrashing" as it tries to handle too many tasks at once (see chapter 6). Does agency center on the programmer who tinkered with lines of code to make them do something she imagined? Does a program act as a vehicle for the agency of someone who runs it, "the user"? Or does it lie with the corporation whose enforcement of intellectual property rights radically curtails different uses of software? We recognize other people as agents (to a lesser or greater extent) because they have the capacity to act. But in milieus populated with bodies, things, systems, conventions and signs (and this is virtually everywhere), agency distributes itself between people or between people and things in kaleidoscopic permutations. Agency exists in events and ensembles that generate different attributions. If events were not open or variable in some way, the attribution of agency would be uncontested and thus pointless.

From formalism to a neighborhood of relations

Does this mean that software is culture? Equating software with "culture," as if culture was a given, does not help. So to say that software or code has become culture or to speak of "cultures of software" does not solve the problem of what software does, what it is, and what is at stake in what it does and is. Rather, code needs to be followed as it moves across a terrain where the different forces, formations, dynamisms, knowledges, bodily habits and embodied expertise, institutions, practices, micropolitics, networks, techniques and things associated with code are situated. Software has become intimately bound up with a new sensibility that accommodates constant changes, including changes in the material texture and sensation of cinematic, televisual and photographic processes; in the organization of collective work in open-source software; in struggles over outsourcing programming work to India; in the virtualization of many transactions, interactions, exchanges and types of information and property; in archiving difficulties in new media artworks; in profound changes in the scale and intensity of biotechnological research and conceptualizations of biological life; in radical transformations in the production and circulation of popular music. In short, almost anywhere that perception and movement are seen as especially flow-like or eventful, software animates.

Agency is distributed unevenly, and it entails widely divergent transactions (Gell 1998, 24). However, even if software participates in the transactions of social agency, that participation in no way distinguishes it from any other object. Is there not more specificity to the agency of software? From the perspective of an ontology of software modeled on Gell's anthropological theory of art as index of agency, at least four different entities stand in relation in software: code, originators, recipients and prototypes.

1. Code as index

Code provides one way to specify transactions more precisely. Code combines marks, symbols and other software, and refers to objects such as computers, conventions, protocols, networks and peripheral devices. Much hinges on how code hangs or concatenates relations together. The general definition of code given earlier describes code as a "rule for transforming a message from one symbolic form (the source alphabet) into another (the target alphabet), usually without loss of information." The "symbolic" forms are highly variable and include programming languages, hardware platforms, styles of programming, patterns of distributions and circulation, and functions or operations. The idea of code as a rule that transforms messages without loss of information represents an abstraction; in the definition above, replacing "usually" with "never" would be more realistic. However, as long as rules are not understood too narrowly, this definition provides an interesting angle from which to analyze some different modalities of software.

Gell's anthropological theory of art focuses on how indexical signs or "the index" found in art-like situations permit "abductions of agency," that is, nonlinguistic inferences of social agency. To understand the adhesiveness of code, the rules comprising any body of code can be treated as indexical, as a "natural sign from which the observer can make a causal inference of some kind" (Gell 1998, 13). Code as rule-governed transformation between source and target symbolic forms (or alphabets) is itself part of a wider software nexus of social relations within patterns of calculation, logic, counting, listing and other algorithmic processes.

Code itself has a specific texture and materiality. Software constantly verges on collapse because code is fragile and precariously subject to *bitrot*: "Unused programs or features will often stop working after sufficient time has passed" (Raymond 1996, 69). Like anything else, software does not grow or exist in isolation. Left alone, it tends to fall apart because all around it hardware platforms and other software change. Software, despite its algebraic-ideal image, needs carefully maintained niches. Examining code over time (as we shall in chapter 4) shows how much hospitality work is needed to maintain the niche, a niche that itself is inevitably changing shape along with changing hardware platforms (short term), network protocols (relatively long term) and operating systems (medium term). Code is being constantly superseded. The constant arrival of new versions, updates and patches both conceals and highlights the brittleness of software.

Code verges on disappearance in another sense. As later chapters will show, software participates in a more general invisibility of technical infrastructures and enters into a certain historically specific "technological unconscious" (Thrift 2004b). Social and material processes that organize and co-ordinate movement and perception within Euro-American-Asian cultures actively render software invisible. The process of *backgrounding* forms a deep part of software and code. Much work in since 1980 has been carried out (particularly in the social studies of science and technology) in order to understand why technical mediations are at once intimately woven into the social-material fabric of everyday life and yet often not represented as such (Latour 1993, 1996, 1999).

Bitrot and backgrounding raise a host of problems refractory to analysis. Circulating, fragile and backgrounded: these characteristics position software on the edge of disappearance and prevent it (for better or for worse) from being analyzed as object or as expression of subjective intention. Software dwindles into the interstices of fine-grained syntheses of gestures, laws, property, habits, images, machines, networks, infrastructures and devices. Software figured large in the rise of network culture and the Internet during the 1990s, and for a moment—a moment which still resonates—code attracted visible cultural, political and economic attention. Software was the subject of strident claims over invention and property, and residue from the resulting debates is not hard to find. From Y2K, to browser wars, to court cases around patent and copyright infringements in Linux and between Sun Microsystems and Microsoft Corporation over Java, to the Digital Millennium Copyright Act (DMCA)-based case against deCSS (DVD-playing software), many of public struggles over software concerned how code existed over time as an object of value and how it became visible.

However, for every controversial or well-publicized event concerning software, so much more was taking place less visibly and introducing algorithmic processes into the infrastructural backgrounds of movement, perception and memory. Only occasionally did the software at work in a DVD-recorder or a car, deep in the architecture of the object, become an object of contestation (as it would if, for instance, a Bluetooth-enabled automobile computer were infected with a virus transmitted from a Bluetooth-enabled telephone). Hardware production and commodification relentlessly backgrounded code. Constant exchanges, translations and shifts moved code between hardware and software. Semiconductor design appropriated software-initiated features and practices. The architecture of commodity CPUs made by Intel or Advanced Micro Devices (AMD) adopted features that afford certain calculations associated with 3-D graphics. More mundanely, computer keyboards now have buttons dedicated to software user tasks once carried out by issuing commands onscreen. Computing hardware has not been subject to anything like the scholarly interest that it merits. Its production is largely hidden in chip fabrication plants in Southeast Asia, and semiconductor design is hard to study ethnographically. While I'll return to issues around hardware in later chapters (chapter 4 on Linux, chapter 5 on Java and chapter 6 on telephone networks), my general point is that software and computing hardware have an unstable, changing relation. This makes software harder to isolate.

There are no guarantees concerning the visibility of code (for instance, viruses rely heavily on the invisibility of code, as does much of the code embedded in infrastructures and various operating systems). What is visible to a programmer working on a piece of software may be almost totally invisible to users, who only see code mediated through an interface or some change in their environment: the elevator arrives, the television changes channels, the telephone rings.

2. Originators

Software also refers to its producers. Someone or something codes it; there is an *originator*. Whether the originator is a programmer, webmaster, corporation, software engineer, team, hacker or scripter, and regardless of whether the originator's existence can be forgotten, sanctified or criminalized, software originates somewhere. Makers of software are ambivalent figures. The figure of the programmer often vacillates between potent creator of new worlds and antisocial, perhaps criminal or parasitic (hacker, dark-side cracker or monopoly capitalist). The incurable ambiguity of the term "hacker" in popular representations of software as both criminal and creative attests to conflicting ideas of what making software entails.

Such confusions are interesting. Several chapters will later address the unstable relation between different modalities of producers (see chapter 4 on Linux; chapter 5 on Internet programming and Java). In cultural and social studies of technology, production is often downplayed because it is not regarded as a place where everyday practice can be found at work (Couldry 2000). Because of this isolation, production of technologies is sometimes seen as less important or interesting than consumption of technologies. The producers of a given contemporary technology are regarded as part of an engineering, corporate or research elite whose activities lie outside the domain of popular culture or everyday life. While this divide between elite and popular cultures may exist for some kinds of production, it does not accurately describe the production of software.

In the wake of the commercial success of open-source software, for instance, constant arguments rage over whether "hacking" is a proper way to produce software. The polemic between corporate or institutional software engineering and hacking concerns not only how software is designed and coded, but how the work is done, who does it, under what conditions and in what places. In a defense of hacking against university-taught and corporate-supported software engineering, Paul Graham (2004) writes: "What we can say with some confidence is that these are the glory days of hacking. In most fields, the great work is done early on" (33). His argument that hackers are more like Renaissance painters than engineers or scientists is based on the efficacy of programming methods, on the creativity of programming as a cultural practice, and ultimately on the value of software itself.[6] We will address other complications and uncertainties in the production of software, but for now the question remains: How can software be understood or made intelligible?

3. Recipients

The answer lies in the ways code indexes people or machines as recipients. Things that receive or execute code could include an environment or milieu in which code circulates and does something. Just as a painting indexes its viewers in various ways, software too points towards its recipients. Everything—from the shrink-wrapped package of commodity software with the end-user license agreement (EULA) attached to the act of opening a box or clicking on "install," to the intricacies of user interface design, to the elaborate communities of reception found around open-source software— refers to recipients. On all occasions of reception, someone or something undergoes something or does something with code.

Software objects, systems or practices—such as the Linux kernel, software art, the Java Virtual Machine, extreme programming, Perl and BioPython—call for different approaches to account for their reception. In other words, code solicits different concepts of social processuality. It is difficult to analyze code as a text whose meanings can be contested, resisted or revised. The concepts of signification and meaning that have guided much work in social sciences and humanities for decades lack purchase on the structures, patterns, relations and operations that constitute code objects. Although reading and writing are key practices attached to code, and although the "readability" of code has consistently concerned programmers since the 1950s, what is at stake in reading and writing code is not "meaning" in any commonly accepted sense. Rather, the readability of code relates to execution, to how it circulates, how quickly it can be read and understood by other programmers, and how it affords revisions, modulations and modifications. A focus on processes of circulation of code shifts away from the meaning that code objects may have for particular groups of social actors. An exploration of how human communication and interaction are introjected into software through reorganization of production in extreme programming (chapter 7) or open-source software (chapter 4) suggests that code as a material might be more multifaceted than it is usually thought to be. When software becomes artwork as in code poetry and software art (chapter 2), it becomes relevant to ask how code functions and feels as a material in art objects.

4. Prototypes

Finally, software sometimes resembles or represents something else, a prototype. A chess program represents, albeit not visually, a chess player. Image manipulation software such as Adobe Photoshop or GIMP (GNU Image Manipulation Program) presents a set of operations relating to a photographic workshop equipped with instruments such as scissors, brushes, pencils and paint. Similarly, a music or sound editing program (CuBase, ProLogic) presents a set of operations related to recording studios (mixers, tracks, tape recorders, instruments, effects, and so on). Many people who use such programs would never have worked in or even seen a photographic workshop or recording studio, but the software relies on an image or prototype of it. The prototype may reflect highly fictive imagining, as in software for artificial life (Kember 2003; Helmreich 2000), or it may represent something as prosaic as a desktop. Sometimes, even other software is the prototype for software (as in clones).

Permutations of agency

Social science and humanities research, including research into technology, implicitly pre-fabricates objects as social or cultural (Sterne 2003). This book does not demonstrate the social dimensions of information and communication technology. Rather, it regards software and code as an analytical challenge for prevalent understandings of social or cultural processes based on concepts of language, meaning, discourse, communication and media. Taking software seriously means revisiting concepts of "social," "cultural" and "technological."

It would be easy, perhaps, to frame software as technology. Because of the way it moves and percolates through so many other domains, software, it might be said, has become a prime contemporary technology and the most ubiquitous contemporary technical artifact. Software can be represented using the concepts of technology theorised in so much twentieth-century social, media and philosophical theory (Heidegger and Lovitt 1977; Mitcham 1994; Feenberg 1995; Lyotard 1993; Virilio 2000). In the apprehensions concerning technology that guided critical thought in those years, code and information technology were threateningly salient because they alienated, instrumentalized or captured human capacities. However, the distancing effects attributed to technology in these accounts sit very awkwardly with much of the contemporary "codescape" on which programmers, code narratives, coding practices and products move about. The sheer abundance of coding languages, educational and pedagogical activities related to code, and code-related events such as tradeshows, academic conferences and publications (books, journals, websites, newsgroups) is hard to reduce to alienated instrumental reason, "enframing" or simulation (Baudrillard 1994). Nonetheless, in one sense software is deeply technological: it is a *logos* or reasoned discourse of the technical. It can be seen as a corpus of methods, techniques, exercises, practices and judgments concerning information, in which information can be associated with almost any event whatsoever. But compared to other *logoi*, software is somewhat excessive and vexed. It overflows its own context and creates new contexts. In many instances software is so complicated, so distributed and convoluted in architecture that it defeats comparison with any other technical object.

As a result, the boundaries of each of the entities in the software ontology—code, originator, recipient, and prototype—are hard to define. The relationships constituting software coalesce in convoluted, compact formations whose dynamics are not well understood. The important point is that the patterns of relations that unfold in the neighborhood of software are agential. Sometimes the prototype acts on the originator to produce code, as when a design brief presents scenarios in which users carry out certain operations (a scenario is a prototype which programmers must implement in code; see chapter 7 on extreme programming). Sometimes the originator acts on the recipient through code, as when a program constrains a person or machine to perform as a "user" (some of the examples of software art discussed in the chapter 2 illustrate this). Sometimes an originator becomes the recipient and undergoes the action of code (for instance, when programmers working on the Linux kernel write bits of code to allow the kernel to run on new hardware, they constantly oscillate between running the code and producing it; see chapter 4). Sometimes recipients change code in some way, thus acting on the prototype and/or the originator. Pressure points, slippages and collisions arise when we attempt to attribute agency. Sometimes multiple attributions appear within the software itself. Different recipients, prototypes and makers compete for agency (as when, for example, the "user" finds herself struggling to make the solicitious Microsoft Clippy, a help agent included with Microsoft Office products, go away). At times these contests arise over the circulation of code (as in different distributions of Linux/GNU operating system; see chapter 4). They also figure heavily in attempts to organize the production of software along different lines.

As symbolic forms coalesce in massively networked code formations, the agential relations in software become highly involuted and recursive. Just as Gell argues that the work itself (the "index") is only rarely the primary agent in artworks (Gell 1998, 36), we could argue that only rarely is code itself the primary agent in software. The shifting status of code—an ideal expression of an operation, something to be written, something to be run, something to be circulated, something to be upgraded or forgotten—attests to the involutions of agency attached to software. The resulting instabilities lead to many different kinds of dispute, contestation and mutation of code.

Involutions of agency: Force, value and feeling in software

How should such a densely populated neighborhood of relations be studied and analyzed? Unlike art-like objects, for which the term "recipient" usually correlates with a human viewer, it is not clear that code always has people as its recipient. Individuals using software are configured as users, but they are only one species of recipient. Other machines, technical systems and other pieces of infrastructure can be recipients of code, and sometimes originators of code (for instance, integrated software developments usually include code-tools that automatically produce generic code for user interfaces and other template designs). Equally important, non-code-like entities inhabit the environment. Some act as prototypes for software: for instance, an office desk is a prototype for certain user interfaces as well as a place where computers can be found; various forms of record-keeping and bureaucracy are prototypes for databases and information archives, as well as something that supports software. Some regulate the movement of code (licenses, patents, legislation, prices), and some affect how software is represented and consumed (branding, design, product marketing). How then to make sense of the impossibly complex social relations present in the neighborhood of software?

This book treats software as a multi-sited associative or concatenated entity. The anthropologist George Marcus (1995) describes multi-sited ethnography and research as "designed around chain, paths, threads, conjunctions or juxtapositions of locations in which the ethnographer establishes some form of literal, physical presence, with an explicit, posited logic of association or connection among sites that in fact defines the argument of the ethnography" (105). Accordingly, rather than treating the context of software as separate from code, the logic of association posited in the following chapters comprehends chains, paths and juxtapositions in software environments as legible in code and coding; it treats the sociality of the software, the relations that obtain in its neighborhood, as mutable, involuted agential relations indexed by code. Substitutions, translations, attributions and displacements of agency in and through code constitute a nexus out of which software comes. Significant differences in agency arise from the involutions and distributions of relations in code.

From this perspective, each of the following chapters can be seen as tracking a recursion of agency associated with software. At stake here is an account of software as a highly involuted, historically media-specific distribution of agency. This account diverges from a general sociology of technology in highlighting the historical, material specificity of code as a labile, shifting nexus of relations, forms and practices. It regards software formally as a set of permutable distributions of agency between people, machines and contemporary symbolic environments carried as code. Code itself is structured as a distribution of agency.

Why is it hard to pin down what software is? Is there some kind of dynamism or mobility associated with software that doesn't allow it to stand still long enough to be figured, imagined, diagrammed, plotted or mapped out? Is the relation between code and machine inherently unstable, such that deciding what belongs to the thing and what belongs to the practice, the representation or the sign is just too hard, and perhaps impossible? The following chapters map some involutions of agency running across conventional analytical divisions between code as expression and code as action. These involutions reconfigure relations between production, consumption, representation, identity and circulation that bedevil social science and humanities accounts of contemporary cultures. By understanding code-like situations as involutions of agency, it becomes possible to situate these debates in relation to other questions of power, identity and democracy.

Chapter 2

Opening code: Expression and execution in software

Baring the code or revealing the unseemly openness of technical and social operating systems augurs an alternative kind of biopolitical production—one that defies any easy recuperation and sale and that contests the production of subjectivity by means of an open cultural practice.

Berry, "Bare Code: Net Art and the Free Software Movement," 2003

During the 1990s, making the code in software visible or "open" became a significant and diversely manifest project taken up by artists, hackers, corporations, government and non-government organizations. Making code visible or "open" was a political project that sought to introduce a new interest in or sensibility to software into human affairs. This new sensibility also unfurled in the development of open software, in the idea of a programmer's life-style as geekish but cool, and in the increased visibility of code as an object of economic, legal, political, artistic and academic interest.

However, "baring the code" is not always easy. Attempts at openness have encountered legal, aesthetic and technical obstacles. So many things are associated with code—so many different social relations, patterns of cooperation and relationship with others are sewn together in software—that finding the boundaries of what is open can be difficult. Even if code can be made visible or legible, how could baring the code predicate an "alternative kind of biopolitical production," as Berry suggests above, in reference to Foucault's account of contemporary formations of power?

Code itself has become both a material and a problem in the production of some software art. Following the model of the software nexus outlined in the previous chapter, the opening of code in these artworks can be generally understood as a contestation of agency focused on the substrate of software: code. Examining the production, circulation, relation to other software, and commentary on several different code-like artworks, this chapter examines one instability of the code nexus: Is code is a form of expression or an operation? The code present in these works stages a collision between different trajectories of code as speech or action, expression or function/operation. The different trajectories have implications for what actions are intentionalized, that is, who is granted agency. Examining how code has figured in some recent artworks—including Perl poetry (Winterbottom 2000), the deCSS gallery (Touretzky 2004), *forkbomb.pl* (McLean 2002) and web-based works of jodi (1997, 1999, 2002, 2003)—is only one approach toward the broader question of code and contemporary forms of life. Later chapters will examine what computer science itself says about code, what programmers of different kinds make of it, either using their own accounts or ethnographic approaches. For now, the virtue of using code-based artworks as a way into software cultures is that they simplify the problem of analyzing software in some respects.[1] They often involve a small number of lines of source code, making them easier to analyze than the relational databases or enterprise resource planning systems described by Campbell-Kelly (2003).

Even as they narrow the field of analysis, software artworks make instabilities and slippages in agency associated with code more obvious. They slow the slippages down enough so that they can be situated in relation to other norms, forms and conventions associated with law, power, communication and language. When the 2003 Ars Electronic Festival for Art, Technology and Culture held in Linz, Austria, for instance, adopted the theme "Code, the language of our time. Code = Law Code = Art Code = Life" (Stocker and Schopf 2003), the three equations between code and law, code and art, and code and life designated fields within which code has become a problem, something to be contested as well as taken for granted. That is, these equations define fields in which the contraction of practical habits of electronic communication encounter extensive forms of governance, regulation and commodification, fields in which code seems to offer some traction, resistance or tool.

The uneven visibility of code

Since 1995, studies of digital culture, information culture, information society and cybercultures have focused on the forms of new media (Manovich 2001; Lunenfeld 2000) and how new media are used (Poster 2004). These studies identify changes in the production of images and in the kinds of communities, representations, governmentalities, interactions, ideologies, subjectivities and corporealities attached to information and communication. Many artworks associated with "new media," itself an unsatisfactorily loaded term in many ways, have thematized embodiment, identity and indeterminacies in spatial location.[2]

In comparison to the high-profile aspects of cyberculture (virtual reality, artificial intelligence, the web, gaming, online communities), code objects have had uneven visibility and significance. Because these objects form a large part of the material fabric of information systems and new media, some have called for new media studies to begin analyzing information infrastructures (S. Graham 2004). These calls highlight the role of "information mythology" (Bowker 1994) in disguising the material bases of new media and information technologies. They point to the practical embedding and interweaving of code objects into everyday life:

> [N]ew media technologies are being woven so completely into the fabric of
> everyday urban, social and economic life that they, in turn, are becoming more and
> more ignored in cultural and media discourse. At this point, paradoxically,
> technologies are more important than ever. For at this time, the sociotechnical
> configurations of politics, representation, spatiality and power that tend to be
> embodied by, and perpetuated through them, tend to be even harder to unearth and
> analyse. (Graham 2004, 23)

There are many aspects to this increasing invisibility of the interface to code objects, and their opacity has not itself been well analyzed. The quote from Graham simply mentions everyday life without differentiating the different kinds of weaving and without specifying which software is becoming harder rather than easier to analyze.[3]

Code and ordinary language

How did code become opaque or illegible? German media theorist and
literary historian Friedrich Kittler suggests that the opacity of software or
code stems from competition between software and "ordinary language":

> Programming languages have eroded the monopoly of ordinary language and grown
> into a new hierarchy of their own. This postmodern Tower of Babel reaches from
> simple operation codes whose linguistic extension is still a hardware configuration,
> passing through an assembler whose extension is this very opcode, up to high-level
> programming languages whose extension is that very assembler.... What remains a
> problem is only recognizing these layers, which like modern media technologies in
> general, have been explicitly contrived to evade perception. We simply do not know
> what our writing does. (Kittler 1997, 148)

In this passage, which summarizes a complex argument, the problem of
code hinges on the way it competes with ordinary language. Kittler writes
that "we simply do not know what our writing does." The general problem of
code, he argues, is that "it seems to hide the very act of writing"; in fact, the
inscriptions that result from this writing "are able to read and write by
themselves" (Kittler 1997, 147). Amplifying Kittler's take on code would
mean tracing, on a smaller scale, what kinds of "ordinary language"
articulations are being eroded.[4]

One dimension of erosion of "the monopoly of ordinary language,"
according to Kittler's argument, can be located in code's "evasion of
perception." The surfaces on which code is inscribed are heavily
technologically sedimented and layered. The contraction of electronic
circuits into increasingly compressed convolutions, a process stimulated by
the strenuous market competition between semiconductor manufacturers in
the United States and Southeast Asia, means that as inscriptions shrink down
on the semiconductor substrates, layers of code pile up. The path from the
high-level interfaces to machine level becomes more and more torturous and
involuted as it runs through switchbacks up and down Kittler's postmodern
Tower of Babel.

A second challenge to the monopoly of ordinary language stems from
that fact that code makes no pretension to be a common language. Despite
the quasi-universal resonance of the term "code," programmers have not
invented any Esperanto. Rather, code has dispersed into a cacophony of
different coding languages, sometimes hierarchically related, sometimes not:
FORTRAN, Perl, Prolog, C, Pascal, Applescript, Javascript, Actionscript,
Hypertalk, LISP, Python, Java, C++, C#, etc. The spawning, mutating and

cloning of different idioms of code, and indeed of different versions of similar software applications or "solutions" generates code babble. There are many banal manifestations of this disintegration. The need to constantly upgrade software to fix bugs and ensure compatibility, the struggles to standardize protocols, and the proliferation of clones and variants of the same application all attest to this code babble and to a multiplication of coding dialects.

Kittler diagnoses code as something that people read and write yet cannot comprehend because it has been encrusted with a layered architecture that sequesters code in inaccessible interior spaces. The inaccessibility is also temporal, as the duration between reading and executing code falls beneath the threshold of perception (that is, millions of instructions per second). This is usually analyzed in terms of an opposition between lived human time, the time of language and perception, and the instantaneity of technological execution or digitally clocked circuit switching. Thus the problem of code's opacity can be focused on those who read and write code. Code is so ubiquitous that it should be an important material for cultural practices and representation, but it is relatively invisible, backgrounded and forming part of what Thrift (2004b) terms a "technological unconscious," an "atomic structure" that produces forms of positionings and juxtapositions (177). Most people don't spend time working, reading or playing with code as such.

Making code readable

Recent artworks have begun to address some of the issues concerning who reads and writes code, and under what conditions. Net art and software art are particularly useful in exploring code because they usually present relatively simple configurations of software, they have an interest in rendering visible or readable their own workings, they are exhibited in various festivals, museums, galleries and online repositories and they attract commentary and criticism. Rather than theorizing these artworks in terms of what they represent, it makes sense in this context to treat them as participating in contests occurring around the agency of software. In each of them, code becomes the subject and material of the artwork. The works show a sensibility to the contestations of agency associated with code and a willingness to experiment. In each case, code is not just used as an inert material. Like canvas and paint, code as material becomes visible as a problem, as something whose visibility or readability is questionable from different angles, including those of "law" and "life."

One problem for artworks that make use of code as a material is conveying how code can be read. As we will see, certain coding practices attempt to get beyond the opacity of code in different ways, and with different motivations. The first work we'll examine, an example of "Perl poetry," definitely lies at the banal end of contemporary art and literature. It explicitly links code to a highly valorized form of writing and reading ordinary language, poetry:

If light were dark and dark were light The moon a black hole in the blaze of night A raven's wing as bright as tin Then you, my love, would be darker than sin.

```
if ((light eq dark) && (dark
eq          light)          &&
($blaze_of_night{moon}    ==
black_hole)                &&
($ravens_wing(bright)      ==
$tin(bright))){   my  $love  =
$you = $sin{darkness} + 1; };
```

(Winterbottom, A. 2000)

The poem on the left is from Edgar Allan Poe, the code on the right is by programmer Angie Winterbottom, who won the Perl Poetry Prize in 2000 with this entry. It is written in the popular programming language Perl. The work transliterates the poem line by line into a compound conditional if-then statement. Aptly, Perl was developed by system administrators to allow programs to be quickly written for ad-hoc purposes, such as renaming a large number of files or tidying up the formatting of a text document. It became particularly important in the development of early interactive websites since it allowed web servers to generate HTML webpages in response to requests from browsers.

From most standpoints, Perl poetry is kitsch art, the computing equivalent of dabbling in paint-by-numbers. It does, however, touch on two issues around reading and writing code: whether code is a craft, and just how much creativity is involved in it. Programmers sometimes present the process of coding as creative. There is a folklore and hagiography of famous programmers and hackers (Lohr 2002). Some famous figures in computer science, such as Donald Knuth, are known for the elegance and beauty of code fragments they have written (Knuth 1968) or as proponents of aesthetically formalized styles of programming (Knuth 1992). Many popular accounts of hackers valorize concise or compact code that tends to be opaque. The rules of the International Obfuscated C Contest (IOCC 2004) prize obscurity and illegibility as indicators of the highest aesthetic value. The source code for typical IOCC entry is a reading puzzle, even for experienced C programmers; the rules encourage the most arcane, or esoteric formulations that still execute reliably.

The domain of code poetry seems a relatively innocuous and inconsequential activity that has more to do with programmers' self-identification as "creative" than with any problematization of code per se. The quite banal judgments about the merits of one code poem over another reflect values from the domain of ordinary language. Reading and writing code are governed here by norms and notions of agency derived from literary art forms.

Who is allowed to read and write code?

In code poetry, of which Winterbottom (2000) is just one example, the creativity of programmers stands in for larger claims over who can read or write, for a wider cultural and transnational contestation of agency. These notions of agency find other echoes on the highly kinetic surface of the contemporary codescape, as when programmers in the United States and the United Kingdom mount industrial action against the outsourcing of programming work to India and other offshore labor markets (Pink 2004). This is an ironic twist since programmers have long been intensely involved in building the communication networks and systems of collaboration now facilitating their own obsolescence. One of their key claims is that while the

Indian programmers are extremely technically proficient, they lack the creativity to bring about the next generation of innovations in software, in interfaces and in new media applications. "What comes after services? Creativity," writes Chris Anderson (2004), *Wired* magazine's editor-in-chief, implying that this is an essential component that the Indian or Chinese software industry lacks. Whether code can be brought back to ordinary language after it becomes poetry, Kittler's explanation pivots on the competition at the core of contemporary information systems. The layered structure, the tower of code babble, affords no panoptic view on what is inscribed in software or what software does.

Sometimes code is obfuscated for other reasons. Many of the debates over open-source software have taken issue with controls imposed on code legibility. Legal constraints on the visibility of code lie at the center of some significant legal events. One of the first applications of the U. S. Digital Millennium Copyright Act of 1998 (U. S. Congress 1998) concerned decryption software for DVDs. Under the act, breaking or circumventing the encryption on any software program is a federal crime. Encryption of the content of DVDs to prevent them being copied is carried out by the CSS, the Content Scrambling System. In 1999, the hacker magazine *2600* posted on its website a piece of software called deCSS written by Jon Johansen, a Norwegian teenager. The software breaks the encryption on DVDs, enabling Linux-based computers to play DVDs (when encrypted, DVDs can only be played on commercially licensed operating systems such as Microsoft Windows). Representing the American movie industry, Universal Studios sued *2600*'s publisher. In 2000, the court ruled against the magazine (2600 2002). A later case against Johansen, filed by the Motion Picture Industry Association of America in Norway, failed; in 2003 a Norwegian court found that Johansen had done nothing illegal in writing the deCSS software. Meanwhile, the case inspired programmers to produce many different expressions of the algorithms that deCSS instantiated. In so doing, the programmer/artists argue that computer language is speech and should be protected under the First Amendment of the U. S. Constitution, the right to freedom of speech.

Following is a fragment from Seth Schoen's long poem "How to decrypt a DVD: in haiku form":

Arrays' elements
start with zero and count up
from there, don't forget!
Integers are four
bytes long, or thirty-two bits,
which is the same thing.

To decode these discs,
you need a master key, as
hardware vendors get.
(This is a "player
key" and some folks other than
vendors know them now.
If they didn't, there
is also a way not to
need one, to start off.)
You'll read a "disk key"
from the disc, and decrypt it
with that player key.
You'll read a "title
key" for the video file
that you want to play.
With the disk key, you
can decrypt the title key;
that decrypts the show.

(Schoen 2000)

In another version of the DVD decryption code, the algorithm for decrypting DVD is written in much lower level machine code. The code was printed on t-shirts and turned into various kinds of images, such as the DVD logo (Touretzky 2004). Code meant to be read by machines is made readable, in principle, to a literate public. The poem and the t-shirts are two of the many "artworks" arguing that code should be protected under freedom of speech. All of the artworks make the same point: that code should be understood as form of expression, not as a technological object, mechanism or a function (Touretzky 2004).

Code is execution

This argument was not successful in court. The trial judge said that code was a function, not speech:

> Computer code is expressive. To that extent, it is a matter of First Amendment concern. But computer code is not purely expressive any more than the assassination of a political figure is purely a political statement. Code causes computers to perform desired functions. Its expressive element no more immunizes its functional aspects from regulation than the expressive motives of an assassin immunize the assassin's action.[5]

Executable source code was not subject to First Amendment protection because its "functional aspects" need to be regulated in the same way that any gesture or act is. Execution is equivalent to assassination.

The court's attempt to regulate the "functional aspects" triggered many creative responses. These responses presented instructions for decrypting in ways that blurred the line between coding and ordinary language, between expression and execution. Although Universal Studios threatened to sue websites publishing the proliferating versions of deCSS, it didn't. The question of whether code is speech (and therefore art) or merely a technology has not been tested in higher courts. An appeal against the deCSS decision was not mounted, despite massive support from academic and research-based computer scientists, cryptographers and hackers who almost unanimously argued that code is a form of speech. An amicus curiae ("friend of the court") brief deposed by a group of prominent American computer scientists, cryptographers and programmers argued their point:

> It cannot seriously be argued that any form of computer code may be regulated without reference to First Amendment doctrine. The path from idea to human language to source code to object code is a continuum. As one moves from one to the other, the levels of precision and, arguably, abstraction increase, as does the level of training necessary to discern the idea from the expression. Not everyone can understand each of these forms. Only English speakers will understand English formulations. Principally those familiar with the particular programming language will understand the source code expression. And only a relatively small number of skilled programmers and computer scientists will understand the machine readable object code. But each form expresses the same idea, albeit in different ways. (Abelson et al. 2000)

Works like "deCSS haiku" attempted to problematize the notion of code as technical function, to resist the legal regulation and consequent obfuscation of code. When transformed into an artwork or other form of expression, code would become something whose circulation would be indisputably protected, at least in the United States, by constitutional guarantees. Most of the responses supporting the defendant in the deCSS case maintain that code is on a continuum with "human language," even if not exactly "ordinary language," even if only a "small number" of skilled people will understand the machine-level formulations of it. The question of code's functional aspects, the effects or events associated with execution, remained unaddressed. In an echo of Kittler's mordant "we do not know what our writing does," the defendant's case was seemingly argued through a repudiation of any effects for language or expression beyond the act of saying itself: as if language, even in the relative precision of computer code, has no effects, as if language does and can do nothing.

Code is law

Around the same time as the Digital Millennium Copyright Act and the deCSS court case of 2000, other forms of competition were changing the nature of the Internet, the web and cultural formations of cyberspace. The Internet was being heavily commercialized by dotcom enterprises. The production and circulation of code were taking on a key significance in the new economy of information. Lawrence Lessig's influential *Code and Other Laws of Cyberspace* appeared in 1999. For Lessig, software was no longer another object of regulation, but itself a form of regulation or law. Rather than being part of an invisible infrastructure that allowed people to communicate or consume through the Internet, or being a form of expression of ideas, code, Lessig argues, is the sociolegal fabric of cyberspace: "In real space we recognise how laws regulate—through constitutions, statutes, and other legal codes. In cyberspace we must understand how code regulates—how the software and hardware that make cyberspace what it is regulate cyberspace as it is" (Lessig 1999, 6). He goes on to say, "We live life in real space, subject to the effects of code. We live ordinary lives, subject to the effects of code. We live social and political lives, subject to the effects of code. Code regulates all these aspects of our lives, more pervasively over time than other regulator in our life" (Lessig 1999, 233). Thus Lessig equates code in the sense of software with code in the sense of law: rather than being regulated by government legislation or international agreements designed to protect intellectual property, code itself is law, it is an authoritative norm. The second equation of *Ars Electronica* festival's subtitle—"Code = Law"—was quoting Lessig (Stocker and Schopf 2003).

Lessig's book struck a chord with "technolibertarian" programmers in North America, Europe and Australia because it ranked code itself as one of the foremost political sites in cyberspace. It was widely promoted by leading figures in the software industries, such as computer book publisher Tim O'Reilly. Enthusiastic responses confirmed the perception that coding, far from being just another relatively well-paid form of new media or engineering work, was becoming a site of significant contestation between technology and law. When O'Reilly, an open-source software evangelist, reviewed Lessig's book under the title "You Must Read This Book" (O'Reilly 2000), his readership was principally composed of programmers and hackers, professional and nonprofessional. His injunction was very closely linked to the book's promotion of programmers' own agency and contributed to the subsequent fame of Lessig as a cyber-advocate. Whereas

the deCSS contest was framed heavily in terms of U. S. constitutional law
and the right to free speech, Lessig's argument took a step further.
Accepting that code is a form of expression, he also proposed that code or
software (the distinction was not always clear) had an associated force. In
almost outright contradiction to the eminent amicus curiae brief, Lessig's
argument framed code as something that possessed authority.

The authority of code: Executing software art

The assimilation of code to law remains problematic. In what sense is code
law? Is it just because it includes classifications and conventions that
support social legal norms governing people's behavior? Or is there
something else in its very mode of existence that is law-like, that possesses
some force? How, in short, does code accrue any authority? The new-found
equation between code and law present in Lessig's analysis hinges on
something that machine execution adds to expression. The relation between
code as speech and code as something that exercises authority lies at the
core of some software art. Some "software artists" (as distinct from
programmers who write code poetry) trenchantly criticize code art or code
poetry because it does little or nothing. In their view, code poetry is pallid
and deracinated because it separates execution of code from its description.
When executed, the code of Winterbottom (2000) does nothing special:

> All that has been demonstrated is an act of translation from an existing text, simply
> 'porting' existing poetry into perl. It produces poetry in a conventional sense,
> possibly expressing some clever word order and grammatical changes, but does
> little to articulate the language of perl in itself. When you execute perl poetry in this
> way, it simply repeats itself but does not acknowledge its execution. It is this
> operative function that is an essential of part of the experience of poetry. (Cox,
> McLean, and Ward 2002)

"Acknowledging execution" is the critical difference between code
poetry and software art. A short piece of computer code called *forkbomb.pl*
that does acknowledge its execution won the 2002 Transmediale Art Prize in
Berlin. It was written by British artist Alex McLean in Perl, the same
language popular with code poets. "Forkbomb" refers to a system crash
caused by an exponential growth of processes. The entire source code, the
code written by the programmers, for *forkbomb.pl* is listed below:

```
die "Please do not run this script without reading the documentation"
  if not @ARGV;
```

```
my $strength = $ARGV[0] + 1;
while (not fork) {
        exit unless --$strength;
        print 0;
        twist: while (fork) {
                exit unless --$strength;
                print 1;
```

(McLean, 2002)

The presence of code in an art object is not unique. Computer artists have been working with it since the 1960s.[6] McLean's *forkbomb.pl* is distinctive, however, because the code itself, as well as any effect it might produce in execution, is presented as the work. As a contemporary art object, code here becomes something that overflows production, use or exchange value and explicitly seeks to pose itself as the object of attention, as an index of different agencies in relation in a social network.

In their judgment, the Transmediale jury wrote that "*forkbomb.pl* was awarded [the prize] as a crafted code which is transformed into an art of technical transgression" (Transmediale 2002). It can only be transgressive if it puts norms or conventions into question. What norms or conventions does *forkbomb.pl* transgress? What aspect of the code is transgressive? Do those transgressions tell us anything about how code could gain a law-like authority? The jury's comments contrast with other, less celebratory responses to *forkbomb.pl*. Hacker Eric Raymond wrote, "Creating [a forkbomb] seldom accomplishes more than to bring the just wrath of the gods down upon the perpetrator" (Raymond 1996, 203).

How does software run?

The code quoted above has to be executed as Perl code on an operating system furnished with a Perl interpreter. When it is run, it simply prints out a string of 1s and 0s like the following:

```
011101111100011111110001110101111111111110000011110011110000111111100111
101101011111101011000011011001010001011011010000010100111101100111111111
00111010100101000101100111111
```

The marks both provide an undecipherable snapshot of the operating system as it is currently is and in some ways change that system. Judging by this modest output, the perceptual complexity of the work and the aesthetic sensations it immediately elicits are minimal, to say the least. It hardly rates against the iconic density, color and carefully designed layout of the average computer interface or the spectacular visual detail seen in the latest generation of console computer games. In the case of *forkbomb.pl*, the executing process has no clear political or aesthetic significance. The output of an executing process generates ordered 0s and 1s. Just as coding involves editing text according to rules expressed syntactically by a programming language, the work done by executing code is mundane, not mysterious: it generates sequences of marks.

Where does the "function" of software occur, if not within such sequences of marks? Function, "doing something," executing, running—all need to be analyzed here in relation to an authority associated with inscription. Cultural theory has argued that the authority of any utterance depends on how it invokes and repeats a prior set of conventions (Butler 1997, 51; Derrida 1982). The concept of performativity, doing through saying, became prominent in cultural and political theory as a way of untangling the mixtures of naming, acting and expressing found in any utterance founded on such conventions. If we accept that all code indexes some utterance (as per the model of expression propounded in the deCSS case, and as per the more general model of the software nexus described in the previous chapter), then all code-utterance is associated other functions, including those associated with the power of legal authority (as per Lessig's influential argument).

Some useful purchase could come from analyzing the prior conventions invoked in code. (A fuller analysis of the performativity of software awaits the following chapter.) What would this approach mean in terms of analyzing *forkbomb.pl* as piece of code and addressing the question of how code exercises authority? The artist Alex McLean suggests that *forkbomb.pl* be seen as producing a "watermark" of the functional coupling of an operating system and hardware platform. Every operating system and platform will produce a different output. Even the same computer will produce different outputs depending on what other processes are running at that time (Cox, McLean and Ward 2002). Running it a few times bears this out. On some occasions, *forkbomb.pl* "bombs" a computer by colonizing the operating system with an exponentially growing number of clones of the *forkbomb.pl* process. Like viruses such as LoveBug, each clone recursively generates copies of itself: hence the Transmediale jury refers to *forkbomb.pl* as "transgressive." As this suggests, *forkbomb.pl* is somewhat self-referential; all it does is copy itself. At the same time, its work relies on two distinctive features of contemporary multi-user interactive operating systems. The key lines that point towards both material singularities within the computing environment and traits of expression within the code are directly readable from the code itself:

```
while (not fork) {


    exit unless --$strength;
```

In effect, *forkbomb.pl* relies on the presence of a "fork" operation within the programming language Perl (not all programming languages have such a construct).

Fork: The interpenetrating contexts of code

Perl's fork operation owes its existence to the fact that Perl was originally designed by a computer system administrator for use by other system administrators. Unlike many programming language designers working in academic computer science departments or in large corporate or institutional research environments, Larry Wall, the language designer, was working during the 1980s as a system administrator in a corporate environment on the West Coast, somewhat removed from the theorematic agenda of computer science as an academic discipline (Moody 2001, 132). The motivation for Perl, according to Wall, stemmed from an unoccupied "ecological niche" in existing computing environments:

> When I started designing Perl, I explicitly set out to deconstruct all the computer languages I knew and recombine or reconstruct them in a different way, because there were many things I liked about other languages, and many things I disliked. I lovingly reused features from many languages…. To the extent that Perl rules rather than sucks, it's because the various features of these languages ruled rather than sucked. (Wall 1999)

Dating from 1987, Perl attained almost unrivaled popularity, first as a Unix system administrator's tool and later in the mid- to late 1990s as a web programming language (largely because it lies midway between low-level programming languages such as C and high-level software tools and applications).

Perl has a fork operation because the fork was the basis of the multiprocessing capabilities of the Unix operating system, something that nearly every operating system today shares. As one of the designers of the Unix system writes: "The system call fork creates two nearly identical copies of a process. One copy is called the parent and the other the child. In the parent process, fork returns the process number of the child. The value returned in the child is 0. If fork cannot create a new process, it returns -1. This can happen, for example, when the system process table is full, or if the fork call is interrupted" (Bourne 1987, 135).

The transgression embodied in *forkbomb.pl* is not purely technical. The use of Perl to express and execute the forkbomb implicitly relies on conventions that schedule the order of competing computing processes in operating systems. The work becomes transgressive in relation to the modes of ordering and governing of work and action nearly taken for granted as the operating system. If, as sociologist Scott Lash points out, operating systems are one of the most important "lifted-out" spaces within contemporary technological cultures (Lash 2002), *forkbomb.pl* can only be transgressive within a system of norms already practically understood as a form or regulation. The question here is: What nexus of norms and authority does something like an operating system entail today?

Just like code poetry, software artwork like *forkbomb.pl* could be criticized for its formalism. It has certainly been dismissed as a "hack attack." One irked response, echoing Raymond's skeptical view of forkbombs, runs: "Do hack attacks now count as art? Viruses? Wouldn't an obfuscated program to completely erase the disk of the subject system be even more 'crafted' and an even greater 'technical transgression,' and therefore, even better art? Will seeing it as art be a defense in computer crime trials now?"(Permungkah 2002). This objection, although suggestive of some other software artworks that have or will be created, privileges execution at the expense of code itself. The artists themselves insist on this point: "code and the execution of the code need to be experienced in parallel. This is both necessary and impossible for generative or autonomous systems" (Cox, McLean, and Ward 2002). Going beyond the Perl poetry and the deCSS haiku, *forkbomb.pl* seeks to hold speech and action, text and function together. Rather than code as speech, it combines speech with action. That execution, like the deCSS code, can be read as transgressive. Here the transgression concerns not so much a state-supported legal system to regulate the reproduction of digital media but rather the operating system as a privileged technological site regulating conduct within contemporary technological culture.

Works such as *forkbomb.pl* register the impossibility of simultaneously experiencing the execution of code and code as expression or utterance. This is an important point: the impossibility of experiencing code as both expression and operation at the same time attests to a singular instability in the mode of code's existence. Software and struggles over how it is intentionalized are rooted in the impossibility of reading and writing code at the same time. If there is no coincidence between expression and function, between text and execution, between word and thing, then rather than crashing operating systems, a forkbomb's disruptive effects include having raised the question of the performativity of code. Judith Butler, a leading theorist of performativity, writes that "in speaking, the act the body performs is never fully understood" (Butler 1997, 11). In any act of speaking, the body of the speaker does something more than what is said, something not fully understood and not analyzable. This conclusion of contemporary social theories of power resonates in software, a domain of technically styled expression directed at doing things.

Code is life

A final set of code-based artworks offers one response to the impossibility of experiencing code as both expression and operation. The work of two Dutch artists, Dirk Paesmans and Joan Heemskerk, collectively known as jodi, became famous for disruptive websites beginning in the late 1990s (jodi 2004). Much of their work—roughly contemporary with *forkbomb.pl*, the deCSS works and the Perl poetry—uses HTML script to counter the norms and habits of user interfaces, or what Manovich (1996) terms the "labour of perception" (183) associated with browsers, computer games and operating systems. On screen, jodi's works often appear as sparsely populated sets of random characters, punctuated by small flashing boxes, inappropriate font-sizing, garish colors, awkward screen layouts and uncontrollable numbers of pop-up windows. They veer away from the highly crafted graphic and interaction design conventions that quickly accreted around websites in the 1990s.

Jodi's work illustrates the third equation from the theme of *Ars Electronica* 2003, "Code = Life." If previous artworks treat code as speech (deCSS haiku) and code as law (*forkbomb.pl*), jodi's work turns to the relation between code and interface. It treats code as a material that lies at the boundary between machines and human life, at least in the sense of "everyday life."[7] In equating life with code, the *Ars Electronica* 2003 catalog links software to biology and more generally, to biopower, the regulation and normalization of the capacities of human bodies as individuals and as members of populations or sets (Foucault 1991). Life came to be understood in post-World War II biology as an information system or as a program executing instructions laid down in a genetic code, as discussed in Kay (2000). Even today, concepts of important biological processes rely on metaphors of computational architectures: "if we wanted to keep the computer metaphor, we could describe the fertilized egg as a massively parallel and multilayered processor in which both programs (or networks) and data are distributed throughout the cell" (Keller 2000, 52). More importantly, however, linking code to life might involve exploration of how communicative processes are invented, produced, regulated and controlled through power relations present in code. This would mean understanding how "users" are objects governed within regimes or biopower (Terranova 2004; Lunenfeld 2005).

Usually viewed through a browser, jodi's works since 1995 have displayed a range of programming and scripting languages and techniques including HTML, cgi scripts, Java, Flash, ASCII codes, C and others. Jodi is famous for disruptions and miscodings and for making self-immersed generators of contingent datastreams. Rather than performing any kind of innovation involving code, this work can be regarded as a creative misuse of code. Jon Ippolito, a curator of new media art of the Guggenheim Museum in New York, says that "artists like Paesmans and Heemskerk, after intentionally entering faulty code into their works, have been likened to the painter Robert Rauschenberg, who applied paint to the back tire of his truck and then ran over paper rather than using a brush" (quoted in Friedman 2003). These works challenge the framing of code through interfaces that intentionalize code in the name of a user.

Jodi's works rarely look the same twice. Chance or random functions change what happens at the user interface, particularly the web-browser interface. A typical spectator/user initially thinks something is wrong with the browser software or the website's HTML markup. What counts as a fault or error is related to norms, to existing functions of software, and to the social and technical agencies software is meant to perform. Disruptions of a transaction, communication or representation are normally experienced as system errors or technical faults.

Error does loom large in the reception of jodi's works: "We get a lot of email. In the first couple of weeks after we put up the site we got a lot of complaints. People were seriously thinking that we made mistakes. So they wanted to teach us. They sent us emails saying: You have to put this tag in front of this code. Or: I am sorry to tell you that you forgot this or that command on your page" (jodi quoted in Baumgärtel 1997). But the artists are not causing computers to crash to highlight how everyday habits concerning interfaces carry ingrained expectations about users as "productive." Error or fault in the sense of transgression does not account for important visible features of their work.

Code moves inside and outside the computer

While *forkbomb.pl* assumes that some person or computer somewhere will run the code, jodi struggles more directly with who runs which code where. In interviews, the artists talk about trying, through their work, to get inside the personal computer. They locate their work by saying, "Our work comes from inside the computer, not from a country":

> It is obvious that our work fights against high tech. We also battle with the computer on a graphical level. The computer presents itself as a desktop, with a trash can on the right and pull down menus and all the system icons. We explore the computer from inside, and mirror this on the net. When a viewer looks at our work, we are inside his computer. There is this hacker slogan: "We love your computer." We also get inside people's computers. And we are honored to be in somebody's computer. You are very close to a person when you are on his desktop. I think the computer is a device to get into someone's mind. (jodi quoted in Baumgärtel 1997)

It would be possible to interpret these works as hack attacks, since the artists explicitly echo the hacker slogan, "We love your computer." However, given these works are publicly displayed on the web and in public art galleries (jodi 2003), a different interpretation is needed. The artists' statements link computers and personal identities, and present their work as concerned with that relation between person and computer. Rather than being about code as such, or computers as such, jodi's work deals with the contemporary relations between computation and personhood, but at a low level. Just as Rauschenberg and other twentieth-century artists addressed the framing and support of the image in order to render visible hitherto unseen historical conditions of visuality, jodi's work with code can be read as seeking to make visible some hidden conditions of computability.

The notion of being inside "someone's computer" structures the works themselves. Often they have hidden order associated with them, which viewers discover only accidentally or by persistent clicking. In the baffling screen full of blinking punctuation characters shown in the work *%Location| http://wwwwwwww.jodi.org-http://wwwwwwww.jodi.org*, using the "view source" command on the browser produces something more comprehensible. The HTML source code for the incomprehensible web page turns out to be an ASCII art image of a nuclear weapon. Rather than being totally disordered or random, what appears in the browser window hides a different layer of order at the level of code. The underlying image turns out to be iconic and representational: ASCII art images are a genre of computer art analogous to Perl poetry. In the code, order accompanies disorder at the level of the user interface.

Other jodi works make code more explicit. The work *SOD.1%* (jodi 2002) uses HTML to publish low-level assembly language code on a webpage. This code is usually not read by programmers at all—it is the product of a compiler and meant for machine execution. It lies near the base of the Tower of Babel Kittler speaks of. Graphically, the webpage mimics a Borland C++ code editor from the 1980s, a time before bit-mapped displays and font-scaling software were readily available on personal computers. Again, what is usually visible and invisible are explicitly inverted here since this is the scene of production of code, not its execution or consumption by users. There are just two hyperlinks to be discovered on the page, pointing to Mac and PC versions of what is by today's standards a very primitive 3-D first-person shooter game written in C++. The code on the page is part of the game. Downloading these components of the work through the links and then executing them as programs tends to crash contemporary operating systems. With *SOD.1%*, the interface in question is no longer the web browser (although the work is displayed in a browser), but the interface to a proprietary coding environment (Borland Turbo C) that lies behind the visual dynamism of a 3-D first-person shooter-style game.

Some of jodi's works push code further toward greater visibility. The work *%Statistic | HQX* (jodi 1997) looks like a system crash, again scripted in HTML. Screens like this once occurred on personal computers when software crashed the operating system to the point of flooding even the graphics area (video-RAM) with meaningless data. This work has many layers leading through different visual organizations of code fragments, images, maps, diagrams, blocks of color and text. Again, what is inside the computer is made visible on a webpage. In this work, as in the simpler case of *%Location* and in *SOD.1%*, some aspect or surface "inside the computer," behind the interface, is rendered onscreen. In each work, this inside, an inside valorized because of its intricate linkages with contemporary subjects of information—communication, biopower-constituted subjectivity—can only be made visible by recourse to code. The inside of the computer is identified with code in these works. Rather than disrupting expectations of usability, the artists substitute different interfaces for the commonly visible ones—the diagram of an atomic weapon, the assembly code editor for a computer game, fragments and layers of code thrown up by a system crash.

What is at stake in locating forms of order at the level of code, beyond the level of more immediate or everyday perception? The artists who call themselves jodi say, "Many people try to dissect our site, and look into the code" (Baumgärtel 1997). Reading code is a way of trying to make sense of what they are doing, and perhaps to copy it. But why do their works disrupt expectations of usability by pointing to code? To make connections with other political or cultural contexts which appear remote from new media or outside the personal computer?

Jodi's work adds a final permutation to the code nexus explored in this chapter and a final gloss on the impossibility of simultaneously experiencing code as expression and as action. The artists' works play directly on the instable mode of existence of code as both text and execution, as instruction and process, as speech and action, as something embodied in habits, half-perceived and worked on. Many of jodi's works can be seen as driven by the impossible coincidence of expression and execution. Their "errors" muddy the boundaries between interface and code by showing that code is another interface, one often less visible, but nonetheless always concomitant.

Lives crossing into code

Mathew Fuller (2003) proposed the notion of "blips" as a label for the dense relationality of certain events associated software: "the enormous spread of economies, systems of representation, of distribution, hiding, showing, and influence as they mesh with other systems of circulation, of life, ecology, resources—themselves always both escaping and compelling electronic and digital manifestation—can be intercepted, mapped, and reconfigured precisely by means of these blips" (30–31). Drawing on Ullman (1997), in which "blip" describes how people's lives cross into code ("there is no other way: human needs must cross the line into code" [14]), Fuller suggests that critical readings of software should be attentive to the "implicit politics" of the concrete arrangements and interactions contained in software.

This chapter has explored some of the ways that various genres of code-based art cross lives with software. An examination of these works' attempts to make code open—available, visible and legible—suggests that code as a material cannot be disentangled from norms, conventions and structures of authority. These norms work at different scales, ranging from state regulation, software industry work conditions and subcultures of Unix and

Perl to the conventions and embodied habits of PC-user interfaces. Across these different scales and distributions of code, the difficulty that Kittler identifies in software ("we do not know what our writing docs") is rooted in a property of code as a material that is read, written and executed. The impossibility of experiencing expression and execution simultaneously is perhaps not unique to code. However, as the next chapter will show in its examinations of the algorithms that structure code, this impossibility triggers many different convolutions and complications in the relations running through software itself.

Chapter 3

Algorithms: Sequence and convolution

Software cannot do without, according to computer science, algorithms and data structures (Wirth 1976). All code, formally analyzed, encapsulates an algorithm. Algorithms—recipes or sets of steps expressed in flowcharts, code or pseudocode—epitomize the operationality of software. It is hard to conceptualize software without algorithms (although there are very different ways to conceptualize algorithms). Algorithms carry, fold, frame and redistribute actions into different environments. As software (and computing) becomes more connective, as it "flows into the environment" (Thrift 2004b, 183), analysis of the mode of existence of algorithms becomes critical. Algorithms move into disparate domains, and disparate domains come together in algorithms. Algorithms have a cognitive-affective stickiness that makes them both readily imitable and yet forbiddingly complex. The orderings of social fields associated with software hinge on formal properties of algorithms that often assume an immutable, general aura. Sometimes algorithms, which specify how to transform a given set of inputs into a desired output, are treated as the formal, static essence of software. This is perhaps why some writers have suggesting using "concepts from computer science as categories of new media theory" (Manovich 2001, 48). Other attributes of software, such as furnishing a user interface or running on a given hardware platform, are treated as more or less contingent in contrast to the essential necessity of the algorithm.

Despite being inherent to software, algorithms are quite difficult to analyze. Typically, computer science textbooks and computer science courses introduce algorithms using a set of well-known examples or model situations. For instance, the famous quicksort algorithm that sorts a sequence of items (Hoare 1961) illustrates the "divide and conquer" approach to algorithmic design. Both the quicksort algorithm and the divide-and-conquer approach can be varied, modified or adapted to apply to any situation where items need to be in sequences. However, to situate algorithms at this level of generality would take for granted the "conventions of address" (Thrift 2004b, 176), the expectation that things will be where we expect them to be (that is, in sequence). A critical analysis of algorithms would start by recognizing that the expectation that things will be in place is historically and socially specific. Order and sequence are the result of much work. For any given situation, there are many possible orderings and actions. What sequences are important? For what purposes?

An algorithm selects and reinforces one ordering at the expense of others. Agency, therefore, is by definition contested in and through algorithms. They affect what can be said and done. The key question for this chapter is: How does an algorithm select and reinforce an ordering? It both naturalizes certain orders and animates certain movements. An algorithm naturalizes who does what to whom by subsuming existing patterns and orderings of cognition, communication and movement. Although algorithmic action is assumed in contemporary everyday life, "the trick," write Bowker and Star (1999), "is to question every apparently natural easiness in the world around us and look for the work involved in making it easy" (39). Position, order and sequence rely on a sedimented background of timetables, routes, directories, address systems, transaction and product codes wrapped into software.

Algorithms also animate certain movements, making them seem lively, imbuing them with celerity and sometimes even grace. They involve certain. As Bowker and Star suggest, practices of positioning and classification mix physical and conventional attributes. This mixing means that algorithms do not simply belong to "us" or the environment. Chapter 2's discussion has suggested that the oscillation between code as expression and code as operation underlies contestations of agency associated with software. Algorithms bring a different level of contestation of agency into software by virtue of what Alfred Gell describes as "cognitive stickiness." In his account of the geometric decoration on certain art-like objects, Gell (1998, 86) explains the visual fascination exercised by Oriental carpets or Celtic knotwork in terms of a set of animating movements induced in the viewer by the art-index. The eye moves constantly as it attempts to make sense of the coils of the Celtic knot or the intricate geometry of the carpet, and in many cases can never resolve or settle the perceptual problem that these geometrical decorations pose. An "agential" effect results from the impossibility of freezing perception: intricacy invites the attribution of agency. Typically, this agential effect is attributed to the art object itself. Hence a labyrinthine decoration on a door turns away unwelcome visitors. Algorithms have similar animating effects on their recipients: they put into question who is moving what.

This chapter tracks how algorithms materialize in a specific domain, bioinformatics, a contemporary knowledge enterprise intensely preoccupied with sequence, position and repetition. As an entry point to the problem of algorithms, bioinformatics is downstream of theoretical computer science. It is also remote from more mundane knowledges of location, sequence, order and repetition found in, for instance, a search engine (Brin and Page 2002) or a barcode scanner at a supermarket checkout. Sequence data is processed at different scales in key bioinformatics algorithms such as the Needleman-Wunsch and Smith-Waterman sequence alignment algorithms. Why track algorithmic treatment of sequence data? Examination of how the dynamic programming algorithms used in bioinformatics temporally and spatially order computation can illuminate a critical feature of software: its generation of singular spatial-temporal composites of order and sequence. Treatment of one significant class of algorithms must stand in place of a more comprehensive exploration of the composite framing intrinsic to all algorithmic design.

Theoretical computer science addresses the time and space of computation through calculations of algorithmic complexity. Viewed practically, every algorithm is framed by the time and space of computation. My central argument here is that even the most abstract formal specifications of algorithms entail contestations of agency. Such contestations can be difficult to recognize because algorithms condense actions in convoluted sequences of spacing and timing. As positioning and sequencing cross all boundaries between cognition and things, between self and world, between thinking and doing, these contestations of agency become invisible. Attachment to these forms is difficult yet important to analyze as they increasingly pattern and coordinate everyday life.[1] Attachment or stickiness occurs through involution of agency, through a sometimes labyrinthine entwining of movements and spaces addressed and condensed in algorithms.

Moving sequences in bioinformatics

In bioinformatics, an "enterprised-up" (Haraway 1997) scientific subdiscipline, the programming languages, patterns of code circulation and organizations of work examined in other chapters coalesce around a very problematic prototype: the intricate spatial and temporal processes of organisms viewed as biochemical systems. Very little of the infrastructure, code constructs, platforms or protocols involved in bioinformatics is new. But like the figuring of code in software art, the concept of code in bioinformatics has a special salience that heightens its singularity as a case study. Of all the situations explored in this book, bioinformatics is the most prototypically code-like. The entities with which bioinformatics software engages, the living systems of contemporary molecular biology, are preconceived as nothing other than code itself in action: "Nature uses algorithm-like procedures to solve biological problems, for example, in the process of DNA replication" (Jones and Pevzner 2004, 14, italics in original). Although bioinformatics may contain nothing new from the standpoint of software, its conception of life as prototypically algorithmic renders it uniquely apposite as an unexpectedly literal way to explore how knowledges and practices of sequence and position become convoluted in software. Algorithms propose solutions to problems, but they are not always simple or quick solutions. In particular, the "algorithmic-like procedures" in nature include many errors, exceptions, missed signals and miscodings that have accumulated over time. In comparison to other code-like situations, living systems, especially in the complicated forms in which they are presently being constituted, such as genomes, offer themselves as at once worst-case and best-case examples of sequenced operations. Life is an impossibly sophisticated and exceedingly bad prototype for software.

After the heavily publicized announcement of the completion of the first draft of the human genome in June 2000, many thousands of people downloaded the complete gigabyte DNA or nucleotide-acid sequence from the Internet. According to *Wired*, many were curiosity-driven. Some reports say people were looking for the letters "GATTACA" (the name of a film about a genetically restricted near-future society) or other hidden messages in the book of life (Philipkoski 2001). Since then, sequence information has undergone much more extensive processing. The highly publicized availability of gene and protein sequence data translated into a variety of software artifacts. Sequence data flowed into systems built to cope with the work of integrating sequence data so that new biological knowledge could be "discovered" through information processing. The algorithms on which biological discovery currently relies intensify and scale-up selected movement in ways characteristic of software more generally. An animating effect precipitates from these movements. This animation could account for the perceptual stickiness of code objects.

As a specialized domain of science at the intersection of computing and biology, bioinformatics was named sometime in the early 1990s in close association with the Human Genome Project (HGP). The first job advertisements for bioinformaticists appeared in the mid-1990s (Farnady 1996), although biologists had sat at computer screens before then since software has been used to analyze sequence data for over twenty years. After the announcement of the HGP, many announcements, funding schemes and opinion pieces in publications such as Science and Nature stressed the urgent need to find ways of organizing, searching and collating the growing tide of sequence data, which in raw form consists of strings of characters representing nucleic acids (for DNA or RNA) or amino acids (for proteins). Vision statements obsessed over computing and information infrastructure as a crucial component of the sequencing project (Gilbert 1992; Lander 1996). Only through extensive computational work could a complete nucleic acid sequence or genome (for humans, chimpanzees, fruit flies, rice, tobacco, etc.) be wrangled out of the overlapping fragments produced by the sequencing robots.

The name "bioinformatics" illustrated the strategic situation emerging as what we call the body lost some of its corpuscular, organismic character and became a nexus of different political, medical, economic and scientific actualities that provisionally congealed as biotechnology. At a general level, bioinformatics could be seen as supporting the more salient intellectual, social, political, cultural and economic events associated with contemporary biology and genetics in the latter part of the twentieth century and early twenty-first century. Under regimes of biosociality (Rabinow 1992), ethicopolitical and ontological questions about living bodies proliferate at many different places: around predictive medicine, agriculture, reproduction and drugs, and beyond. As Thacker (2004) argues, bioinformatics (software and databases) is a significant interface between living systems and biotechnological processes because it concentrates on translating key relations in living media (organisms) into informatic media (sequence data). Not only preserving those relations, bioinformatics, it can be argued, subjects them to repetition and variation in an expanded social field of interactions. At the same time, bioinformatics software is hard to categorize in terms of tools made for users: "Biomedia are novel configurations of biologies and technologies that take us beyond the familiar tropes of technology-as-tool or the human-machine interface" (Thacker 2004, 6). Bioinformatics systems are relatively unobtrusively woven into micropractices within these domains. As with much other software infrastructure, political, economic and social ordering processes work through bioinformatics but do not appear as such.

As sequence data moves through bioinformatics systems, it is arranged and positioned in two ways: first, the biological function and biochemical specificity of sequence data are sought. Second, potential transformations in living bodies are at stake. The cornerstone bioinformatics problems of sequence alignment and sequence matching occur in both processes. Bioinformatics' heavy commitment to lateral transpositions between sequence fragments of different living things re-version living bodies at a fine-grained, partial and concrete level. The practices of bioinformatics version-off living bodies that tend toward a metastable state in which bodies become more susceptible to different determinations. The software manipulation of sequence data opens living systems to subsequent determination, whether as commodities in a biological knowledge economy, as elements in some other assemblage (such as a patented biomedical diagnostic reagent), or as elements in a transformed biological process (such as a genetically modified organism, plant or animal). The versioning of living bodies cannot, at least within the domain of bioinformatics, be divided from property relations.[2] Bioinformatics is representative in its promotion of algorithms to the center of scientific knowledge. These processes can be seen as typical of how code textures worlds more generally. Hence, bioinformatics is treated here as symptomatic of the "soft control" (Terranova 2004, 114), "flow-worlds" (Knorr-Cetina and Bruegger 2000, 141) or "processual contexts" (Thrift 2004a, 590) crystallizing in and through software.

Bioinformatic problems and attachments

The fact that algorithms are often described as "recipes" suggests they are made to be imitated and circulated. However, this circulation is not automatic. Unless attached to a prototype, recipient or producer, an algorithm remains an abstraction. How does an attachment form between algorithm and action? At what level does the action of an algorithm take place?

Since 1955 when the mapping between nucleic DNA base pairs and amino acids in proteins was established, sequence data has come to be regarded as a massive Rosetta stone for understanding living systems (Kay 2000). As the ultimate key to the specificity of biochemical interactions, sequence data promises knowledge of biochemical processes. But in relation to specific biochemical questions, sequence data only yields answers after an intensive labor of recontextualization. For instance, the biochemical function of a sequence of amino acids, the molecules that make up proteins, can only be discerned if either the shape of the resulting protein can be predicted (the protein-folding problem) or if another closely related amino acid sequence of known biochemical function can be found through comparison (the sequence-alignment problem).[3]

Much individual sequence alignment and comparison software runs on individual computers. Programs such as FASTA and BLAST (Lipman and Pearson 1985; Altschul et al. 1990) arguably contain core bioinformatics algorithms. Built around these programs and their core algorithms, a rapidly filling spectrum of networked or Internet-based systems integrates different data sources and processing techniques. Bioinformatics incorporates a multistranded attempt to systematically organize and productively manipulate a body of knowledge concerning living things. Bioinformatics makes claims over the knowledge of "how to do it" (Strathern 1999, 20).[4]

What is bioinformatics' specificity as an algorithmic process? Projects focused on collating and organizing knowledge concerning living things have existed for a long time. Lists, taxonomies, specimen collections, genealogies, encyclopedias, genetic trees and statistical summations have punctuated developments in biological knowledge over the last three centuries. Each shift in our understanding of life has been accompanied by different ways of making the relations between living things, between generations, kinds, species and so forth visible. Already at its inception sometime in the 1970s (see Needleman and Wunsch 1970), what is now called "bioinformatics" dealt with comparing sequence data in terms that seemed quite remote from organisms in vivo. Especially after chemical cleavage methods for DNA became available in 1975, the prospects of large amounts of sequence data became palpable. GenBank, perhaps the major repository for DNA sequence data, was originally conceived as an archive of sequences (Gelbart 1998). Unlike botanical and animal specimens, whose visible attributes are the main basis of classification, sequence data displays no identifying attributes. A given fragment of DNA sequence data could come from almost any living thing since it represents long strands composed of four nucleic acids: adenine (A), cytosine (C), guanine (G) and thymine

(T). Unlike other domains of the social field in which fine-grained schemas of addressability (Thrift 2004a) have entwined with everyday life over the last few centuries, sequence data is unformatted. Other labeling information must be attached. Pure sequence data will not be stored in the databases. Rather, databases store sequence data in standard annotated formats.

For instance, nucleotide data from the nucleotide database at NCBI retrieved via a search on the term "myelin" comes in GenBank format:

```
LOCUS    BI711680   561 bp mRNA     EST    19-SEP-2001
DEFINITION id96c12.y1 Human insulinoma Homo sapiens cDNA 5'similar to
    TR:Q01585 Q01585 MYELIN BASIC PROTEIN ;, mRNA sequence.
ACCESSION  BI711680
VERSION   BI711680.1 GI:15687375
KEYWORDS  EST.
SOURCE   human.
ORGANISM Homo sapiens
    Eukaryota; Metazoa; Chordata; Craniata; Vertebrata; Euteleostomi;
    Mammalia; Eutheria; Primates; Catarrhini; Hominidae; Homo.
REFERENCE  1 (bases 1 to 561)
AUTHORS  Melton, D., Brown, J., Kenty, G., Permutt, A., Lee, C., Kaestner, K.,
    ...
TITLE   Endocrine Pancreas Consortium
JOURNAL  Unpublished (2000)
COMMENT   Other_ESTs: id96c12.x1
    Contact: Douglas Melton, Klaus H. Kaestner, & Hiroshi Inoue
    ....
    High quality sequence stop: 429.
FEATURES     Location/Qualifiers
   source    1..561
        /organism="Homo sapiens"
        /db_xref="taxon:9606"
        /clone_lib="Human insulinoma"
        /tissue_type="insulinoma"
        /lab_host="DH10B (phage-resistant)"
        /note="Organ: pancreas; Vector: pBluescript SK-; Site_1:
        XhoI; Site_2: EcoRI; Constructed with lambda ZAPII system
        (Stratagene) by Dr. J. Ferrer, in vivo mass-excised to
        pBluescript SK- by Dr. H. Inoue following the Washington
        University protocol
BASE COUNT   136 a 138 c  172 g  115 t
ORIGIN
     1 gcacgagcca gaccatccaa gaagacagtg cagccacctc cgagagcctg gatgtgatgg
    61 cgtcacagaa gagaccctcc cagaggcacg gatccaagta cctggccaca gcaagtacca
   121 tggaccatgc caggcatggc ttcctcccaa ggcacagaga cacgggcatc cttgactcca
   181 tcgggcgctt ctttggcggt gacaggggtg cgcccaagcg gggctctggc aaggtgagct
   241 ctgaggagta gaggagtttt agtttaaatg gaaaaagcaa aggagaaatc agtaggtgaa
```

301 ctcagccatt agaggaagaa ctggcacgta gcctcttgct gtctaaggtc tcgttccgtg
361 ctggagaatg catatgagcc caagagtgtg ggcctgagtg gctgcttagg acgttttcgt
421 ttaactcacc ccctcttttc ctcacaaggg atggtggccg gggtgtggct caggaatgta
481 aggacatgct gaattctgga tctctaaggg tgcctggaca tgggcgttgc agaaagagag
541 ccacattctc agggtctctgg

Only in the last ten lines does any sequence data appear: 561 base pairs. The preceding sixty lines hold accession numbers (BI711680), taxonomy information for the source organism (Homo sapiens), publication references showing work that lies behind the raw sequence data, as well as important information about how the sequence was derived. For instance, this sequence is an EST, an expressed sequence tag, which means that the sequence data comes from a cDNA or complementary DNA library derived from RNA (Lesk 2002, 77). The EST has a reference number (id96c12.y1) that can be entered directly into the search facility of any other library that contains ESTs. Rather than sequence data itself, the indexing, referencing, annotating and cross-referencing of the sequence data stands out. The annotations and surrounding links seem more important because they furnish human readers with a key to other parts of a knowledge infrastructure. That key includes references to how the sequence data was produced, who produced it, what experimental protocols were used, and an entry point into a taxonomy browser.

The time frames of an algorithm

Within the biological knowledge economy, these attributes attached to the raw sequence data are vital, yet they say little about the sequence data itself. What is it, and how can it be read? Sequence data can be characterized as a relatively inert, flat representation of biological knowledge "reduced to a linear code in an archive outside time," as Haraway (1997, 245) puts it. From the perspective of critiques that life is being reduced to information, sequence data looks like a fetishized abstraction in relation to living bodies. However, rather than existing as linear code outside time, sequences exist within what might be called "algorithmic time," the computational time required to find relevant patterns within the sequence. Algorithmic time is framed by the computational resources supplied from the biological knowledge economy, and in this respect, algorithmic time is social and machine time. The practices of working with sequence data treat it as an accretion of past biological knowledge production. "Sequence databases are great tools," Claverie and Notredame (2003) point out, "because they offer a unique window on the past. They make it possible to answer today's biological questions by enabling us to analyze sequences that may have been determined as many as 20 years ago, when the whole technology emerged. By doing this, they connect past and present molecular biology" (73).

From the standpoint of bioinformatics as a work process, no sequence stands alone since it invites comparison with all other sequences investigated by biology. An early standard textbook of computational biology remarks: "Sequence comparison is the most important primitive operation in computational biology, serving as a basis for many other, more complex, manipulations" (Setubal and Meidanis 1997, 1). Why is sequence comparison important? Sequence alignment and comparison become important as biological knowledge undergoes piecemeal transformation into a field of potential determinations of living systems. In that transformation, sequence comparison plays a crucial operational role.

A history of that transformation would need to attend in particular to the molecularization of Darwinian evolution (Keller 2000). The most important feature of that reconfiguration for present purposes concerns what happened to the genetic classification trees of species. These phylogenetic trees first began to emerge during the nineteenth century and expressed evolutionary relationships between species. Genetic trees showing how species diverged from each over the course of time carried a strong historical directionality. The height of a tree (that is, the number of branches running from root to leaf) represented historical depth. If understanding how branches had grown apart over time was the primary achievement of evolutionary biology, jumping between branches is the central goal of contemporary bioinformatics. Through this lateral movement, the historical depth of genetic trees undergoes a temporal flattening as sequence date is collocated in the same databases. Amid today's increasingly fevered imagining of horizontal leaps, the depths of historical divergence collapse into a strange contemporaneity; sequence comparison flattens genetic time. Reading nucleic or amino acid sequences, themselves abstract fragments of living systems, turns out to be far less important than reading the sequence alongside other sequences.

Consequently, despite its production by increasingly mechanized nucleotide and amino acid sequencing systems, sequence data is rarely treated in isolation. The Smith-Waterman and Needleman-Wunsch algorithms respond to the problem of how to compare different sequences and express the relation between them. Different sequences potentially belong to different branches or leaves on the genetic tree, but sequences are not completely different. By finding an optimum alignment, similar or related biological functions can be inferred. As Lesk (2002) puts it, "the basic principle is that the origin of similarity [in sequence] is common ancestry" (196, italics in original). While sequence comparison can be done by hand, research published during the late 1970s began to show computers could discover sequence similarities simply not visible to the most astute human eyes (Setubal and Meidanis 1997, 48). In order to gain significant results, sequences must be compared at two levels. First, they must be matched against the extensive background of large public and private sequence databases like GenBank and SwissProt. Without sinking into the "flood-of-data" rhetoric that has permeated bioinformatics since its inception in association with the Human Genome Project, we should note that the size of these sequence databases cannot be fixed for long: since 2000, important databases have been growing daily. The practice of releasing sequence data into databases prior to its publication in scientific journals has become well-established. For instance, the Entrez Nucleotides database at the U. S. National Center for Biotechnology Information (NCBI), which collects sequences from other databases (such as GenBank, RefSeq and PDB), contained at least seventeen billion bases in September 2001, but thirty-eight billion by December 2004 (NCBI 2004). Other genomic and proteomic databases such as TIGR (The Institute for Genomic Research) show similar growth (TIGR 2005).

The sequence databases' "exponential rate" of growth poses many informatic challenges of organization, redaction, updating and access (Smith 1990). But the key problem for the biotechnological vision, as graduated evolutionary descent flattens out into continuous transformation and recomposition of subsegments of living things, is how to navigate laterally between sequences from different phyla or species. The history of life once gave irreversible direction to movement. Bioinformatics, when it works on comparing sequences, cuts across genealogical descent and historical unidirectionality, albeit at the cost of restricting its focus to biological fragments such as proteins, enzymes and genes. Working with sequence data does make it possible to imagine cutting across a historically sedimented and corporeally embodied set of norms, but only along very specific pathways.

Imagined movements and alignments

Every algorithm specifies movements, albeit often very intricate ones.

Moving between different sequences is problematic for bioinformatics because sequence alignments express relations between subsegments of living things. Thus "the discovery of sequence homology to a known protein or family of proteins often provides the first clues about the function of a new sequence gene" (Altschul et al. 1990, 403). Practically speaking, the relations between different living things (or between fragments of organisms) can be expressed in measures of sequence similarity, and most concretely in the numerical scores produced by sequence alignment software. How is sequence similarity calculated? Here is a protein sequence in standard FASTA format:

>GTM1_HUMAN GLUTATHIONE S-TRANSFERASE MU 1 (EC 2.5.1.18) (GSTM1-1) (HB SUBUNI

PMILGYWDIRGLAHAIRLLLEYTDSSYEEKKYTMGDAPDYDRSQWLNEKFK
LGLDFPNLPYLIDGAHKITQSNAILCYIARKHNLCGETEEEKIRVDILENQTM
DNHMQLGMICYNPEFEKLKPKYLEELPEKLKLYSEFLGKRPWFAGNKITFV
DFLVYDVLDLHRIFEPKCLDAFPNLKDFISRFEGLEKISAYMKSSRFLPRPVFS
KMAVWGNK

The long string of letters represents amino acids. The various software tools that prepare sequences for processing emerged during the 1970s, 1980 and 1990s[5] and originally ran only as command-line tools on Unix computers used to process text files. Currently software usually compares local sequence files against web-accessible databases such as SwissProt, GenBank or EMBL. BLAST and FASTA software remain heavily used, and software developed in the mid-1990s still runs on servers behind large bioinformatics websites such as GenBank.

Sequence comparison algorithms treat sequence alignment as an editing problem: how many single-character edit operations are needed to transform a given sequence into another given sequence? The edit operations are simple: delete character, replace character, insert character. Edit distance, the number of edit operations separating different sequences, expresses a degree of similarity. A smaller edit distance implies greater similarity between sequences. But although the concept of edit distance (also known as the Levenshtein distance (Jones and Pevzner 2004, 167) reframes sequence comparison as an information processing task, it does not say anything about how to do it.

After enough edit operations, any text can be transformed into another. After enough inserts, deletes and replaces, any amino acid or DNA sequence can become another. However, any two sequences are linked by many different series of edit operations. For long sequences, huge numbers of possible transformations exist. The edit distance could take on many different values. The real problem for bioinformatics becomes the calculating the "optimum alignment," the minimum number of edits needed to move from one sequence to another. Analogous to physics' principle of conservation of energy, bioinformatics holds as a founding axiom that optimum alignment expresses similarity or kinship between biochemical entities.

Finding this optimum alignment, however, is hard and takes time even for short sequences. As a recent manual of bioinformatics writes, "What sounds simple in principle isn't at all simple in practice. Choosing a good alignment by eye is possible, but life is too short to do it more than once or twice" (Gibas and Jambeck 2001, 173). Unlike some code-like situations, the patterns and relations conveyed in sequence data suffer from convolutions and complications. If only the data showed regularity in its relations, if only the history of life were not a history of accumulated errors, then bioinformatics might not be needed. The problem with moving across a molecularized genealogy is that so many movements are possible. Which movement is best? Which is biologically significant?

Abstract movement in algorithmic time: "Build an appropriate Manhattan"

The Needleman-Wunsch algorithm, dating from the 1970s (Needleman and Wunsch 1970), provided an early and critical intervention in the sequence alignment problem. Versions of its algorithmic approach still lie behind much sequence-alignment software. The strength of the Needleman-Wunsch algorithm is its facility in dealing with DNA sequence irregularity and rampant "replication errors" (Jones and Pevzner 2004, 167). Bioinformatics cannot assume a one-to-one relation between characters in two sequences; any number of insertions or deletions could have occurred in the course of evolution, reproduction or growth. Consequently, finding the optimal alignment necessitates many shifts in alignment between the sequences.

Needleman and Wunsch's approach to the problem of sequence alignment and the later, more widely used Smith and Waterman (1981) variation are presented in contemporary bioinformatics textbooks as examples of the core approach to algorithmic design called "dynamic programming" (a term without any direct connection to programming or software per se). Bioinformatics has no monopoly on the use of dynamic programming in algorithmic design. Many logistical and communication problems, ranging from flight scheduling to voice searching, make use of dynamic programming approaches. Interestingly, dynamic programming models all problems in terms of traversals of directed acyclic graphs (DAGs), or networks in which movement can never go in circuits. This is an expressed in the injunction to algorithm designers to "build an appropriate Manhattan" (Jones and Pevzner 2004, 160). By transforming problems such as sequence comparison or text searching into a graph/network data-structure, and carefully planning the order in which computations are carried out, dynamical programming algorithms massively reduce the time needed to find the optimal alignment and thus a relationship.

Algorithms organize informatic time. We could more say more generally that the "creative production of abstraction" (Wark 2004, 71) in software is not based on a better representation of something (for instance, of the prototypical situation modeled in software). Nor is it based on a solution that puts an end to movement. Rather, the quite small repertoire of algorithmic design techniques used in contemporary software—dynamic programming, exhaustive search, divide and conquer, graph-based approaches, heuristic techniques, genetic algorithms, probabilistic algorithms—contains different forms of movement that can be propagated or concatenated across different domains. The transformations in computational time wrought by dynamic programming proceed via a process of abstraction that needs to be explained rather than simply attributed to software. The dynamic programming technique has been applied many times in bioinformatics and other fields because it lays down an especially effective trajectory of computational movement between inputs and outputs; no technologically determined acceleration in hardware or processor speed is at stake in this movement. Rather, by virtue of the abstraction implicit to dynamic programming algorithms, inputs move differently through software. They undergo topological transformations and reordering in time. When a bioinformatics textbook claims "development of new sequence comparison algorithms often amounts to building an appropriate 'Manhattan'" (Jones and Pevzner 2004, 160), it emphasizes the intimate connection between space (data structures) and itinerary (algorithms). The movement of tourists visiting attractions dotted on the grid of Manhattan's streets provides a useful spatial metaphor for other forms of movement. For instance, in the Needleman-Wunsch and Smith-Waterman algorithms, the sequences to be compared become vertical and horizontal axes on a grid. Series of edit operations lay down paths in the grid, and the task is to find the shortest path from the top left corner of the grid to the bottom right.

Dynamic programming avoids repeating calculations that have already been performed or returning to points on the grid that have already been visited. Rather than trying to solve the specific problem of how to get from one point to another most directly (for example, the minimum number of edit operations needed to transform one sequence into another), dynamic programming algorithms build a table or array containing the best scores for all possible movements (or transformations between characters of the sequence). Expressed in the most elementary form, by solving the general problem of movements between every point, dynamic programming makes finding the best movement between two chosen points more efficient. Somewhat paradoxically, by tackling all possible problems to start with, it accelerates solving a particular one. The creative hack is to reverse the intuitive approach that would start with the particular and then generalize from it. Put more loosely, dynamic programming reverses normal or everyday temporal orderings of action.

History as directed traversal of information

By analogy with the perceptual animation of geometric decoration, we could say that algorithms enliven movements lifted out of everyday or existing social orderings. Not just in bioinformatics, but in software more generally, algorithms reconfigure computational operations in ways that animate movement. They engender agential effects that capture not just visual perception (as in geometrical decoration), but whole social fields of action in cognitive-motor performance. What is sometimes felt as the "inhuman time" of the machine is experienced by programmers as a "cut-diamond-like state of grace" (Ullman 1997, 21). Coding is an abstraction that spatiotemporally reorders existing movements. Well-known code constructs such as loops, conditional tests and data structures (arrays, queues, stacks, dictionaries) in popular programming languages afford this concentration or intensification of movements. But neither the code constructs nor the principle of abstraction intrinsic to algorithm work have any traction without a social framing. Nearly all algorithms are concerned with coordinating computation within a relevant framing of social time. The most abstract measures of algorithmic complexity are also the most prosaic in their concern with computational time and its management.

For contemporary biological scientists at their computer screens, the sequences databases supply free flows of annotated sequence data, and sequence-alignment software allows fast computation of the relationship between sequences. Sequence-alignments algorithms make available knowledge that hand and eye alone would take days to produce. As Thacker (2004) writes of sequence data, "it is there as data to be worked on" (44). The information may be highly fragmented, but the software at well-known bioinformatics websites such as those for the National Center for Biotechnology Information or the European Bioinformatics Institute is frequently upgraded, modified and enhanced. It encourages continuous testing of relations to other contexts, other organisms and relevant taxonomic classifications. Although the software provides little by way of automatic interpretation, these tools configure highly intertextual recipients, able to slip quickly along intertextual links between bodies of biological data, noting shifts in context on the fly, gathering and refining relationships as they go.

Finding sequence alignments is routine biological-knowledge work today. The first step in evaluating any newly obtained DNA or amino acid sequence is to BLAST it against a relevant database. Sequence comparison cuts short many other kinds of biological research. Stories of how years of research have been cut down to weeks abound in the bioinformatics literature. Researchers at the pharmaceutical company SmithKline Beecham were searching for drugs effective against a particular kind of bone cancer. They enlisted Human Genome Sciences in Maryland to isolate some potential candidates. When Human Genome Sciences

> found near-matches for the sequences, they carried out further analyses and discovered that one sequence in particular was overexpressed by the osteoclast cells and that it matched those of a previously identified class of molecules: cathepsins. For SmithKline Beecham, that exercise in bioinformatics yielded in just weeks a promising drug target that standard laboratory experiments could not have found without years and a pinch of luck. (Howard 2000, 49)

At some point, the biological function of sequence data needs to be redetermined. It needs to be mapped back onto living bodies or some lifeform, no matter how "cultured-up" in laboratories. The level of abstraction that allows sequence data to be moved across species differences works against any *ab initio* computation or visualization of its biological function. Since the 1950s, biology has mainly manipulated actual fragments of living bodies within living systems. As Lily Kay (2000) and others have shown, despite the metaphors of code and information, nearly all important developments in biological understanding resulted from bench-work, not computation. For instance, careful biochemical assays, as well as X-ray crystallography or NMR spectroscopy, ascertained the function and shape of DNA, the amino acid sequence of proteins or the mapping between DNA codons and amino acids in protein synthesis (Kay 2000). Postgenomic science circumvents the laborious and tricky convergence between sequence and living bodies as much as possible, instead "creating a context in which certain biological components and processes may function as they do 'naturally' in vivo or in vitro" (Thacker 2004, 21). Bioinformatics suspends recourse to living bodies in laboratory systems, instead searching in the sequence databases for similar contexts.

Moving sequences into alignment with other sequences seems relatively formal and abstract in comparison to working with live cultures. However, every sequence-alignment algorithm incorporates a history of prior alignments. Editing operations such as substitution, insertion or deletion are scored accorded to matrices that distill the evolutionary likelihood of particular substitutions. Matrices such as BLOSUM (Blocks Substition Matrix; see Lesk 2002, 174–5) incorporate accumulated biological knowledge into the algorithm. In all actual algorithms, a second, more concrete spatiotemporal order shadows the abstract "hack" that orders computational time and space. Scores generated by alignment and comparison software are used to decide whether a chosen sequence might have a similar function to that of known proteins or sequenced genes, thus sidestepping much of the work of evaluating biochemical function on the laboratory bench. But this sidestep relies on the distillation of previous laboratory work encapsulated in the scoring matrix. Sequence comparison seems easy because this work has been subsumed into the algorithm.

Algorithm and enterprise

Much of this entwining of concrete and abstract orderings in algorithms is difficult to access. In the field of bioinformatics, however, the concatenation of sequence-comparison-alignment algorithms with other information retrieval systems is still proceeding and can be tracked. By annotating, cross-linking and reformatting biological information sources so that connections between them become accessible on the space of a single computer screen, bioinformatics potentiates living bodies as knowable and transformable. Bioinformatics envelops them in a field of possible transformations and substitutions of living fragments, although as a material practice ("point and click biology"), it does not get its feet wet in lab cultures. Decisions about similarity and relatedness are being resituated through enterprise-wide information systems. A new class of infrastructurally sophisticated software is adding many new connections between many biological data sources.

Bioinformatics software producers such as Lion Bioscience, InforMax, DoubleTwist, Inpharmatics and NetGenics promise enterprise-wide control over biological information in corporate research environments. NetGenics' website proclaims, for example, that "NetGenics DiscoveryCenter is a software environment that provides an integrated view of chemical and biological information held in both internal and external repositories. By providing an intuitive and comprehensive view of research information, wherever it is held, DiscoveryCenter improves decision-making in discovery research at all levels."[6]

"Discovery" is a key term here. Enterprise-wide systems figure heavily in the "new" mode of "discovery science" following in the wake of large-scale gene- and protein-sequencing projects. Many current research programs and highly capitalized projects for drug discovery, for instance, promise the detection of hitherto unknown features and properties of biological molecules through computer database searching and comparison. Computer systems, and in particular, software systems designed to integrate sequence, functional and evolutionary knowledge, have begun to abound. The names of such software—ISYS (integrated system), Ensembl, Apollo, GeneOntology, DiscoveryCenter, BioNavigator, SRS (sequence retrieval system)—highlight contemporary imaginings of fly-through, in-the-round, drill-down, scaled-up biological-knowledge synthesis.

The visual interface for expert users of these systems, often presented as either a webpage or an intricately color-coded bar graph, organizes pathways through biological information sources. Tree and list visualization of relations between different kinds of data abound. Postgenomic tools such as GeneOntology turn to hierarchical trees and data models to organize and present information. These systems, with their dynamically updateable GUI (graphic user interface) controls, anticipate direct mouse-driven manipulation. DiscoveryCenter, ISYS, GeneOntology and LionBiosciences' SRS present themselves as ways of blazing new paths between genes, proteins and chemical compounds. New research institutes crop up around new bioinformatic techniques. The Institute for Systems Biology at the Pacific Northwest National Laboratory in Seattle and the Biomolecular Networks Initiative (PNNL 2005) push towards integrating diverse kinds of biological data. At the Institute for Systems Biology, a May 2001 press release claims:

> The Institute for Systems Biology is formed around the realization that advancing biology in the 21st Century will rely on using advanced biological and computational technologies to generate and correlate many different levels and types of biological information. Unlike traditional scientific approaches that

examine single genes or proteins, systems biology focuses on simultaneously studying the complex interaction of vast numbers of biological elements. (Institute for Systems Biology 2001)

Recruiting researchers across biology, computing and astrophysics, the Institute seeks to couple different kinds of biological and biochemical information and move between them.

Efforts to link diverse biological databases strongly resemble "enterprise" information systems in domains like e-business and e-commerce, in which coupling databases and processes (customer-data warehouses, billing and auditing software, just-in-time scheduling and inventory systems, reporting systems, delivery-tracking processes, online web sales, etc.) has been the object of intense activity since the mid-1990s. Significantly, the project of building enterprise-wide systems now transpires as a new mode of doing science or producing knowledge. Haraway's (1997) phrase "Nature enterprised up" emphasizes the inseparability of business and biological problems. For instance, reflecting back on a meeting at the inception of the Human Genome Project during the 1980s, Leroy Hood (inventor of an important kind of sequencing robot at CalTech, among other things), says that the "genome introduced to biology a completely new approach, which I've since come to call 'discovery science.' It's the idea that you take an object and you define all its elements and you create a database of information quite independent of the more conventional hypothesis-driven view" (Hood 2001). The idea that sequence-driven biology could adopt a "completely new approach," which Hood calls "discovery science," underpins hopes and expectations associated with bioinformatics. Although cloning, germ-line and somatic therapy remain very problematic and hardly nearer any clear technical resolution, that kind of work—"discovery science"—has a high priority in new domains of knowledge and business.

The notion of "discovery" becomes very complicated under these circumstances. As Marilyn Strathern (1999) writes, "Euro-Americans witness on the one hand an increasing emphasis on corporealisation (biology), and on the other hand an increasing value given to conceptual or mental effort" (21). Discovery science strains to encompass an increasingly fine-grained technical plying of living processes ("corporealisation") on one hand and an increasingly mobile, abstracted set of property arrangements validating "mental effort" on the other. The torsions flow from the interfacing of mental effort embodied in the person of the researcher-corporation with living processes figured as highly distributed information systems. At the same time, as the concept of gene fragments (Keller 2000) and genetics become entwined with development biology, property relations attach intellectual legal rights to the "invention" of individual genes.

Articulating diverse realities

Like most software, enterprise biology information systems emerge from torsion between biological life and intellectual property, which articulate diverse realities. Attempts to integrate biological data—sequence, molecular shape, metabolic function and characteristics—focus on producing a locality where the chaotic merging of datasets takes on clearer shape for researchers. These systems marshal a comprehensive corpus in whose heavily annotated, cross-hatched margins many different sources of biological data can be traversed via the itinerary-making capacities of bioinformatic algorithms. At a distance from animal bodies that live and die in research facilities, and from people struggling to comprehend the implications of individualized predictive medicine, these systems reanimate biological data within the highly organized space of computer screens connected to private and public data repositories. The very design of the user interfaces, with their profusion of windows, trees, tables, lists and diagrams, suggests the potential for repeated searches, comparisons and annotations. At these interfaces, an inventor-researcher's mental effort and authorial personhood closely accompany movements across biological data. Any promising connection or similarity can be quickly named, stored and retrieved. Enterprise biology systems seek to fertilize the ground for hybridization between different data sources—a hybridization largely focused on ensuring that registered proper names and property relations stick to any new relation between (fragments of) living things. Somewhere in all the point-and-clicking at the interfaces, a moment of discovery might surface, an event that implies a new capacity for some living thing might become visible. These systems help biological-knowledge enterprises nurture, name and claim a connection that others have not yet found. In their tracking and recording of paths between data sources, in all the mechanisms for searching, labeling and annotating these systems provide, moments of invention or hybridization became nameable.

In relation to an earlier phase of heavy business/organizational informatization, Geoffrey Bowker (1994) addresses this articulation of diverse realities through the concept of "information mythology," arguing that "there is a clear link between the nature of the universe and the way to run a business. Information mythology is not an epiphenomenon generated out of thin, hot air: it describes an integral part of the economic process of ordering social and natural space and time so that 'subjective' information can circulate freely" (245). According to Bowker, recurrent claims that the universe, matter or life itself is information cannot be fully decoupled from an economic ordering of space and time accomplished over centuries (through transport infrastructure management, record-keeping and organizational practices). The more ambitious claims made for bioinformatics since the mid-1990s have been followed the slipstream of other forms of "information mythology." Following Bowker, any claim that life is information covers over the complicated social, technical, political and economic nexus where exchanges among living bodies, technical practices and economic value occur. Extending his argument figures bioinformatics as an intellectual-economic process of ordering certain abstracted determinations of living bodies (sequence data) so that information can circulate (more) freely through them. Today, any account of bioinformatics as an enterprise must countenance an intersection between the mobility of "lateral alignments" and the vertical anchoring of such movements in intellectual effort and creativity attached to property relations. Nature and business intersect there in specific ways. Most of the claims made for the potency and centrality of bioinformatics in decoding the book of life (e.g., Gilbert 1992) simultaneously concern "life itself" and how to organize property relations so that they circulate more freely through living bodies.

No doubt, bioinformatics must be understood as substantial scientific knowledge project, but its workings cannot be evaluated without reference to nature "enterprised up." Bioinformatics synthesizes social and organic spaces and times in a hybrid economic-informatic manifold. The software tools, interfaces and website portals built around the sequence databases potentiate movements. The software ensembles of postgenomic discovery science symptomatize cross-cutting collective imaginings animating contemporary biopolitical cultures. They shed light specifically on how biological corporealization and the generation of new forms of property and innovation attach themselves to movements of data, and in particular, through movements of data modulated by enterprise property relations.

Agency of algorithms

For an account of the contestations of agency associated with software, three general implications can be elicited from how bioinformatics treats sequence and order. The first concerns the process of abstraction intrinsic to algorithms. Algorithms do not simply speed up computation; they institute a composite time and space in which existing orderings and sequences are both preserved and reconfigured. Algorithms naturalize and animate order and sequence. The cornerstone problem of bioinformatics, sequence alignment, approaches living systems as a problem of where and in what order to place events or times for organisms. Dynamic programming techniques map a problem as a set of possible itineraries in a network and then generalize the itineraries to cover all possible starting points and destinations in a network. The abstraction generalizes the possible calculations and thereby makes space for many different transformations. It also makes itself generalizable, which is why the dynamic programming algorithm is said to have been discovered a number of times in different domains (operations research, bioinformatics, telecommunications and signal processing).

The second important implication concerns the entwined framings at work in algorithms. Every abstraction is relative to a concrete framing (for instance, the scoring matrices that distill previous laboratory-produced biological knowledge). Considerations of computational space and time can be found at each level of abstraction in algorithmic design, ranging from theoretical estimations of algorithmic complexity (linear, polynomial, exponential) to optimizations in the flow of code that individual programmers implement in well-known algorithms. The crafting of computational time, especially within the bounds of real-time perception, is a key aspect of this framing because it allows software to flow into everyday life. However, the time and space of computation organized by any algorithm is always caught up in conventions of positioning and sequencing. The injunction to "build an appropriate Manhattan" envisages applications of dynamic programming to other domains (for instance, signal processing in cellular phone networks), but only insofar as those domains are already imagined as spatially ordered and temporally sequenced. The incorporation of prior knowledges, codings and practices within the sequence of operations attaches specific frames and patterns to the relatively abstract space and time of algorithmic process. Just as sequence data is hardly ever treated in isolation from journal references and scoring matrices, all algorithmic processes blend historically disparate practices, knowledges and conventions. Regarded algorithmically, even the most sophisticated, distributed, multitier software is nothing other than a coalescence of positioning and sequencing conventions, some relating to social conventions, some, as in the case of bioinformatics, relating to physical processes.

The third implication concerns the points of attachment between algorithms and other movements and spaces. Algorithms are not neutral formal procedures. In algorithms that predict or correlate sequences of events in living systems, the treatment of living systems as algorithms in process is enmeshed with the broader promises of bioformatics as source of scientific knowledge and economic value. The positioning knowledge produced by bioinformatics forms an intersection between axes of biological knowledge and the political economy of biotechnology. Algorithms themselves are animated: they induce movement between inputs and outputs, and are themselves caught up in diagonal movements between biological knowledge and property value, movements characteristic of the new media biotechnology economy.

Whereas the previous chapter argued that instabilities in the mode of existence of code as expression and action set software up a field of contested agency, this chapter has proposed a second trajectory that departs from the mode of existence of code as algorithm. The contestation of agency here concerns how action is both naturalized and animated, made to seem ordinary and extraordinary. Here the contestation of agency pivots on the composite, concatenated patterns and orderings that algorithms condense. No algorithm, it could be argued, is ever safe from being transported to a different context, but neither is any actual algorithm unattached from the orderings, positionings and sequencings that increasingly weave software into environments. In the next chapter, the zone of contestation widens as we follow how code circulates on the shifting terrain of commodity hardware.

Chapter 4

Kernel: Code in time and space

The kernel of an operating system is its essential component.[1]

Martin Campbell-Kelly (2003) divides the history of the software industry between 1950 and 1990 into three phases: "software contracting, corporate software products and mass market software products" (3). These sectors developed as software production slowly drew apart from computing hardware development. In the 1950s, software was written by in-house programmers with intimate knowledge of hardware specificities. In the 1960s, it was contracted out to programming services companies, which were themselves later replaced by "corporate software products" such as the airline reservation, document and file management, banking, billing and accounting systems. Mass-market software products like Microsoft Office, Adobe Photoshop and Macromedia Dreamweaver are a more recent development, emerging sometime in the late 1970s. In a small historical irony, the first mass-market software product was a programming language, Microsoft Basic (Campbell-Kelly 2003, 205) in 1975. It was later followed by many personal computer operating systems (CP/M in 1976, MS-DOS in

1979) and applications: spreadsheets (Visicalc, 1979), word processors (WordStar, 1979), databases (dBaseII, 1980) and games (Zork, 1980). As an economic-cultural products, mass-market software for personal computers in the 1980s "had almost no connection with the existing software industry and therefore established most of its development and marketing practices de novo" (Campbell-Kelly 2003, 227).

Would that disconnect hold throughout the 1990s, when mass-market software, corporate software products and software contracting came into proximity as new forms of connection (the Internet) and generic, commodity computing hardware (the personal computer) proliferated? In the novel *Distraction*, author Bruce Sterling (2000) describes a future scenario in which the software industries have keeled over. By 2044, China has flooded the world's computer networks with pirated copies of commercial software. The American economy, long propped up by monopolistic intellectual property arrangements, has consequently collapsed. Bands of unemployed technicians, programmers and engineers calling themselves Moderators roam through splintered urban and rural zones of North America harvesting technological junk and waste products, extracting energy, discarded components and materials and recycling them into tools, energy and materials for their own use. At the center of postconsumer nomadic Moderator life stands an important infrastructural component: the servers. The Moderators' servers monitor, collate and record the status of members of the community. Individual status fluctuates in real time in response to continual server polls of the community to evaluate individual contributions to the life of the collective.

In certain respects, Sterling's scenario is not too far from some contemporary realities of the software industries. Although software developers do not in any large measure regard themselves as a disenfranchised nomadic underclass, and property rights have not collapsed (in most domains), software increasingly attracts the complex collective orderings that Sterling describes. Important sectors of software production are in migration, transnationally between the United Kingdom/Europe/the United States and Asia, and transinstitutionally between corporations, universities and loose aggregates of paid and unpaid workers. Software workers move from Asia to Europe and the United States under special immigration quotas, just as European and American companies outsource their software development to software houses in India or the Caribbean. At the same time, distributed software projects relying on networked computers generate large-scale code objects such as operating systems and web servers that leading corporate and personal computer enterprises such as IBM and

Apple take up, sponsor and promote. Individual programmers such as Linus Torvalds, Larry Wall, Alan Cox and Richard Stallman reach celebrity status within programming cultures and minor stardom in the mass media, including books, magazines and cinema.

The agency of distributed objects

Previous chapters highlighted some slippages in the distribution of agency associated with software artworks and algorithms. Those chapters assumed that code objects (in the form of artworks or algorithms) could be analytically isolated in a more or less discrete, static form. They also bracketed the question of whether code can be "intentionalized" as the product of an individual. This chapter explores a more extensively distributed object and its associated agencies, the Linux kernel, the core code component of GNU/Linux operating systems. Although at times Linux has figured as an art object (for instance, when it was awarded the *Ars Electronica* 1999 Golden Nica prize), it complicates notions of individual software production and of software as algorithm expressed in code. This chapter investigates some involutions in agency associated with the polymorphous Linux kernel.

   In many academic and nonacademic accounts, Linux is often cited as the epitome of free software or "open-source" software, a term coined by commercial software producers and computer book publishers in 1998 to dispel the more financially disturbing connotations of "free" software during the dotcom boom.[2] Linux has made the cover of *Time* (in addition to frequent editorial discussions elsewhere) and generated substantial speculative activity on financial markets during the late 1990s (Taylor 1999). It has enrolled tens of thousands of programmers and software developers in (mostly) unpaid software development projects. At the same time, Linux and the other major open-source software project, Apache, a web server, have rapidly slotted into corporate software industry at companies such as IBM, Compaq, Hewlett Packard, Oracle, Apple and Sun Microsystems. All the while, open-source software has generated huge quantities of metacommentary about software (of which this chapter forms a part), and challenged the blackboxing (the process whereby the workings of technological commodities are closed against outside interference) of commercial software in important domains. Many aspects of Linux are ripe for analysis; my discussion focuses on Linux as a distributed code object.

The problem of understanding distributed, "open" objects is not new. Alfred Gell (1998), in an innovative treatment of Polynesian funerary artworks and of artists' oeuvres (221), handles such ensemble entities— entities with components widely scattered in space and time—by attaching them to a cognitive process, itself distributed in time. The core idea is that the temporal modifications of mental states (for instance, of a social group or an artist over the years) are externalized in the relations between the objects composing the ensemble (the paintings composing the oeuvre; the gradually modified production of funerary carvings in Marquesan cultures). Echoing general findings in phenomenological investigations of time consciousness (Husserl and Brough 1991), cognitive anthropology (Hutchins 1995), science studies (Law 1994) and cognitive science (Clark 1997), but supplying a detailed model of their application to art objects, Gell argues that the ensembles in question isomorphically correspond to the temporality of cognition "writ large and rendered public and accessible" (Gell 1998, 236). Although the hypothesis that technical systems externalize human cognitions or practices is staple in new media and cultural studies (especially those influenced by the work of Marshall McLuhan (1994), Gell's detailed analyses of specific stylistic features of Marcel Duchamp's work or carvings on Maori meeting houses in terms of the temporality of cognition heads in a different direction, suggesting how collections of objects modified over time and distributed widely in space might be conceptualized differently.

From the standpoint of the temporality of cognition, code objects are not to be read as static forms, but as temporal entities made up of relations between different mental states. Code itself, as mosaic of relations (see chapter 3), carries some of the relationships that exist between mental states of its producers in time. As later discussion will emphasize, the Linux kernel, dating from late 1991, is not an original or totally new thing. It explicitly clones a well-known operating system, Unix, dating from the late 1960s. At any moment in time, as Linux provisionally stabilizes in a "release," the source code undergoes constant modification, with "patches" appearing every few days, and major releases at least every year. Spatially too, Linux is a highly distributed object. A loose corpus of source code, it consists of several thousand files organized in an intricate tree-like hierarchy (Linux Developers 2004). When compiled for execution on a particular hardware platform, these files are transformed into a single large object (the "kernel image") and a cluster of associated modules. Modifications of the kernel source tree usually concern a small number of files located along some branch. Occasionally, the tree itself is reorganized. Programmers work on specific regions of the source code, and their work is "committed" to the kernel through a series of steps moderated by "code lieutenants." The very term "kernel" (or "core") implies a centering. Even after more than a decade of development, the code that flows into the latest versions of the kernel from the work of many individuals scattered around North and South America, Europe, Southeast Asia and Australia is closely controlled by and identified with one person, the Finnish programmer Linus Torvalds.

Neither the quasi-celebrity status of Torvalds nor the relatively conventional architecture or technical features of the kernel itself constitute radical innovations. So how does something such as Linux become the object of intense feeling? How does it manage to enlist hackers and programmers to work inordinately hard on it, and at the same time become something that Wall Street, West Coast venture capital, the Pentagon, the European Union, schools in Goa, the Japanese government, antiglobalization protesters in Genoa and many other institutions, organizations, groups and individuals see as a common solution to their problems?

Exacerbating slippages in agency that we've seen code can trigger for law, life and art, the ongoing development of the Linux kernel can be understood as a partial solution to a more general problem of the relation between information infrastructures and the cultural life of software. Linux represents software-associated collective agency in the process of constituting itself in the production and circulation of code. Because coding does something, this ongoing constitution is performative. The performative constitution of collective agency associated with Linux is complex. Just as the Linux kernel coordinates and schedules computing processes in time, so too the ongoing development of Linux coordinates and schedules many different programmers' work in time. The social organization of code work, and the operating system itself as operational object, constitute a coupled process in which describing, and enacting what is described, coalesce. The earlier analysis of code as performative in relation to authorizing contexts (see chapter 2) is developed here in two key respects: code underpins the efficacy of Linux as an operational technical object, and code facilitates the emergence of Linux as a cultural formation that elicits affirmative and negative identifications on the part of programmers, consumers, institutions, organizations and corporations. Put more abstractly, the mechanism to externalize the temporality of cognition in Linux is "a self-reflexive use of reference that in creating a representation of an ongoing act, also enacts it" (Lee and LiPuma 2002, 195). Glossing Gell's suggestion that collections of objects are an index of cognition in time, it can be argued that the Linux kernel functions as an intricate indexical icon, something that recursively refers to a description of itself, and in doing so performs what it describes.

The operationality of software

Operating system software has since the 1950s provided a way to circumscribe and conceal computing hardware specificities. However, as the sociologist Scott Lash suggests, platforms constitute zones on which "technological forms of life" depend (Lash 2002, 24). Linux constitutes one such zone. An operating system operating at tens of millions of different installations, it is a particularly important platform as a server, a basic component in the construction and extension of the Internet. As in Sterling's futuristic *Distraction*, contemporary servers multiply relations in information networks because they offer services: they provide modes of access and channel data through information networks. Some servers send webpages, some receive and send email messages, some transport or stream audio or video. Dozens of protocols (IP, TCP, ICMP, FTP, IRC, SSH, SSL, and so on) regulate this movement of data (Galloway 2004). Because it quickly came to operate as an Internet server, by the 1990s, Linux inhabited a domain where contemporary problems of work, property, commodification, communication and production were played out intensely.

Like other operating systems produced by Microsoft, IBM, Sun Microsystems, Novell or Apple, Linux puts layers, many layers in fact, of code between the loosely assembled commodity hardware (CPUs, motherboards, disk drives, network interface cards, graphics and sounds cards, and so on) and the application software (web servers, databases, word-processing programs) on which users of the Internet (email, the web, UseNet) focus, using individual graphical desktop user interfaces. Linux differs from proprietary mass-market operating systems sold by Microsoft and Apple in that it spans different hardware platforms, ranging from handheld computers (Shah 2002) to game consoles (such as Sega Dreamcast and Sony PlayStation) to IBM supercomputer clusters. In the late 1990s, Linux "ports" or adaptations began appearing for many embedded or real-time platforms used in controlled noncomputing devices or systems.

Which operating system runs on a given hardware platform would not normally appear as a pressing cultural issue. Although Linux originates in the relatively affluent domains of university computer science departments, corporate IT departments and research labs, and various American software companies, in the network cultures of the 1990s (Terranova 2004) Linux quickly migrated out of the elite domains of computer science. This move is symptomatic of contemporary technological culture. Lash (2002) suggests, "In the representational culture the subject is in a different world than things.

In the technological culture the subject is in the world with things" (156). Within technological cultures, operating systems and server software become cultural by virtue of the density of the mediations and relations that run through and texture them. As culture becomes "operational," information technologies, software in particular, become more lively and convoluted. Software merges into wider circulatory practices of ordering and differentiating value. Increasingly representing and regulating differences in some ways and not others, once-infrastructural matters (like operating systems, protocols, algorithms and code) figure as singularities.

An operating system is hardly a mass medium in the sense that television or newspapers are media. Nor is an operating system a message whose content or meaning can be analyzed semiotically in the way that advertising sign-systems might be. Certainly, operating systems are branded, packaged, circulated, regulated (as in the U. S. attorney general's antitrust action against Microsoft's Windows operating system) and consumed in global mass markets. Yet at the same time, as Linux indicates, an operating system also resists reduction to a conventional commodified object. It constantly modulates as it moves through a distributed collective of programmers and system administrators. The same thing cannot be said for computer hardware. Almost without exception, computer hardware is commodified and its mass production is highly industrialized. The very existence of an operating system such as Linux, which cannot be easily located within any existing sector of the software industry, challenges the analytical distinctions among production, circulation and reception (consumption, use, spectating or audiencing) relied on by social sciences and humanities. If much social and cultural theory relies on that separation de facto, the question remains: What kind of cultural object is Linux?

Technical performance and performativity

The principal claims made for Linux—that Linux performs better than comparable commercial products of the software industry because it is "free" and produced by a loose federation of programmers—have been remarkably consistent. Leaving aside for a moment the question of whether or how Linux is free (a question that has preoccupied most analysts of free and open-source software), Linux has been and continues to be heavily figured in terms of its technical performance. Measures of the performance of software are complex, contested, and very dependent on context. In infrastructural applications, reliability is paramount. For instance, an advertising campaign for the database and "enterprise infrastructure" company Oracle claims that Linux and Oracle together are "unbreakable" (Oracle Corporation 1999). Computer companies such as IBM, Compaq, Hewlett Packard, and Dell, as well as retailers like Wal-Mart, all currently sell Linux on this basis. They market Linux to corporate and government clients. In China, where legal controls on intellectual property are beginning to be enforced as a condition of membership in the World Trade Organization, the TurboLinux distribution outsells Microsoft Windows (Turbolinux 2002). We could say then that Linux's popularity figures largely in terms of performance combined with low or zero cost. How can that performance—denoted by terms such as "unbreakable," "proven performer" (Redhat Corporation 2004) or "stability"—be analyzed without falling back on a naturalized or technologistic understanding of performance?

Technical-economic performance of the software is coupled, in ways that need to be analyzed, with performativity, a mode of constituting social agency. The technical performance of Linux is situated within a context that figures information and communication processes as the epitome of postindustrial power and productivity. The productivity of the digital economy frames any perception of the technical performance of Linux. As power becomes performative—"power itself is no longer primarily pedagogical or narrative but instead itself performative" (Lash 2002, 25)— information and communication networks become important venues in which power materializes. But what does it mean to say that a code object becomes performative? Given the many ways, sites and levels at which performativity works, and the problems of class, race, gender and sexuality for which the concepts of performativity have been most often used, how does an object like Linux participate in power?

Performativity rests on extralinguistic dimensions of linguistic praxis. The wide ranging discussions in social, political and cultural theory of performativity over the last decades (Butler 1997) have sought to emphasize this pragmatic dimension. Something speaking does something because its utterances are "redoubled" (Butler 1997, 11) by acts which cannot be fully recognized or made audible in the utterance. No statement is utterly dissociated from bodies, places or times. Although utterances sometimes have a "divine" agential effect, that is, they sometimes make things happen, such occurrences necessarily elide something attached to the utterance. As we saw in the analysis of forkbomb.pl, the practices and singularities of an authorizing context transport a speech act and lend it force. In principle, computer code, an exemplar of formal clarity and univocity, presents an unlikely candidate for performative analysis since it so emphatically abstracts from ambiguities of place, location, time and bodies. This abstraction effect depends on the production and circulation of code remaining invisible. Linux's singularity consists in how it valorizes practices of coding or programming, configuring and executing code. But its uneasy relation to different commodity hardware computing platforms remains in the background.

From the standpoint of hardware platforms, Linux would have to be understood not just in terms of the meanings ascribed to it, or in terms of operational function in moving data and information in communication networks, but in terms of how it moves across platforms. In their modified version of the concept of performativity, the anthropologists Benjamin Lee and Edward LiPuma (2002) write: "The analytical problem is how to extend what has been a speech act-based notion of performativity to other discursively mediated practices, including ritual, economic practices, and even reading. What is interesting about performatives is that they go beyond reference and description - indeed, they seem to create the very speech act they refer to" (193). What would be the Linux "act"? How does it enact the act that it represents? The technical-economic performance of Linux is an effect produced by the widely distributed practices of reading and writing kernel source code. Technical performance and being free are linked because being free means that source code is widely legible. But these linked claims about superior technical performance and being free constitute, I would suggest, only the public face of the "speech act" in question. These narrativized claims about Linux, abundantly backed up by origin stories (Himanen 2001; Lohr 2002; Moody 2001), hover above the mediated coding practices that constantly modify the Linux kernel. Insofar as it appears as free and technically superior to other operating systems, Linux succeeds as a speech act. However, the success of Linux as speech act is contingent upon another layer of performativity attached to code, to what Lee and LiPuma (2002) term "circulation": "Performativity has been considered a quintessentially cultural phenomenon that is tied to the creation of meaning, whereas circulation and exchange have been seen as processes that transmit meanings, rather than as constitutive acts in themselves. Overcoming this bifurcation will involve rethinking circulation as a cultural phenomenon, as what we call cultures of circulation" (192).

Lee and LiPuma argue that circulation also produces performative effects. That is, processes of circulation themselves objectify praxis, albeit in different ways. They enact something. If information and communication networks constitute a central venue for the performativity of important contemporary forms of power, then the circulation and exchange of software and code participate in that performativity. From this perspective, explicit claims about Linux's technical performance as they appear in advertisements, editorials, newsgroups, how-to manuals and popular press accounts spin off the primary, collective performativity of practices circulated as computer code.

Circulating, distributing and coordinating code

As an operational object, a platform, Linux literally coordinates the encounters between specific social actions pertaining to information and communication networks. Just as floor managers in an airport spend much time moving people through gates and redirecting passengers on canceled flights to ticket desks, an operating system constantly schedules, queues, allocates and reallocates events flowing across the edges of the platform through networks, peripherals, application software, mass storage devices and system users viewing their screens. At the same time, in distinction to the airport, coordinated actions centered on Linux constantly modulate it as an object in self-referential ways. A set of practices produce, circulate and consume Linux as an object distributed in space and time. Development work done by programmers on the Linux kernel gradually modifies the very platform on which they do their programming. Added features or modified versions of old ones appear at a high rate as new communication and computing hardware (CPUs, network cards, peripherals, storage devices, graphics and sound cards) comes onto the market.

These modifications affect how the ensemble itself moves around. Because it operates differently, Linux circulates differently. Each new release of the kernel (there have been dozens since 1991) performs and circulates slightly (sometimes substantially) differently because features have changed or been added. New hardware configurations, new communication protocols and new kinds of connectivity are merged into the kernel. Each modification of the kernel potentially extends its circulation and thereby heightens the coupled effects of technical performance and political-economic freedom. A feedback loop between technical performance and performativity mentioned above plays an important role in the life of Linux because it triggers constant modulations both in the object itself and the practices associated with that object. Linux gains increasing traction as a platform partly on the basis of the high-level linguistic performative ("Linux works better because it is free"). Yet that traction itself relies on the performativity of the practices associated with Linux.

The agential effect of performatives rests on their capacity to objectify some kind of praxis, most often linguistic practices, but also as Lee and LiPuma argue, circulatory practices. This objectification, however, only succeeds provisionally or partially. Judith Butler writes:

> If a performative provisionally succeeds (and I will suggest that "success" is always and only provisional), then it is not because an intention successfully governs the action of speech, but only because that action echoes prior actions, and accumulates the force of authority through the repetition or citation of a prior and authoritative set of practices. It is not simply that the speech act takes place within a practice, but that the act is itself a ritualized practice. What this means, then, is that a performative "works" to the extent that it draws on and covers over the constitutive conventions by which it is mobilized. (Butler 1997, 51, italics in original)

Could the analysis of performatives extend to the repetition or citation of a prior authorizing set of practices in software? How would attending to "repetition or citation" found in Linux afford understanding of its circulation? What is cited or repeated? What is covered over? What extra purchase would the idea of the partial workability of performatives provide in understanding the distribution of Linux?

"Distros": Repeating and citing Linux

A salient feature of Linux is its propensity to circulate source in many different forms and versions. At one end of the contemporary spectrum lie distributions of the kernel source code as artwork. For instance, an online and radio broadcast performance of Linux occurred during the first half of 2002 called "RadioFreeLinux" (Radioqualia 2002). The performance consisted solely of the source code (the program as written and read by programmers) of the Linux kernel (the central part of the operating system that interfaces between hardware and applications) being read, line by line, over various radio and streaming web-radio sites.

As in the software artworks discussed earlier, in making the source code visible or in this case audible, "RadioFreeLinux" signals a change in the status of code as "source code." On the one hand, Linux is free because it is available to be copied and distributed under the terms of the GPL license. It is often given away on the CD-ROMs bundled with popular computer magazines. On the other hand, source code possesses to a greater or less

degree some social or cultural value apart from economic value. The title of
the work, "RadioFreeLinux," suggests that source code could circulate or be
broadcast like radio news. This piece is not an isolated aberration. In 1999,
Linus Torvalds was awarded a significant new-media art prize at *Ars
Electronica* art festival. Linux had almost become an object whose
distribution in time was being recognized:

> The Jury of the .net category awards the 1999 Golden Nica to Linus Torvalds as
> representing all of those, who have worked on this project [Linux] in past years and
> will be participating in it in the future.... It is also intended to spark a discussion
> about whether a source code itself can be an artwork. (ArsElectronica 1999)

Art-show prizes are somewhat problematic forms of recognition and
certainly should not be read as unequivocal seals of cultural value. However,
they do prompt the question, What does it signify when source code
becomes an artwork, as in "RadioFreeLinux" or the kernel itself? Given that
source code for programs has been around for at least fifty years, why has
source code only now become something which people want to "read"?

At the other end of the spectrum, early in 2002, Sony announced that it
was releasing a version of Linux for the game console PlayStation2 (PS2).
Typically, gaming development environments, such as ProDG for the
PlayStation, cost between five and ten thousand dollars for restricted
developer licenses (SN Systems 2002). Sony itself licenses games
development in order to control the quality of the games commercially
released for the console. In a shift of licensing policy, Sony announced
Linux for PlayStation by saying:

> The PlayStation 2-specific libraries will be released under the LGPL; there are no
> proprietary licenses involved. Sony's distribution of Linux is based on Kondara,
> which in turn is based on Redhat. The documentation with this kit will give all the
> same information about the PS2 hardware that Sony provides its licensed game
> developers (but it won't give access to the system's anti-piracy mechanisms). This
> will include full details on the PS2's proprietary Emotion Engine core instruction
> set, the Graphic Synthesizer, and the Vector Processing Units. (Wen, 2002)

The migration of open-source code onto the proprietary hardware PS2
platform is not unique. As mentioned above, Linux has been ported to many
different proprietary hardware platforms, ranging from PDAs to
mainframes.[3] This announcement points to something else. Sony's
distribution of Linux is based on a Japanese Linux distribution, Kondara,
which in turn is based on Redhat: Linux exists in many different "distros" or
distribution versions. Kondara and Redhat distribute or repackage the Linux

kernel along with associated software. While it is possible to visit various websites and FTP servers (Linux Developers 2004), download the source code and compile it to build a complete operating system, almost all contemporary users of the Linux kernel adopt one of the many Linux distributions, such as Redhat, Mandrake, Debian, SuSe, or Gentoo. Distributions emphasize different features. Often distributions recirculate an existing distribution in a somewhat modified form. Kondara modifies the Redhat distribution to adapt it to the hardware specificities of PS2. The PS2 distro figures as just one of around at least a hundred different commercial and noncommercial distributions of Linux (Distrowatch 2002). Some of these, such as PS2 Linux, have the specific purpose of making a hardware platform more widely programmable and less of a blackbox. Some concentrate on particular application domains, such as "desktop users." The European Commission-funded Agnula distribution focuses on sound and music processing (Agnula 2004). Others have specifically a national or language focus: Turbolinux focuses on selling Linux in China and was the first Linux distribution to provide Chinese language support (Turbolinux 2002). New distributions of Linux appear and sometimes disappear at a high rate.

The Linux kernel exists in multiple incarnations, ranging from an art-like radio broadcast, to a quasi-proprietary platform-specific Sony distribution, across dozens of branded distributions, all linked back to some version or release of the kernel source code itself, widely available on websites, FTP servers, CD-ROMs and DVDs. Linux circulates as artwork, as a commercially packaged commodity sold by many different companies, and as freely available source-code files, constantly worked on and exchanged using sophisticated software mechanisms of coordination, scheduling and organization, mechanisms usually running on Linux servers.

Linux: An object out of control?

Commercial distributions, it could be said, have largely come into existence as a way of capturing the "free labour" (Terranova 2000) embodied in Linux. Without violating the GNU (an acronym for GNU is not UNIX) Public Licenses (GPL, a legal document specifying conditions under which the code can be copied, altered and distributed) attached to the Linux kernel, new and established software industry companies such as Redhat and IBM effectively give away Linux distributions, but charge for support services needed to configure and maintain them in operation (Taylor 1999). At the same time, work on the various components of Linux continues, and the changes constantly made to it by numerous programmers are successively incorporated into new releases of the commercial and noncommercial distributions. The economics of this process were subject to strong stock market speculation during the late 1990s (Taylor 1999; Redhat Corporation 2004) and extensively analyzed by academic researchers (Tuomi 2000).

The Internet-based coordination mechanisms that permit collective development work on the kernel have been described in both semipopular and academic accounts of open source (Moody 2001; Bezroukov 1999). The analytical problem lies in connecting the circulation of Linux in dozens of different distributions to technical performance and the performativity of Linux as code ensemble. Distributions permit Linux to transit between hardware platforms and between cultural, institutional and national domains. Each new distribution and each successive release of an existing distribution incorporates and repeats the conventions embodied in the Linux kernel, but adapts those conventions to a slightly different situation: a different hardware platform, a different language grouping, a different kind of computing task (supercomputing, office productivity, e-commerce transactions, genomic sequence searching and alignment, etc.).

Social and cultural studies of science and technology (Latour 1996; Haraway 1997) have sought to analyze why certain contemporary technological objects are "out of control," why they generate unexpected consequences. They attract unexpected levels of investment, financially and affectively. They percolate into popular culture, and they proliferate at an unexpectedly rapid rate. Technical objects like Linux become unstable and proliferate as a consequence of the translation or objectification of social and cultural relations into and through them. Lash (2002) argues that such objects get out of control as an unintended consequence of modern rule-regulated reflexivity, which "involves the reflexive monitoring of the object by the subject, in which the subject subsumes the object under rules.... The more we monitor the object, the more the object escapes our grasp.... This moment of contingency, where the object, or the self, escapes the cognitive categories of the subject, is indeed aesthetic" (50).

From this perspective, the Linux kernel can be understood as a heavily matted web of rules, conventions, standards and protocols pertaining to information and communication networks, as well as specific features relating to commodity computing hardware. The conventions range from the electronic clock-based timing disciplines on which binary logic circuits rely through to the highly conventional protocols for transactions and messages on the information networks. The latter are defined by regulatory and standards organizations such as the ISO (International Standards Organization), the W3C (World Wide Web Consortium), the IEEE (Institute for Electrical and Electronic Engineering) and ANSI (American National Standards Institute). The conventions and protocols on which nearly all computer code relies attempt to subsume information systems under rules that render those systems inspectable or reportable—so, for instance, Linux "aims for POSIX (Portable Operating System Interfaces) compliance" (Linux Developers 2004).

Does the spectrum of conventions explain Linux's proliferation, its propensity to "escape our grasp"? If, as in the earlier quote from Lash, "the more we monitor the object, the more the object escapes our grasp," it could also be added that the object's escape from "the cognitive categories of the subject" is not an accident or a result of risk and uncertainty. Rather, monitoring the object necessitates its circulation. The analysis of the performativity Linux hinges on this point. The kernel code "succeeds" as a performative to the extent that in connecting commodity hardware and convention-governed movements of information, it also makes a social arrangement for the ongoing production of code.

What Linux covers over

Ultimately, the line between code object (the kernel) and code subject (the hackers and programmers centrally personified in Linus Torvalds) wavers. As Linux became publicly visible during the 1990s, hacking or programming with or on Linux came to be seen as a form of life that challenged norms of property ownership and corporate organization of work (Moody 2001; Himanen 2001). This style of programming is not confined to free or open-source software projects, but also affects digital, knowledge and information economies and new media more generally (see Terranova 2004). As Linux began to spin off versions and distributions, it exceeded the prerogative of any individual to control its meaning. The agential effect of performativity arises first through repetition and citation, and Linux repeats itself across platforms and in different contexts.

Performatives work not only by citing, or enacting through describing, but by also "covering over," as in my earlier quote from Butler, the "authoritative set of practices" that lend force to what they do. What "authoritative set of practices" or "constitutive conventions" does Linux cover over? The "authorizing context" is the set of conventions and practices whose repetition lends a performative act its force. Judging by what was said in advertisements, in newsgroups or in editorials and essays about Linux since the mid-1990s, there would be some justification in seeing the history of Linux as a technical object and commodity as brief, linear and uncomplicated. Around November 1991, the Internet first began to enter into public awareness, so the history of Linux is often presented as a consequence of the coordination and circulation of code that the Internet permitted in the late 1980s and early 1990s (Moody 2001). Because source code could be uploaded and downloaded from FTP servers via dialup modem lines and PCs, source code circulated much more rapidly and widely than in the 1970s and 1980s, when only institutional and corporate computing facilities had network access. Available fresh source code was mentioned and discussed in UseNet newsgroups such as computers.os.minix.

However, as mentioned earlier, Linux clones an earlier computer operating system, Unix. By copying or citing Unix, Linux sediments a complicated relation to proprietary hardware and software. But Unix was and remains not just another piece of software dating from the late 1960s; it adapts and continues a set of coding, software design and system administrative practices sometimes referred to as the Unix philosophy. These could well amount to an authorizing context for Linux, but Linux's authorizing context is complicated since Unix combines regulatory practices and coding-hacking practices (Salus 1995) quite distinct from the norms and patterns of the software industry of the 1960s–1980s (Campbell-Kelly 2003). As an event, Linux is temporally complex or distributed in ways that the popular narratives of invention (Himanen 2001; Moody 2001; Lohr 2002) somewhat occlude.

Kernel archive sites (such as ftp://ftp.kernel.org) show that Linux has been through dozens of major release cycles and hundreds of minor patches or updates. A file of a few hundred kilobytes in 1991 grew to thirty-four megabytes by mid-2004. Analyzing how Linux begins to accumulate agential force means asking what that growth involves and covers over. One side of Linux faces back towards Unix as an authorizing set of practices, but the other faces towards the Internet, the digital economy and proliferating new media.

Authorizing context I: Interaction and economy

The README textfile found in every release of the kernel source code since 1991 begins:

> "WHAT IS LINUX? Linux is a Unix clone written from scratch by Linus Torvalds with assistance from a loosely-knit team of hackers across the Net. It aims towards POSIX compliance" (Kernel 2002). In compressed form, this description points to almost all the elements that need to be held together in order for Linux to materialise. First of all, although "written from scratch," Linux heavily cites another operating system or software platform, Unix.[4]

All distributions of Linux currently circulating and performing with various degrees of commercial and noncommercial success are versions of systems loosely grouped under the name "UNIX," "a Trademark of the Bell Telephone Laboratories" (Kernighan and Ritchie 1978, ix). Unix itself dates from the summer of 1969, when two computer scientists (Dennis Ritchie and Ken Thompson) at the Bell Telephone Laboratories in New Jersey developed an interactive operating system. Although there may be other elements and practices within the authorizing context from which Linux draws its performative force, it would be hard to argue against the centrality of the Unix philosophy.[5]

The Unix philosophy is precisely the heterogeneous mixture of practices, names, strictures, conventions and habits characteristic of any performative nexus. By the early 1990s, when the Linux kernel first appeared, Unix was widely used at universities and research institutions in North America, Australia, Asia and Europe. Why was it so popular? The technical lineages of operating systems and the constant trade-offs and exchanges between academic computer science, computer manufacturers, U. S. military research funding, telecommunications companies and the software industries are detailed in Salus (1995). The first academic report on Unix by Dennis Ritchie and Ken Thompson (Ritchie and Thompson 1974) emphasized the combination of the power of "interactive use" and economy in relation to hardware ("equipment") and labor ("human effort"): "Perhaps the most important achievement of UNIX is to demonstrate that a powerful operating system for interactive use need not be expensive either in equipment or in human effort: UNIX can be run on hardware costing as little as $40,000, and less than two man-years were spent on the main system software" (Ritchie and Thompson 1974, 365, italics in original).

The "interactive" character of Unix stemmed from a "desire for programming convenience" (Ritchie and Thompson 1974, 374), rather than any predefined operational or conceptual objectives for the system. In other words, the kind of work that programmers do pervaded the design of Unix. Not only were the features and functionality available in Unix suited to programmers, Unix was itself coeval with a particular programming language, C, which became an academic and software industry standard language. C, not coincidentally, is used to write Linux code. In contrast to many other commercial operating systems of the time, Ritchie and Thompson explicitly set out to design a system for programmers' convenience. Unix's design was shaped by two major abstractions. These abstractions strongly affect not just the design of Linux, but also how it has grown and circulated. The notion of everything (printers, keyboards, diskdrives, network connections, displays, other programs or users) as a "file" (Kernighan and Ritchie 1978, 2) and the notion of "the process," plus many discrete tools and utilities for accomplishing specific programming and system development tasks, still pervade Linux. By the early 1990s, just before Linux emerged, Unix was in widespread use. A standard undergraduate textbook on operating systems of the time, Tanenbaum's *Operating Systems: Design and Implementation* (1987), writes: "UNIX has been moved ('ported') to more computers than any other operating system in history, and its use is still rapidly increasing" (11). Unix migrated to many different hardware platforms because of its specific architectural features, the "file" and "process" abstractions and the loose assemblage of software tools. Consequently Unix forms a constitutive convention for clones such as Linux, Minix, HP/UX, A/UX, and others.

The history of distribution of Unix lies at a complicated conjunction of organization of capital, state regulation of communication, and the technical work of programming. Unix's circulation between 1969 and 1983 was also strongly affected by an antitrust case initiated in 1949 by the U. S. Department of Justice against Western Electric and AT&T, companies that jointly owned Bell Telephone Laboratories. Between the first public release of Unix in 1971 and 1983, AT&T had been bound by the terms of a 1956 court judgment to distribute UNIX at a nominal fee to anyone who wanted it. As a telephone company, AT&T was legally prohibited from profiting from computer software. As a result, AT&T provided no support and no fixes for bugs in the system: Unix was "unsupported." As Salus (1995) writes, "The decision on the part of the AT&T lawyers to allow education institutions to receive Unix, but to deny support or bug fixes had an immediate effect: it forced users to share with one another. They shared ideas, information, programs, bug fixes, and hardware fixes" (65). However, in 1983, a second antitrust action (similar to the one mounted against Microsoft in various

North American and European jurisdictions between 2000–2004) divested AT&T of the Bell Operating Companies and thereby changed the status of Unix. In the aftermath of the second antitrust action, the newly formed AT&T Bell Telephone Labs, no longer legally a part of a telephone company, could license Unix and set any price. The charge for the all-important source code rose steeply, to the order of several hundred thousand dollars, and prohibited the source code from being studied in university courses (Salus 1995, 190), where Unix had been a standard teaching platform for computer science students.

Unix existed for a long time as software that U. S. government legislation prohibited a telecommunications company from commercializing, so AT&T Bell was compelled to give Unix away for free. At the same time, because there was no maintenance support, adopters of Unix did their own maintenance and development, turning Unix into an experimental and pedagogical platform used to teach computer science students about operating systems during the 1970s and 1980s. Because it came with and was written in its own programming language, C, Unix was highly mutable and reconfigurable: computer scientists used it to explore new protocols, data structures and hardware architectures. Unix was crucial to infrastructures of networked computers in the late 1970s, infrastructures that grew during the 1980s into the Internet. One fundamental layer of Internet communication protocols, TCP/IP, was first incorporated into Unix in the late 1970s, mainly through military research funding (Abbate 2000, 133). Since the 1980s, these protocols have come to almost universally regulate the flow of data between hosts or servers on the Internet by providing a way to connect many computers and order the movement of data between them without making many assumptions about the content or internal structure of the data.

Authorizing context II:
Coordinating and communicating

One primary component of the authorizing context underpinning the performativity of Linux code comes from the highly contingent mixture of abstractions, practices and legal arrangements associated with Unix as a noncommercial pedagogical-experimental platform. These practices intimately linked producers and users/consumers of operating systems. Given that Unix had, as Tanenbaum's textbook states, already been ported to more platforms than any other operating system in history, what was at stake in having it cloned by hackers? Linux bears the marks of Linus Torvalds's close reading of Tanenbaum's academic textbook on operating systems during 1990. In the mid-1980s, Tanenbaum, a computer science academic in Amsterdam, wrote a Unix clone called Minix as a companion to his textbook and in order to teach students about Unix without incurring AT&T's newly imposed licensing fees (the Minix source code was available for a small fee). Thus, by 1990, as an undergraduate computer science student at Helsinki University, Linus Torvalds himself had access to a pre-existing clone that could run on an Intel-based PC, and a textbook that gave a complete account of the architecture of the Unix operating system. But why then did Linux come into existence, given that Minix already ran on personal computers and provided Unix-style computing to almost anyone, students included? Tanenbaum's Minix (which had tens of thousands of users) was designed to support teaching about operating system design. It downplayed hardware specificities to keep the system simple and easy to understand and was only slowly enhanced to deal with a wider range of hardware devices. If Minix emerged in response to the licensing restrictions on Unix source code, Linux was defined in relation to the proprietary nature of commodity hardware.

There resides the second crucial component of the authorizing context undergirding Linux's performativity. Linux, according to Torvalds, was also a "program for hackers by a hacker" (Torvalds 1991), just as Unix was, according to Kernighan and Ritchie, a system by programmers for programmers' convenience. The first pieces of code recognizable as Linux were experiments with a particular feature of the Intel 80386 chip called "task-switching." In a 1994 interview, Torvalds said, "I was testing the task-switching capabilities [of the 80386], so what I did was I just made two processes and made them write to the screen and had a timer that switched tasks. One process wrote 'A,' the other wrote 'B,' so I saw 'AAAABBBB.... Gods I was proud over that" (Moody 2001, 36). Although a clone of Unix, Linux took root as a test of the task-switching capabilities of the i386 family of microprocessors produced by Intel, capabilities that themselves borrowed ideas from interactive or time-sharing software such as Unix. Why was task-switching of interest? The "process," one of the fundamental abstractions in Unix and in computer science more generally, lies at the core of Unix's shape-shifting portability. By using the task-switching capabilities of the Intel platform, Torvalds could build a concrete implementation of the fundamental "process" abstraction. With that in place, Unix culture could move off the industrial and academic hardware platforms on which it had been developed to commodity consumer computing hardware. In its grafting onto mass-produced consumer computing hardware, the conventional object Unix metamorphosed into something more dynamically distributed. Linux promised to uncouple mass-produced commodity computing hardware from mass-market software, by opening a window onto the authorizing context embodied in Unix.

In Linux, a new mode of commodity consumption occurs through coding: the proprietary hardware specificities of different computational devices and peripherals are addressed in a demarketized form. The first release of the kernel in late November 1990 contains a warning about relations to proprietary devices: "LINUX 0.11 is a freely distributable UNIX clone.... LINUX runs only on 386/486 AT-bus machines; porting to non-Intel architectures is likely to be difficult, as the kernel makes extensive use of 386 memory management and task primitives" (Torvalds 1991). The proprietary features of hardware are often not documented in technical manuals published by semiconductor manufacturers such as Intel. So, in the first publicly released version of Linux, a key piece of code in the "main.c" file sets the operating system time from a hardware clock:

```
/*
 * Yeah, yeah, it's ugly, but I cannot find how to do this correctly
 * and this seems to work. If anybody has more info on the real-time
 * clock I'd be interested. Most of this was trial and error, and some
 * bios-listing reading. Urghh.
 */
#define CMOS_READ(addr) ({ \
outb_p(0x80|addr,0x70); \
inb_p(0x71); \
})
Kernel 0.11, main.c (Kernel, 1994)
```

As the code comments say, this is "ugly" material because information about how the Intel 80386 CPU hardware clock works is not readily available. The lines of code are executed when the operating system starts up. They actually refer to some other lines that relate to hardware specificity. If we trace the line "outb_p(0x80|addr,0x70);" to its definition in another source file, we find it defined as:

```
#define outb(value,port) \
__asm__ ("outb %%al,%%dx"::"a" (value),"d" (port))

#define inb(port) ({ \
unsigned char _v; \
__asm__ volatile ("inb %%dx,%%al"::"=a" (_v):"d" (port)); \
_v; \
```

})

kernel 0.11 /include/asm/io.h (Kernel 1994)

The code becomes even uglier and less easily readable. The increasing illegibility shows something important. These instructions read and write to specific spatial locations on the Intel x86 family of CPUs: the input/output (IO) ports. Some of the very first lines of the Linux kernel are very closely tied to the deeply embedded specificities of the Intel 80386 chip. Frustrated by the opacity of the hardware, Torvalds comments, "I cannot find out how to do this correctly."

If the process abstraction was key to Unix programmers' convenience and its implementation on consumer computing hardware, the other Unix abstraction, "everything is a file," was essential to the growth of Linux. During early 1991, postings on newsgroups such as comp.os.minix soliciting programmers to work on Linux were framed in terms of the difficult specificities of hardware devices. Here is Linus Torvalds, inviting people to work on what would later be called Linux:

> Do you pine for the nice days of minix-1.1, when men were men and wrote their own device drivers? Are you without a nice project and just dying to cut your teeth on a OS you can try to modify for your needs? Are you finding it frustrating when everything works on minix? No more all-nighters to get a nifty program working? Then this post might be just for you :-) (Torvalds 1991)

This first announcement and call for volunteers—"men"—focuses on the all-night pleasures of low-level system programming of "device drivers," the parts of an operating system that speak to specific pieces of hardware rather than higher level abstractions. The mention of a time when "men ... wrote their own device drivers" presumes, first of all, a time when men had access to the device in question. Since then, as the source code for the kernel has grown from a few hundred kilobytes to approximately tens of megabytes in size, code that addresses thousands of proprietary device specificities (CPUs, graphics cards, audiovisual, network and storage devices) has been added to the system. Releases of the kernel encompass widening circles of commodity hardware and consumer electronics such as set-top digital video recorders. As Linux is ported onto different platforms, new hardware specificities have to be addressed. Assumptions about hardware specificities built into previous versions of the code have to be rendered explicit and then moved out of shared code into specialized areas. As widening streams of kernel code encircle new proprietary hardware specificities, a patchwork of subprojects and parallel development fold into the kernel.

A final facet of the constitutive conventions at work in the performativity of Linux should be mentioned, although it has not been explicitly theorized or developed in this chapter. The Linux kernel is deeply tied to a gendered corporeal set of practices of programming work. The mention of "all-nighters," of a time when "men wrote their own device drivers," reminds us that Linux is above all a program by men for men who like to play with computing hardware. The specificity of the commodity computer hardware for which Linux hackers write device drivers correlates directly with the desire to "modify an OS for your [own] needs." Anthropologically speaking, these desires remain somewhat unexplained.

Moderating the movement of code

A condition of China's entry into the World Trade Organization is strengthened regulation of intellectual property law. The growth of Linux in China and its recent adoption by the Beijing city government (TechCentral 2003) suggests that some of details of the opening scenario from Sterling's *Distraction* might miss the mark. However, the broader point of his narrative probably does hold: a transformation in the organization of material culture is signalled in the emergence and dynamism of code-objects such as the Linux kernel. If a shift from a register of meaning to one of operationality (Lash 2002, 216) is underway, operationality will need to be understood not in mathematical-technical terms but as an articulation of diverse realities.

The Linux kernel raises the problem of how software exists as object distributed in time and space. Background to the question of distribution comes from more general accounts of the operationality of "the information order" (Lash 2002, 4) or of network societies (Castells 2001). The Linux kernel displays symptomatic features of the material culture of information. The technical performance of Linux versus other operating systems is a matter of endless contestation. Its capacity to enact what it represents or describes, however, depends on an isomorphism between distribution of work and distribution of code. The proliferation of distros, sites, enterprises, products and designs associated with Linux attests to that circulatory force. This analysis of Linux treats the action of software as an effect of patterns of circulation, in space and time, patterns that modify code in a double-facing cognitive process that synthesizes Unix's authorizing conventions with a proliferation of commodity digital hardware. Linux stands at the confluence of coding practices in academic research and software industries (embodied in Unix) and the large-scale production, circulation and consumption of computers as consumer electronics.

Extending performativity from spoken or written texts to technological objects is not new. Sociologist of science Bruno Latour implicitly relies on a concept of performativity when he writes, "Programs are written, chips are engraved like etchings or photographed like plans. Yet they do what they say? Yes, of course, for all of them - texts and things - act. They are programs of action whose scriptor may delegate their realization to electrons, or signs, or habits, or neurons" (Latour 1996, 223). In claiming that "programs" do what they say, Latour attributes performativity to objects because they "realize" specific social actions. The complicating gloss that Linux adds is that realizing "programs of action" is provisional and open-ended in both time and space.

The concept of circulatory performativity developed in this chapter examines an objectification of social praxis accompanied by a collective subjectification. Augmenting the claim that objects act and speak by virtue of delegation, the performativity of a culture-object such as Linux might be further glossed as a partial solution to a problem of social identity or authority for information elites. Caught between highly commodified hardware production, the stringent regulation of intellectual property and an ethos of free-wheeling experimentation with and collaboration on code, hackers seem to have radically reorganized some things—the production and consumption of software—and stabilized others (gender norms, for instance). Linux constitutes a partial solution to the problem of how different authorizing contexts coming from the quasi-academic ethos of Unix computing and its coding conventions, proprietary licensing of software, the plethora of commodity computing hardware and protocols for networking can be articulated together. It remains a partial solution since the programming collective has been unable, for instance, to overcome limitations in regard to gender. The obvious feature of Linux in this respect —the credits listing is almost without exception male—shows that performativity synthesizes some things with great novelty but keeps others static.

Chapter 5

Java: Practical virtuality

To abstract is to produce the plane upon which different things may enter into relation. It is to produce the names and numbers, the locations and trajectories of those things. It is to produce kinds of relations, and relations of relations, in which things may enter.

Wark, *A Hacker Manifesto* 2004, §083

Until now my treatment of software has proposed that code, the primary material of software, becomes an involuted nexus connecting people, platforms, reading and writing conventions, power, law and creativity, distributed in space and time. If this nexus or knot holds, it ties people together, but not seamlessly, effortlessly or without tensions. In association with wider claims, hopes, expectations, fears and speculation about communication, media, democracy and capitalism, some twists in this knot around software became visible during the 1990s. I turn, then, to argue against the "software repressive hypothesis" found in many accounts, academic and nonacademic (Lohr 2002; Ullman 1997; Campbell-Kelly 2003). According to the software repressive hypothesis, software remains invisible, infrastructural and unspoken, although it should be brought to light (Graham 2004). In contrast, this chapter explores the "steady proliferation of discourses," as Foucault (1984, 302) put it, emerging around software. These discourses of software have specific forms and objects that reconfigure the code nexus and permit different attributions of agency to software.

In the early to mid-1990s, new media associated with the Internet sometimes appeared as "spaces or places apart from the rest of social life ('real life' of off-line life), spaces in which new forms of sociality were emerging, as well as bases for new identities, such as new relations to gender, 'race,' or ontology" (Miller and Slater 2000, 4, italics in original). Examples of new media and ordinary life in separation came from cyberpunk fiction, popular books (Rheingold 1994), cinema (*The Matrix, Strange Days*) and early academic work on cyberspace (Heim 1993). Theories and versions of the virtual—virtual community, work, identity, classes, time, space, gender, cultures, society—flourished in attempts to analyze the "newness" of new media. Manuel Castells, in one of many examples, wrote that virtuality is "a system in which reality itself (that is, people's material/symbolic existence) is entirely captured, fully immersed in a virtual image setting, in the world of make believe, in which appearances are not just on the screen through which experience is communicated, but they become the experience" (Castells 2000, 373). On the basis of that separation, a radical discontinuity between identities, bodies, relations and ontologies associated with old and new media could be postulated.

From the standpoint of 2003, the post-dotcom crash and 9/11, understanding the Internet (including email, Usenet groups, chat rooms, IRC, MUDs/MOOs) as something separate from other economic, cultural, media and political processes seems plainly inadequate. Today the principal objection to such notions of virtuality is precisely their tendency to separate experience of new media from another world, the real or ordinary world of social, cultural, economic and political activity. This widely voiced objection can be found in semipopular accounts of new media (Mitchell 2003) and in academic treatments. Miller and Slater (2000) write, "By focusing on 'virtuality' as the defining feature of many Internet media and then moving on to notions such as 'cyberspace,' we start from an assumption that it is opposed to and disembedded from the real" (4). In the main, notions of the virtual now look like exaggerated representations of certain relational potentials of computer-mediated communication. As more recent studies of new media have shown, the identities, relations, politics and ontologies associated with new media are not radically different or disembedded, but intimately interconnected with older media, older institutions, places, spaces and forms of sociality. Instead of insisting on the virtual, new media assume the Internet is no more transcendent than markets, nations, cultures, institutions or identities.

If the equation between new media and virtuality was mistaken, obfuscatory or hype, what motivation remains for an analysis of virtuality in software? Since the mid-1990s, an alternative theoretical understanding of virtuality has gradually surfaced, and although subject to much misunderstanding, it continues to extend its scope and relevance. Principally associated with Gilles Deleuze's thought (and elaborated in Shields 2003; Lister et al. 2003; Grosz 1999; Delanda 2002; Massumi 2002; Rodowick 2001; Lévy 1998; Wark 2004), in this new understanding, the virtual designates something real that involves an unstable relationality or difference. As Rob Shields (2003) writes, "The virtual troubles any simple negation because it introduces multiplicity into the otherwise fixed category of the real. As such the tangible, actually real phenomenon ceases to be the sole, hegemonic examples of 'reality'" (21).

Virtuality in this theoretical sense has no necessary connection with information systems, new media, digital technologies or the Internet. Shields discusses virtuality in art, economics and religion; some writers strenuously resist the equation between virtuality and digital technologies. The cultural theorist Brian Massumi (2002), responding to over-enthusiastic identifications of digital technologies with virtuality, argues, for instance, that

> nothing is more destructive for the thinking and imaging of the virtual than equating it with the digital. All arts and technologies, as series of qualitative transformations ... envelop the virtual in one way or another. Digital technologies in fact have a remarkably weak connection to the virtual, by virtue of the enormous power of their systematization of the possible. (137)

This concept of virtuality as something that continually generates divergences highlights the need to think in terms of ongoing processes of transformation. This definitely seems relevant to software and new media. Even in its mundane sense, "a reference to the virtual includes future states as a part of the real" (Lister et al. 2003, 361). The virtual typically concerns open-ended or incomplete processes, as when someone says "I'm virtually finished." The open-ended temporality of contemporary code-objects has already been mentioned (chapter 4), but here open-endedness, as potential novelty and as a sense of something about to be completed, appears in a different form.

The trajectory of a specific quasi-technical process of "virtualization" began in the mid-1990s. In examining this trajectory, rather than transposing the concept of the virtual from cultural theory or philosophy onto new media, I undertake some "fieldwork in philosophy," as Pierre Bourdieu termed it (quoted in Rabinow 2003, 84–5), via Java, a programming language and software platform dating from the mid-1990s. Virtuality, I would argue, is a practical project of detachment, lifting-out or disembedding actions from existing social, organization and communicative contexts—a project that produces new forms, practices, interpretations and subjectifying effects in response. The process of abstraction in Java code and programming, as we shall see, removes or brackets some things (such as hardware or operating system specificities), but makes other relations possible.

This case study draws on diverse materials, including ethnographic observation of programmers and software developers; the "grey literature" of technical specifications, programming manuals, tutorials and magazines; the software tools and development environments associated with Java; and some of the many published interviews, news and opinions concerning Java's significance. As per Marcus (1995), my discussion will treat materials in terms of the "chains, paths, threads, conjunctions or juxtapositions of locations" (105) that link them. While questioning any direct equation between new media and the virtual, in following these chains I explore how a specific case of virtuality entails both abstraction or separation and constitutive incompleteness, open-endedness, relationality and forms of attachment. My methods are influenced by recent social studies of science and technology (Latour 1993; Haraway 1997) that treat technical concepts, objects or practices as hybrid social-material entities to be investigated by following the "thing" as it shifts contexts, changes in status, enters into a variety of discourses and practices, and is subject to distinct modes of participation and circulation. Consequently, rather than identifying the virtual as an abstract concept, fieldwork in practical virtuality needs to ask how processes of abstraction have been implemented, interpreted and resisted.

Code as practical virtuality

Dating from 1995, the Java Virtual Machine and the Java programming language (together known simply as Java) gradually gathered more and more components, enrolled millions of programmers, was embedded in all the major web browsers, and triggered imitations and competitors (such as Microsoft's .NET products). In 2003, Java was being built into approximately twenty million mobile phones per month (according to some sources), came preinstalled with every copy of Windows and Mac OS, was found running on most web servers, and was distributed in various more esoteric forms (such as smart cards). Java is the standard programming language taught to university computer science students. While it would be difficult to exhaustively list the applications of Java, the breadth and variety of its circulation suggests that Java embodies a concentrated scaling-up of a particular kind of technical mediation (Latour 1996) within contemporary new media and information cultures. Although technologies as objects or commodities have been black-boxed, branded and marketed for a long time, Java, as we will see, is not so much a single thing, object or media, but an unfolding, bifurcating, loosely held ensemble of practices, imaginings, logos, knowledges and artifacts.

In this "Internet programming language" (a description that designates when Java was produced), an explicit technical concept of the virtual is central. "The Java Virtual Machine," declares the *Java Virtual Machine Specification*, "is the cornerstone of Sun's Java programming language. It is the component of the Java technology responsible for Java's cross-platform delivery, the small size of its compiled code, and Java's ability to protect users from malicious programs" (Lindholm and Yellin 1996, 3). More technically, the virtual machine at the core of Java can be defined as a "collection of resources that emulates the behaviour of an actual machine."[1] This definition of a virtual machine emphasizes a "collection" of things and a relation to an "actual" machine. Extrapolating from the technical definition, Java's virtuality involves more than collecting or emulating: it has become a site of attachment for people, practices, products and events.

In the assemblage of code, trademarks, documents, technical models and abstractions, categories, standards, practices and events collectively named "Java," software infrastructures, coding subjectivities and differences of rhythm and speed provisionally coalesce. As in the Linux kernel, they remain partial or incomplete solutions to problems of agency associated with software. This provisional stabilization of identity and platform/infrastructure is akin to the "fluid organizational form" of "permanently beta" described in Neff and Stark (2004). In the sense that it is never finished—always undergoing modifications, fixes, updates—much commercial and free software is in a beta state. "Practical virtuality" differs from "permanently beta" in that it does not rely on a formal notion of variability or on explicit organizational strategies. The dynamics of new media, I would argue, are not always driven by organizational design or by formal attributes, but by irreducible slippages between discourses and practices. Somewhat paradoxically, the abstraction associated with notions of the virtual (both in new media theory and software engineering) turns out to be highly relational, contingent and grounded in practice. The practical virtuality of Java begins from the minimalist technical computer science definition of the virtual as a collection of resources emulating the behavior of an actual machine, and progressively encompasses resonances and interactions between a widening circle of actors. "Virtualization" of the virtual is problematic: the process of lifting out and disentangling connections brings new configurations connected to other realities.

Software as variable ontology

Critics of first-generation accounts of cyberculture such as Miller and Slater (2000) rightly insist on the relation between new media and social context. In Java's case, however, what counts as context is hard to decide. While it can be situated within the history of the software industry (Campbell-Kelly 2003) and the Internet (Abbate 2000), its ongoing development and circulation make it difficult to adopt a purely historical perspective. Too much is still in flux, and without detailed archival work, any brief history of Java risks repeating quasi-journalistic accounts that attribute all agency to key human actors (e.g., Lohr 2002); such accounts should themselves perhaps be objects of analysis. More importantly, in principle, context alone cannot necessarily reveal the specificity of an object regarded as a multiplicity characterized by unpredictable slippages. Context can just as well obscure that specificity by reducing it to a set of familiar terms, meanings, representations or narratives.

If it is not possible to isolate Java as an object, it might be more productively approached as a project. From the standpoint of important strands of contemporary science and technology studies, the shifting ontological status of some things—especially epistemic objects that are both the object of knowledge and technical work (Rheinberger 1997)—complicates any simply notion of context or object. In the process of formation, sociotechnical objects constantly contextualize and decontextualize themselves. Java is a typical variable-ontology object or project (Latour 1996, 173). The term "variable ontology" suggests that essential nature of the entity is unstable. Questions of when and where it is social or technical, material or semiotic cannot be conclusively answered. Even after almost ten years, Java continues to be in formation, and this ongoing process is explicitly part of its constitution. In other words, it is made to be constantly in the process of making itself. For instance, in 1999, at a point relatively late in its rise to popularity, the Java-centric view of new media projected itself well beyond the desktop and screen, as *JavaSpaces: Principles, Pattern, and Practice* reveals:

> By early in the new millennium, a large class of computational devices—from desktop machines to small appliances and portable devices—will be network-enabled. This trend not only impacts the way we use computers, but also changes the way we create applications for them: distributed applications are becoming the natural way to build software. "Distributed computing" is all about designing and building applications as a set of processes that are distributed across a network of machines and work together as an ensemble to solve a common problem. (Freeman, Hupfer and Arnold 1999, 2)

The ambiguities of the last sentence are relevant: not only was Java designed with a view to ongoing changes in information devices and networks, it is conceived as changing the way software is designed and built. The "common problem," the problem to which the practical virtuality of Java responds, is how to make software move around in ensembles of machines. In order to lift itself out of localized contexts, the Java project takes on different kinds of reality, it moves between social and technical registers, and it participates in an ongoing process of contextualization and decontextualization rather than circulating as an inert, stable object.

The trademark of a variable ontology project is difficulty in saying what something is once and for all. Java has long exhibited this trait. In the early 1990s, a software product group at Sun Microsystems in Palo Alto, California was working on Project Green. The software was designed to control entertainment appliances such as video games and television set-top boxes and to allow appliances to communicate with each other. Project Green had involved the design and implementation of a platform neutral programming language, initially named Oak and later changed to Java (Gosling 1995, 1). Oak aimed to overcome the obstacles that the proprietary specificities of commodity electronic hardware put in the way of programmers. If programmers were writing programs for mainframe, mini- or microcomputers, the computing environment was relatively familiar and well-defined, according to widely shared conventions of relatively few operating systems. But during the 1980s, when programmers began to develop software for new programmable devices proliferating in consumer electronics, domestic white goods such as refrigerators and washing machines, communications and entertainment equipment, bugs multiplied. Oak, the new lingua franca, was going to simplify the complexities of existing programming languages like C and C++ and would furnish a new computing platform to smooth over some mundane but tricky pitfalls of programming embedded devices. The vision of many different consumer electronic devices with embedded computers continues in ideas of ubiquitous computing over a decade later (for instance, in the JavaSpaces literature cited above, but also in the Mobile Java technologies) and finds current echoes as computer hardware manufacturers such as Intel and Dell move into consumer electronics.[2]

In the mid-1990s, just as first-generation studies of new media and cyberspace were appearing and the notion of virtuality as radically distinct from the real was most heavily discussed (Heim 1993; Rheingold 1994), the technical problem of platform-specific code that Project Green had addressed reappeared in the guise of disparities between computing platforms increasingly networked together by the Internet. Project Green was newly relevant to the Internet. The new rationale for Java, as told by one of the principal product engineers at Sun Microsystems, James Gosling, in a technical white paper from 1995, substituted "network" for "consumer electronics":

> JAVA was designed to support applications on networks. In general, networks are composed of a variety of systems with a variety of CPU and operating system architectures. In order for a JAVA application to be able to execute anywhere on the network, the compiler generates an architecture neutral object file format—the compiled code is executable on many processors, given the presence of the JAVA runtime. (Gosling 1995, 1)

This goes well beyond anything envisaged in Project Green a few years earlier: Java applications "are able to execute anywhere on the network." A strong challenge to the prevailing mode of existence of software was implicit in this recontextualizing claim. If software applications can execute anywhere on the network, then they are freed or decontextualized from the notoriously localized configurations and specificities of hardware.

Much programming practice and system administration work tries to cope with the problems of platform specificity. An application written for Unix in the language C++, for example, has to be rewritten for Windows. Photoshop users on Windows might have a slightly different version than those on Macintosh because programming teams have trouble synchronizing their work. A game written for Sega's Gamecube will not run on Sony's PlayStation. Many technical innovations and workarounds are used by software developers, system engineers and users to circumvent the obstacles posed by the differences between commodity hardware platforms. These solutions often involve rewriting or modifying software code at some level.

These difficulties might have remained largely invisible to the world outside software development if Java had just offered a practical solution. But when Sun Microsystems trademarked the phrase "Write once, run anywhere," they made a stronger claim.

Solving the problem of the platform?

New media forms such as the web, text-messaging, online gaming and email depend on hardware and software platforms. However, relations among media forms, practices and platforms are often in flux. Technological platforms like Windows or Macintosh tend to define themselves as "lifted-out" spaces (Lash 2002, 24). Platforms are singular sites in certain ways, which can put them at odds with attempts to ground the Internet as a domain of practices and discourses embedded in "real social interactions." Java complicates the picture because it figured itself as a metaplatform, a space lifted out from the already-lifted-out spaces of the Windows, Mac or Unix platforms. The promise of a metaplatform was directed at software developers, not general consumers or markets for hardware or software. Although Java has made many headlines in mainstream newspapers and periodicals from 1995 to date, the core platform components were not directly sold to consumers.[3] From the outset Sun Microsystems freely licensed the basic tools and the Java Runtime Environment or Java Virtual Machine (Sun Microsystems 2005d), while retaining fairly strict control over the later evolution of the language. Issues of commodification, property and branding in software production will return later, but my key point about the "Write once, run anywhere" trademark is that it promised something of practical significance to writers of computer software. The act of writing software, a complicated, highly labor-intensive activity, was detached from one existing context, the proprietary computer platform. As we will see, the program changed, too, becoming an "architecture-neutral object" rather an architecture-specific one.

Changes in programming work associated with Java became more significant only after the advent of another software platform, albeit of a different kind: the graphical web browser. Java's migration from consumer electronics to Internet programming language navigated a narrowly technological but critical passage via the web browser. In 1995, browsers, still relatively new (the first, Mosaic, was released in 1993), could only display static text and static images. Many newspapers reported at the end of that year that Java was going to solve the "problem" of static web content:

> The most significant technical development of the year was Java, an "object-oriented, interpreted, architecture-neutral programming language" according to its developer Sun Microsystems. That understated and unglamorous description hides the real power of Java, which will allow small programs—called applets—to be embedded in Web pages, giving them a life of their own. (Azeem 1995, 12)

If small Java programs or applets could be embedded in webpages, then webpages need no longer be static. The Java-enhanced web browser could execute downloaded programs on the fly without any prior installation or configuration of those programs by a user. This capacity depended on an agreement by Netscape, the makers of Netscape Navigator, to implement and incorporate a Java Virtual Machine, a substantial and sophisticated chunk of code, into Netscape Navigator, a proprietary product. Microsoft reluctantly followed soon after, licensing Java for their Internet Explorer. Unfortunately, the promise of animated, audiovisual, interactive webpages did not really come to fruition in Java. Many difficulties beset Java applets (speed of the virtual machine, download time for Java applets, reliability, incompatible implementations of the virtual machine on different platforms). Today Java applets are relatively uncommon on webpages, even though they have technical capabilities that parallel those of the far-more common Flash animations.

Nevertheless, the promise to programmers of "Write once, run anywhere" became visible in the context of the struggle for domination of the browser market. We could say that in transmuting into a web browser plug-in, Java formed part of an assemblage that included the practices of web browsing and the burgeoning domain of the web itself. The proprietary differences between consumer electronic devices were no longer the central problem; executing "anywhere on the network" was no longer the grand vision. Rather, the linkages between the new medium of the web—with all its associated promises of interactivity, accessibility, hypertextuality, and redistributions of authorship—gave Java visibility as a metaplatform, a singularly lifted-out space amid all the other potential lifted-out spaces.

Installing and implementing everywhere

Java initiated a variation in the mode of existence of software and developers as related to a crucial element of new media's technical context: the platform. First, platform specificity was no longer to be an obstacle to the circulation of computer code. Code's new mode of existence was "architecture neutral" and thereby gained a certain provisional autonomy from existing proprietary platforms. Second, programming work changed. The "write once, run anywhere" branding of Java promised new mobility for software and software developers. Not only could their code move more freely, but software developers themselves could transition more smoothly between projects. By suspending or "neutralizing" proprietary platform specificities, Java gained credibility as a metaplatform; by entering into a domain of intense cultural-technological change, the browser wars of the mid-1990s, Java gained credibility as a coding practice. The advent of Java, which could have been just another of Silicon Valley's innumerable software product releases, became significant in the market contest between Netscape's and Microsoft's graphical web-browser products. At the same time, Java's capacity to alter the mode of existence of programs and to change the character of the technical practices associated with programming required Java, at least initially, to enter that highly contested domain.

As a project involving practices of virtualization rather than virtuality per se, Java could not be completed. As mentioned previously, Java couples a programming language and a platform or software system called the Java Virtual Machine (JVM). Two technical documents published as separate books formally describe these entwined entities: the *Java Programming Language Specification* (Gosling, Joy, and Steele 1996) and the *Java Virtual Machine Specification* (Lindholm and Yellin 1996). Although neither makes much sense without the other, the language and the machine have different modes of existence, and they circulate in different ways.

A significant asymmetry exists between Java as a platform-neutral architecture or abstract machine and Java as a programming language. On the one hand, according to the *Java Virtual Machine Specification*, "The Java Virtual Machine knows nothing of the Java programming language, only of a particular file format, the class file format. A class file contains Java Virtual Machine instructions (or bytecodes) and a symbol table, as well as other ancillary information" (Lindholm and Yellin 1996, 4). Leaving aside technical terms such as "class file" and "bytecode," this quotation explicitly decouples the programming language Java from the JVM: the JVM "knows nothing" of Java the language. On the other hand, the JVM, the specification later continues, "was designed to support the Java programming language" (Lindholm and Yellin 1996, 1). The platform was designed to support a programming language it "knows nothing" about. The coupling between the programming language and the platform, even an architecture-neutral platform such as the abstractly defined JVM, runs from the language to the machine, but not in the opposite direction.

The Java Virtual Machine, or the Java runtime, as it is usually known, was vital to Java's Internet programming claims. Java's promise to programmers that they could write code in Java for different platforms relies on the Java runtime being installed wherever the code is going to run. But this installation presupposes an implementation of the virtual machine. The question of implementation has been a sore point in the installation of Java. In order to retain maximum platform neutrality, the *Java Virtual Machine Specification* remains highly formal in its description of the JVM. The technical specification states: "This book specifies an abstract machine. It does not document any particular implementation of the Java Virtual Machine, including Sun's" (Lindholm and Yellin 1996, 5). The motivation for this level of abstraction is simple. Since different kinds of devices have different technical capacities, "the Java Virtual machine does not assume any particular implementation technology or host platform.... It may also be implemented in microcode, or directly in silicon" (Lindholm and Yellin 1996, 5). Many divergent implementations of the JVM arose in the late 1990s: Java-on-a-chip, JavaOS, JavaPC, PicoJava, Java smart cards, as well as the many implementations of Java for PCs, mainframes, workstations and most notoriously, in the form of Microsoft's implementation for the Windows operating system.

In principle, this arrangement was intended to keep several layers of code apart. Firstly, the programming language Java was to be decoupled from a software platform, the Java Virtual Machine. Secondly, the JVM, an "abstract machine," was to be separated from any particular implementation on a particular operating system or hardware system. Neither of these could be completely accomplished. Although the JVM was in principle supposed to "know nothing of the Java Programming Language," in practice it soon became apparent that in order to work around the various limitations and problems of getting Java code to perform effectively in specific applications, programmers would have to know something about the way the JVM executed code. Programming websites, magazines like *Dr. Dobbs Journal* (DDJ 2005) and *JavaWorld* (IDG 2005), and many books (Cadenhead 2004) were quick to furnish explanations, tutorials, tips and tricks to help deal with performance problems. At the same time, working from the opposite direction, it also became desirable that actual JVM's should know something about the code they were executing. In the late 1990s, in response to long-standing complaints about the speed of the Java Virtual Machine on certain kinds of computation (graphics processing in particular), the leading implementations of the JVM produced by Sun, IBM and Apple began to heavily feature "just in time" and "hotspot" compilers. These compilers measured what parts of the program were being executed most often and "precompiled" those parts of the program to ensure their faster execution. Such highly technical innovations, remaining largely black-boxed inside the JVM, responded directly to the widespread perception among programmers and software developers that the performance of code written in Java could not compete with code written in other languages such as C or even Perl. The separation between the layers—of language, abstract machine and actual machines—were being distorted and blurred. Implementations became shaped by what programmers wanted to code in Java, and programming changed in response to the specificities of Java implementations.

Finally, Microsoft's version of the JVM for Windows operating system diverged in subtle ways from the abstract machine in the *Java Virtual Machine Specification*, which led to Sun to litigate in U. S. courts. The installation of the JVM as a default component of Windows was the crucial issue. Microsoft's decision to include either a nonstandard implementation or no implementation succeeded, according to U. S. District Judge J. Frederick Motz, "in creating an environment in which the distribution of Java on PCs is chaotic."[4] Microsoft's innovations only highlighted that the coupling between Java and commodity computing hardware was abstractly defined, and that Java as an actual, executable code object was inherently unstable.

Books, screens, machines and networks

My earlier argument that software performativity is circulation-based can be developed further here. As a way of writing and running software, Java circulates code across different scenes or surfaces of writing (paper, screen, computer chips, web articles and help sites). In contrast with the Linux kernel, where the interplay between a collaborative Unix philosophy and the momentum of constant commodity-hardware innovation cause code to circulate, in Java's case the process of abstraction called virtualization generates the agential effect of Java software. A performativity centered less on technical performance (in execution speed, Java software has often been judged slower than software written in other programming languages) than on code mobility arises from this circulation.

The Java Virtual Machine and Java programming language impose constraints on the circulation of Java, constraints that played an important role in legal struggles. But the problematic separation between programming and executing Java code also drives Java's practical virtuality. The abstract specifications of the programming language and JVM were reworked and reinterpreted. Interpretive communities (Fish 1980) were built around structured circulations of code and particular forms within code. Cultural processes of circulation linking an object (JVM), artifacts dependent on that object (programs or executable code), and the embodied skills of programmers began to coalesce around the abstract specifications of the language and the Java Virtual Machine. Rather than remaining black-boxed, unrelated abstractions as defined in the specifications, both the programming language and the JVM became complex circulating forms from which other projects, promises and contexts constantly spun off. Sifting through the avalanches of press releases, newspaper and magazine articles, online editorials and website discussions of Java since 1997 gives some indication of the broader scope of circulation associated with Java. As the JVM was installed—unevenly and with frequent updates during the late 1990s—and the Java programming language became known more widely, an "interpretive community" grew up around the relatively abstract forms defined in the Specifications.

One space for interpretive community resides in the gap between Java as machine and Java as language; the gap between architecture and code necessitates circulation of several different kinds. Java had not only to be learned by programmers, it had to become a matter of embodied skill or even habit. To facilitate this, the syntax, lexical structure (the keywords, characters, operators, and separators such as brackets) and idiomatic expressions in Java programs were selected to appear very familiar to programmers. Explaining the design of the new programming language, Java language designer James Gosling wrote that "even though we found that C++ was unsuitable, we tried to stick as close as possible to C++ in order to make the system more comprehensible" (Gosling 1995, 2). While it was diverging from the economically and technically significant programming language C++ on key technical issues in order to fulfill the "Write once, run anywhere" promise, Java was also mimicking C++ through its syntax and lexical structures. Through pastiche, the borrowing of elements from other writers or texts, the JVM could both support a familiar-looking language and yet "know nothing" about it. Existing knowledge of C and C++ syntax could recirculate through Java.

Pastiche is not unusual in programming language design. New languages often explicitly cite features from older, well-known programming languages to make the new languages easier to learn. Popular web-programming languages such as Perl pride themselves on openly borrowing the best features from many different languages (Wall 1999). But the citational practices in Java run deeper and structure a second level of circulation. Not only is the language syntax itself a pastiche of C++ (and other languages, such as SmallTalk and Modula), but writing Java code relies heavily on a controlled form of pastiche. One technical term for this is "code reuse." Another is to say that the language is "object-oriented." The term "object-oriented" is used in varying senses by software engineers and computer scientists. Sometimes it refers to a design metaphor that understands programs as sets of objects with "state and behavior": "an object is a software bundle of variables and related methods" (Sun Microsystems 2005c). More concretely, Java programs are structured around invocations of existing pieces of code (objects) organized in a class hierarchy descending from a single generic class at the top called "Object." "The fundamental unity of programming in Java is the class," write the language designers, Ken Arnold and James Gosling (Arnold, 1998, 29). Each class of objects inherits attributes and behaviors of classes above it in the hierarchy and adds new variations to them. Programming work in Java often entails deciding whether a pre-defined class offers the desired behavior, and then either invoking instances of that class in a program or extending that class by creating a modified version of it (Gosling, Joy, and Steele, 1996 128−133). If no class offers the desired the behavior, programmers must define a new variant of an existing one.

In the process of finding which pieces of code can be recycled, Java programmers spend a lot of time trawling through the application-programmer interfaces (the APIs) that define the pre-existing classes, looking for desired behaviors in the class hierarchy. The APIs are available in printed form (Chan 1999; Flanagan 2002) or more widely as a large collection of online HTML files (Sun Microsystems 2005b). Once programmers have learned Java syntax, much of their programming work revolves around reading APIs and drawing together different pieces to construct a useful program. If there is a commonly interpreted text underlying the production of Java code, it includes not only Java language syntax and idioms, but also, as a central component of that text, the class hierarchy documented in the APIs.

Unlike the relatively static and formally defined Java programming language, since 1998 the APIs have expanded significantly in response to the increasing specialization of computer software. Java code has migrated into different places and onto new kinds of platforms partly because of that expansion. For instance, in 1998, a large class hierarchy named "Swing" was incorporated into Java API (Sands 1998). This class library contained highly configurable and carefully designed graphic user interface (GUI) components so that Java programs could be developed with the kinds of user interfaces seen in Windows-style desktop computing software. At a time when Java applets were losing their appeal, the Swing components significantly increased the complexity of the Java APIs, providing a contemporary look and feel to the visual interface (and hence the functionality) of the Java Virtual Machine. Like many other specialized additions (SQL database connectivity, CORBA functionality, XML capabilities, XML parsing, etc.), these components positioned Java in the rapidly changing domains of Internet and web innovation, albeit at the cost of increasingly fragmenting the technical knowledge-base of Java programmers.

By 1999, it had become difficult for any programmer to know all the Java APIs. Hefty computer how-to books multiplied explanations, examples and tutorials that simultaneously explained and promoted particular aspects of Java. By virtue of the citational practices associated with Java (syntactical pastiche and API code reuse), Java programming forms an anchor point for practices of reading and writing code that extend well beyond the onscreen frame of the code editor and the development environment of the programmer. The APIs solidify and modulate Java both as a coding practice and as a heavily marketed software platform. The slippage between the specific implementations of the JVM and Java language functions not so much as a lacuna as a site of metastability in which sociotechnical problems are posed and receive solutions. In this sense, practical virtuality consists in ongoing incompleteness.

Programmers: Agents of (new media) history or new consumers?

Software developers' fascination with cutting-edge software systems is well known (see Ullman 1997). But this fascination has drawbacks, principally that they will never finish learning software or programming languages, only tire of keeping up with the latest variations. Because of ongoing innovation in languages, libraries and platforms, Java programmers and software developers constantly need to relearn the systems they are programming. Ethnographic studies of professional Java programmers at work observe them frequently shifting between onscreen and printed resources, and between onscreen windows (Ó Riain 2000). One of the windows is likely to be open on an integrated development environment (IDE), a key piece of software that combines text-file management, code analysis, software building and other forms of programming assistance. Several dozen competing commercial and noncommercial IDEs (Borland Jbuilder, OptimalJ, IBM Visual Age, IntelliJ, Visual Cafe, VJ++, Sun One Studio, NetBeans, Eclipse, etc.) are available to professional and nonprofessional Java developers (*JavaWorld* 2003).

An analysis of how Java IDEs are used to code and integrate Java programs with other software would help extend the concept of virtuality to the social relationality of coding work. The "organizing devices" (Button and Sharrock 1996) that IDEs contain augment the processes of pastiche and citation. IDEs automate certain code-development tasks so that programmers do not need to remember exact sequences of steps or look up the exact syntax of a particular code construct. For instance, "code insight" devices automatically suggest possible completions of program code in the same way that auto-spell features on word processors suggest possible word completions. API documents are often available at a keystroke, so writing code and reading about existing reusable code become closely related operations. Often, the designs of complicated software devices (code repositories, check-in/check-out mechanisms, automated build or "make" tools) envisage programmers working in teams more easily. Version control mechanisms and code repositories manage problems of conflicting versions of code. More sophisticated IDEs, such as IBM's Websphere, contain miniature models of Internet infrastructural components like web servers and databases.

Beyond automating mundane manual sequences of keystrokes and onscreen scrolling, IDEs lie on a continuum spanning many other documents, websites, journals, training programs, product launches, trade shows, conferences and even specialty cruises,[5] all of which circulate, promote and marketize practices, detailed knowledge and visions concerning Java. While software production has long been an object of management planning (Campbell-Kelly 2003), Java arguably represents the first occasion on which coding work itself became an object of intense marketization. There are a number of significant facets to this circulation that all cluster around the question of marketization of programming itself. Annual conferences, such as JavaOne, held in San Francisco, are heavily publicized within the software industry. The participants at these events (fifteen thousand in 2003, but up to thirty thousand in previous years) largely come from commercial or corporate IT departments, software industry and the computer trade press. Heavily funded by corporate sponsors such as Sun Microsystems, these conferences combine product promotion, vision statements and training sessions in new or difficult parts of the Java API. Speculations on the future directions that Java will take, and how significant Java is to ongoing processes of technological innovation are legion. Vision statements typically suggest to Java programmers how significant their work is. At a 2003 conference, Sun's CEO, Scott McNealy, announced, "The big message is that it is no longer cool to write for the operating system.... You don't write to Windows or Linux or Solaris or Macintosh. You write for the Java Web services layer. It is so last millennium to write for the operating system."[6] McNealy claims that by coding in Java, Java programmers become agents of contemporary innovation: coding in Java, they inhabit the new millennium. In his understanding, programmers are agents of cultural and technical innovation, subjects of history.

Constant (usually less grandiose) solicitations run through the many ancillary publications devoted to Java. For instance, the monthly online magazine *JavaWorld* (http://www.JavaWorld.com) has been publishing articles on Java since March 1996. Some are introductory tutorials written for beginning programmers, while others publicize recent or forthcoming extensions of Java to new platforms or applications. Often, articles focus on a specific facet of the Java language and demonstrate how it can be applied to a "typical" programming situation. The definition of what counts as typical is highly fluid. An article from 2003 bears the title "A Do-It-Yourself Framework for Grid Computing: Learn to Build Your Own Grid Computing Application Using Open Source Tools" (Karre 2003). Given that it is not likely that average Java programmers will be involved in implementing grid computing applications (the large-scale software installations discussed in previous chapters that network thousands of machines ranging from PCs to supercomputers; the most famous example is SETI, the Search for Extraterrestrial Intelligence, running on half a million PCs), why would *JavaWorld* tutor its readers in how to construct them? Despite the fact that it massively exceeds the typical programmer's purview, grid computing is seen as a way to take the Internet a step further. The article explains how this might be done: "Driven by the success of the SETI project and others like it, researchers have been working to exploit the vast pool of computing resources connected to the Internet, but in a way that is secure, manageable, and extendable" (Karre 2003). Many articles like this one imply that by reading and experimenting with the demonstration applications or code fragments described in the article, programmers become participants in transformations "about to" occur in the Internet. The "vast pool of computing resources" in the quote above hints at these potentials.

In the incessant updating of technical knowledge associated with a bewilderingly wide field of possible applications of Java, programmers and software developers become skilled by accessing training materials found in the trade press, public institutions of higher education, hobbyist magazines and corporate education facilities. In the late 1990s, Java quickly became the teaching language of choice for introductory undergraduate computer science courses at universities across the United Kingdom, Europe, the United States, Australia and Asian countries such as India. Academic teaching departments were quick to respond to the appeal of Java to students as "the" Internet programming language. Academic authors promptly produced programming textbooks based on Java (such as Rowe 1997). These books merged into the stream of trade books flowing from publishers such as O'Reilly, SAMS, and Addison-Wesley; academic books are sometimes hard to distinguish from trade books.

At the same time that Java programmers were being trained in universities and colleges, the identity of "Java Programmer" was being scaffolded by proprietary certification. For instance, the Sun Java Programmer Certification Program administers tests of coding knowledge at Sylvan Prometric testing centers located in major cities around the globe (Sun Microsystems 2003a). At these testing centers, programmers pay a substantial fee to have their knowledge of Java tested through a series of multiple-choice questions downloaded via satellite from a central testing center in the United States. If they answer 85% correctly, they receive a certificate, Java lapel badges and permission to use the Java logo on their business correspondence. These somewhat banal souvenirs receive kudos from some Java programmers. Achieving Java certification tends to be the ambition of younger programmers without much industry or commercial experience, whose employment prospects are uncertain. In user groups, news lists and websites, debate intermittently arises over the value of certification,[7] over the value of "real" experience versus book knowledge. Underlying both sides of the debate is a commitment to the distinct identity of the Java programmer, an identity shared and reinforced through the very act of debate.

Sites of attachment

At the nucleus of the involutions of agency associated with Java, stable and inert textual forms like the *Java Programming Language Specification* and *Java Virtual Machine Specification* remain relatively untouched. As forms, circulation changes them slowly. The Java language only added a small number of keywords from 1996 onwards. The JVM has changed little in specification, although implementations have proliferated. The trademarked promise "Write once, run anywhere" links these singular, relatively abstractly defined forms of Java. Paraphrased, the promise reads, "Write code in Java, and wherever a Java machine is, the code will run." Yet a gap remains between the language and the virtual machine that the trademarked promise does not totally bridge. Bowker and Star (1999) write, "All classification and standardization schemes are a mixture of physical entities, such as paper forms, plugs, or software instructions encoded in silicon, and conventional arrangements such as speed and rhythm, dimension, and how specifications are implemented" (39). Java both confirms this point and complicates it. Although they face each other, the "conventional arrangements" in question here (Java the language and Java the virtual machine) and the attributes of particular implementations (speed, rhythm, dimension such as memory usage) remain in indeterminate and metastable relation. The JVM and Java language are not the same thing at any level. The differences, gaps and frictions between them constantly defer the fulfillment of the write-once, run-anywhere promise, which consequently remains virtual itself.

Another level of circulation attached constantly expanding Java APIs and diversifying JVM implementations to these relatively stable forms of the virtual machine and programming language. Certain aspects of new media culture became "hotspots," attracting a lot of Java programmer interest and coding work during the latter years of the 1990s. Sometimes, that interest became so intense that it led to changes in the form of Java or in some aspect of the work done with it. Java, as we have seen, owes something of its survival to the browser wars. Even as problems with Java applets were appearing, new facets of the Java platform were developed. New points of attachment or identification became available to programmers. If web-based applets were the front-end application that elevated Java to semipopular status via the graphical web browser, Java servlets were the infrastructural software components that allowed increasingly complicated dynamic institutional and corporate websites to move away from the ad-hoc CGI (Common Gateway Interface) Perl scripts that prevailed during the early 1990s. Like many other pieces of software infrastructure associated with growing popularity of the Internet and the advent of e-commerce, Java servlets and Java server pages (JSP) allowed websites to be integrated with existing software such as databases and transaction processing systems. They changed the nature of the programmer's work by abstracting web programming from HTML scripting using built-in code templates. Java developers and software architects quickly found well-remunerated employment during the late 1990s, in part because servlets offered organizations a more easily managed process of implementing complex database-driven websites.

The character of the JVM implementations changed correspondingly. JVMs for specific purposes such as running servers or enterprise-wide functionality appeared. The industry-standard Java Enterprise Edition combined a number of different Java components into a package that could be used for enterprise-wide applications (Sun Microsystems 2003b). These components were themselves incorporated into software industry products for the web (such as IBM's Websphere) or into open-source projects (such as Apache Foundation's Jakarta Tomcat project). Migrating inwards from the publicly accessible side of corporate-institutional websites, Java percolated through the burgeoning and perhaps commercially important structures of business process re-engineering and business-to-business (B2B) applications.

In sum, the relatively stable circulating forms of the Java language and virtual machines are heavily ornamented by layers of documents, manuals and tutorials that modulate the primary layer of installation, implementation and code production. Many different pieces of software such as IDEs were designed to facilitate the writing of Java code. Beginning with graphical web browsers, crucial platform-specific implementations of the JVM were or are being made available by different vendors such as Sun, IBM, Apple, Microsoft, Redhat, and others. Around these relatively slowly evolving entities circulates a much more rapid kaleidoscope of claims, counterclaims, promotions, conferences, press releases, court cases, books, journals and even souvenirs associated with Java. These repeatedly flow back through Java coding practices and the operational deployment of the Java Virtual Machine. None of this occurs without attachments or identifications between Java as a branded artifact and software developers: their work—what they read, the code they write and the things that matter to them—directly affect how Java circulates in the networks of contemporary new media cultures.

Virtuality overcomes separation?

Java is perhaps the most widespread programming language of the Internet (albeit in heavy competition with other languages, proprietary and nonproprietary, such as PHP, Perl, C# and Python). It begins as a variable ontology technosocial project, a programming language coupled to a chunk of software, the JVM. Where this project could anchor itself was uncertain. Initially tethered to the web browser, it successively bifurcates and differentiates as it takes code along new pathways. The pursuit of platform neutrality exposes new sites of attachment and enrolls new practices and processes of consumption and production that modulate Java in turn. The project constantly absorbs innovations arising from its intensively marketized interpretive communities. It unfolds through technical yet deeply cultural processes of circulation associated with coding, networks and machines. Because it remained metastable, always holding out a promise of still-to-come cross-platform compatibility, Java accompanied and at times led the waves of innovation and change that visibly and invisibly channeled information flows during the last decade. Java remained open to divergent realizations, and Java articulated diverse realities together.

What is generalizable from this case study for the purposes of an ontology of software? The simple equation between virtuality and digital technologies that characterized some mid-1990s accounts of the Internet seems hardly tenable anymore. In retrospect, it appears that partial and relatively narrowly understood aspects of online communication were mistaken as total transformations of existing social relations and identities. Struggling to ground an explanation of shifting patterns of communication and sociality, many analyses of new media were premised on a radical disjunction between the virtual/digital and the actual/analog and treated virtuality as a new ground, substance or space. In so doing, however, they ignored some very real continuities and structural elements connecting new media to other social, economic and cultural processes. While remaining wary of universalizing concepts of the virtual, we nonetheless need to explain how a more semiotically limited, technically defined abstraction gained traction. In main, this chapter affirms the virtual as something real, inseparable from the real world(s) of social relations, groups, institutions, production, politics and identities associated with changes in the mode of existence of software: Java enacts processes of virtualization that link software production to the ongoing development of new media and information technologies.

Deeply entwined with the media-multiplicity of the Internet, the process of virtualization by definition cannot be fully completed, no matter how many specifications and implementations of virtual machines appear. The virtuality of Java removes obstacles that proprietary computing platforms pose to the networked flows of information and the mobility of code. As seen in previous chapters, the problem of the platform underlies many debates around software and new media because platforms support technological forms of intellectual property, commodification and identity. Java's virtuality promised crucial contemporary labor, to lift software development out from the proprietary spaces of the operating system platform. It offered software programmers the powerfully attractive opportunity to release their work—the product and the act of their work—from platform specificities.

The practices of experimenting with, building and maintaining Java software suggest that virtuality is more abstract, open-ended and provisional than envisaged in strident proclamations and denials of the technological-virtual identity. In his evaluation of the ongoing usefulness of the concept of the virtual, Robert Shields writes:

> Today's tight connection of the virtual to the digital hardware and software is a new form. It represents a return of "the virtual" in our social activity. Some would just dismiss the term as an overused and underdefined label. However, this ironically recognizes that, at a minimum, "the virtual" is one of the most important marketing terms for the high-tech sector which is claimed to drive the development of a putative high-tech, knowledge-oriented "virtual society." (Shields 2003, 19)

At a minimum, the marketing and strong branding of Java, key adjuncts to its virtuality, need to be analyzed. In its branding of the virtual as "Write once, run anywhere," Java uncouples some connections between digital hardware and software. It does so at the cost of slippage, a critical metastability between Java as platform and coding language that allows other structured circulations to come into orbit around Java.

The attribution of agency to Java code is complicated by these slippages. Usually, software works or does something independently of how the code was written. With Java, that separation between production and consumption comes into question. "Show the world your enthusiasm and support for the value Java technology brings to everyday products and services with this NEW Java 'Get Powered' logo!" suggests Sun Microsystems (Sun Microsystems 2005a). The origin of the software, that fact that it was written in Java, becomes pertinent to its ongoing life. The attachment of programmers and software developers to brands and logos is somewhat novel and suggests a new twist in the distribution of agency in software. No longer is code the bridge between commodity hardware and a collaborative programming ethos; the act of coding itself has been branded and commodified in quite complex ways. Coding becomes something more than work, a way of keeping abreast, of being contemporary within the flow of innovations. The cost of code mobility, however, is attachment to brand.

Chapter 6

"Pits" and "traders": Infrastructures in software

Information infrastructure is a tricky thing to analyze. Good, usable systems disappear almost by definition.... Infrastructures are never transparent for everyone, and their workability as they scale up becomes increasingly complex. Through due methodological attention to the architecture and use of these systems, we can achieve a deeper understanding of how individuals and communities meet infrastructure.

Bowker and Star, *Sorting Things Out: Classification and Its Consequences,* 1999, 33

The growth of software is heterogeneous rather than simply abstract. It addresses commodity hardware, invokes standards and conventions, imposes orderings of space and time, and diffuses modes of identification and subjectification for originators and recipients. Rather than parts being put together, the development of software is a sedimentary process composed of overlapping flows of materials. These materials can be excavated from code and coding, but how do they coagulate or concretize? What gives traction to the relational nexus in software? At some point, code, no matter how virtualized or abstract, encounters obstacles, resistances and gaps it cannot surmount. As Ellen Ullman (1997) puts it, "there are dark, unspecified areas" (21) that software development has to make sense of.

One of these areas is infrastructure. Software is located somewhere in an information infrastructure, and its location has consequences for contestations of agency attached to code. Infrastructures localize software in different ways, and software in turn absorbs and incorporates infrastructural elements. Code is developed at particular places (Palo Alto, Manchester, Taipei, Sydney), and as chapter 4's discussion of the Linux kernel suggested, code circulates according to complicated norms that do not simply reflect market conditions or technical demands. This chapter examines the relationship between code and infrastructural locality, using the software that manages telecommunications infrastructure as a case study. This software crosses boundaries between information networks (the Internet) and telecommunications infrastructures (telephone networks). Telecommunications infrastructure might seem a long way from more well-known coding hotspots such as Linux, peer-to-peer networks or viruses, but as Stephen Graham and Simon Marvin argue, "infrastructure networks, and the sociotechnical processes that surround them, are strongly involved in structuring and delineating the experiences of urban culture and ... the 'structures of feeling' of modern urban life" (Graham and Marvin 2001, 10). As an ethnographic study focused on software in a specific place per Miller and Slater (2000, 21), this chapter asks: How do infrastructures and individuals meet in the context of software development? At the most general level, I argue that an awareness of modifications of an embodied self and its relation to other bodies constitutes an important facet of the meeting between code and infrastructure, and thus of software as a neighborhood of relations.

The notion of locality plays a vital role in linking technoscientific knowledges, practices and things. Yet locality becomes slippery when the things and practices in a given location constantly refer to elsewhere, or are indeed constituted explicitly to resist localization (see Newman 1998). The continual arrival of new programming techniques and languages, protocols and processes of software development suggests that the problem of code's relation to place persists. Protocols, virtual machines and distributed systems are imagined, sometimes explicitly, as vectors of delocalization or decontextualization. In certain ways, software is made to be uprooted. Methodologically speaking, the only way to meet the challenge of self-decontextualizing or "vectoral" processes (Wark 2004, 316–45) such as telecommunications is to reassess the work done by locality itself.

Within poststructuralist anthropology, the notion of locality has been questioned. The anthropologist Arjun Appadurai (1996) suggests, "drawn into the very localization they seek to document, most ethnographic descriptions have taken locality as ground not Figure, recognizing neither its fragility nor its ethos as a property of social life. This produces an unproblematized collaboration with the sense of inertia on which locality, as a structure of feeling, centrally relies" (182). Appadurai invokes a basic conceptual distinction between figure and ground. He argues, in effect, that ethnographic descriptions have treated locality as substrate rather than an active outcome of social life. An ethnography that localizes technical practices and things, for instance, may show how "men [sic] and things exchange properties and replace one another" (Latour 1996, 61–2), or it may help explain how "a person is an effect, a fragile process of networking associated elements" (Law 1994, 33). But it also assumes, inadvertently, that there is a place or context in which such exchanges, articulation work or networking occurs. If, as Appadurai claims, most ethnographies treat locality as ground, then ethnographies of software are particularly vulnerable because the "ground" of software is already figured as deracinated, that is, as the product of "immaterial labour" (Hardt and Negri 2000), as virtualized-commodified operational object (Lash 2002), or decentralized control (Galloway 2004). Where is the "structure of feeling" that Appadurai names "inertia" in relation to software?

Where are "these things they call systems"?

The Rural Access Multiplexing Operational Support System (RAMOSS) was developed at Forge Research, a software development house specializing in telecommunication software in the Australian Technology Park in Redfern, Sydney. RAMOSS existed at the time of my study (February–October 2000) as a software project in process, a collection of disparate documents, code fragments, gadgets, servers, cards and plugs. During six months spent at Forge, Penny O'Hara and I sat in on formal and informal meetings and observed the developers' work areas and work stations, work carried in the server room and testing suite, as well as daily trips to the nearby café where ideas about RAMOSS were often mulled over. I conducted interviews with engineers, project managers, software developers and trainees. RAMOSS was meant to be a piece of second-order infrastructure, an operational control system designed to monitor, control and configure a digital telecommunications infrastructure scattered over rural Australia from a bunker somewhere in North Sydney.

The telecommunications company contracting Forge to develop RAMOSS occupied a powerful but ambivalent position. On one hand, on the strength of RAMOSS's functionality, it could publicly announce that nearly all customers in rural Australia would henceforth have direct access to digital telecommunication services at the cost of a local call and at speeds comparable to those of city data networks. RAMOSS, in fact, would allow existing analog networks to be converted cheaply into digital networks without any new cabling or modification to the remote "local loops," the telephone cables that run from pits to dwellings. That would be a powerful card to play in negotiations with the government over other important contracts and in the ongoing wrangles over privatization. On the other hand, the rural market for telecommunications in Australia had few prospects for growth. Rural populations are declining, and any further investment in rural infrastructure could be a bad bet. Commercial rollout of new cable across the rural landscape seemed out of the question.

Furthermore, since the mid-1990s the legal status of telecommunications infrastructure itself had entered limbo. The telecommunications infrastructure, especially the copper cable running into remote parts of Australia, dates from the mid–twentieth century's state monopoly on communication. As the federal government's monopoly on telecommunication is dismantled, what was once public infrastructure underwent many different kinds of partitioning and carving up through leasing and licensing arrangements. The telecommunications company, whose technical crews once roamed the countryside maintaining infrastructure, was now more interested in scaling down its rural workforce, outsourcing maintenance and concentrating on its newly profitable mobile telephone and broadband services. In this context, the piece of software called RAMOSS could be a trump card or, if the cards were dealt differently, useless. In the latter case, all the engineered complexity of RAMOSS itself could become an expensive technological ornament.

By virtue of its bunkered existence, RAMOSS was to dwell somewhere almost lost to sight. During its development, it was already deeply entwined in infrastructures and other technological systems not usually visible outside the technical worlds of telecommunication and network engineering (see Thrift 2004b). RAMOSS had little to show for itself; it was so thoroughly dispersed and distributed across pieces of normal-looking computing and communication hardware that senior engineers at Forge worried that the several million dollars needed to develop the software would seem unjustified to the client company, a large telecommunications corporation. RAMOSS mainly appeared as diagrams on whiteboards and in numerous documents on the computer monitors of the Forge developers. As a figure, it would never take on a very palpable or distinct form apart from the complicated, densely patterned control screens designed to be viewed by telecommunications technicians. Describing the individuals and things clustered around RAMOSS involves tracing connections well beyond Redfern, and beyond the relatively sparse telecommunication networks of the Australian countryside, to places that the developers of the system had never or only rarely visited, such as the annual JavaOne conference in San Francisco and the Object Management Group.[1] These connections were actively imagined in and around RAMOSS. Through imagining, understood as awareness of bodily transitions to states of greater or lesser activity (Gatens and Lloyd 1999, 77), the project materialized as an encounter between individuals and infrastructure.[2]

Since it "remediated" (Bolter and Grusin 1999) an existing infrastructure (that is, it turns an analog telephone network into a digital Internet network), RAMOSS found its locality already organized along certain lines. When asked "What is RAMOSS?" Greg, a trainee software engineer who worked mostly on parts of the system that displayed information to the technicians and operators using RAMOSS, replied:

> Umm … I guess the whole idea of it is managing these things that they call systems, which are telecommunications hardware. And, umm, there's lots of different things going into that. So basically, we'll be keeping a lot of the information about these systems … and making attempts to deal with that automatically rather than needing user intervention. And the [client] company seems to want that more and more.[3]

This description is very generic. It shows "detectable system awareness" (Marcus 1995), the idea that within any specific locality, individuals are conscious of their connection to other localities (see also chapter 7 on programmers' "system awareness"). The "whole idea" is couched in a single figure: "it" is a system. System talk plays a vital role in connecting RAMOSS to other things. From the engineer's perspective, RAMOSS, itself a system, will manage "these things they call systems," it will keep information about them, and it will attempt to deal with them automatically.

In contemporary technical infrastructure talk, the figure of system looms large. Dozens of systems on different scales crosscut and intersect with RAMOSS. Here already, the figure of system gives shape to what is imagined. The very figure of system entails an imagining of movement. System thinking imagines alignment, integration and connection between things that lack a more substantial or tangible unity or essence. The integrity of a system has to be projected or imagined because it cannot readily be seen. Saying that "the whole idea of it is managing these things they call systems" suggests that for the engineer, the problem revolves around how to establish coherence amongst things that don't spontaneously cohere ("there's lots of different things"). The problem is connecting diverse things. The complications that result from trying to make connections stick will be discussed later.[4] There is also the issue of what "the company seems to want." A note of caution and uncertainty tinges the response. Eliminating "user intervention" sounds like de-skilling of telecommunication technicians and workforce reduction. Is what the company wants what the software engineer wants?

RAMOSS crosses boundaries

Importantly, the different facets of RAMOSS have no common ground. Making RAMOSS entails weaving connections or establishing an ethos in which those facets come into contact. Each brings up gaps, discontinuities, vexations, obstacles or boundaries. The practices of imagining carried in coding mediate these disconnected facets. The ideal of system as integrated whole, the problem of how to connect diverse things, and the compulsion to satisfy what "the company wants" all filter through coding. Elements of the Forge locality refer elsewhere or contain constitutive gaps to which the developers are sensitive. Imagining combines awareness of relations between bodies with a certain inadequacy or incompleteness in knowledge, a sense of limitation. Imagining, in effect, connects different bodies, most powerfully through the medium of images, but also through other forms and materials, including codes and protocols. At the same time, it leaves those connections in question or suspended: what is imagined may not happen.

   RAMOSS as a software system moves in a broader field of relations that Appadurai called "technoscape."[5] As part of Australia's national telecommunications infrastructure, RAMOSS negotiates geographical, economic, social, political, legal and technical boundaries on many scales (Graham and Marvin 2001, 8), boundaries that surfaced in the office suite of Forge Research, the software company contracted to develop RAMOSS at the Australian Technology Park (ATP). Some punctuated the regular telephone conversations between the team leader, Charlie, and the corporate client; some figured daily on the whiteboards in the shape of code fragments, modeling diagrams and database designs; and some crowded into the server-room racks of computing and telecommunication equipment. The very locale of RAMOSS' own production indexed geographical, economic, political and cultural tensions between "bush" and "city" between a vast but sparsely populated rural hinterland and the concentrated telecommunication infrastructure of coastal cities. Outside the converted early twentieth-century railway locomotive workshops housing Forge, a large grassy vacant lot fenced with cyclone wire awaited construction of a hotel by a Japanese developer. Barry, the engineering director, mentioned one afternoon during one of my visits that if the hotel was ever built on that lot, it would mean relocating a telecommunications "pit," a local subexchange from which telephone lines fanned out into the technology park. Since it managed the telecommunications hardware in just such pits, RAMOSS straddled that divide between the grassy lot and the busy Forge office suite, a divide that indexes the torsion between "bush" and "city" in Australia.

As in many other countries, the agricultural population in Australia is acutely attuned to world trade and commodity price fluctuations. If nothing else, access to digital networks in the late 1990s promised instant updates on the latest drop in grain, meat and wool prices. Less pessimistically, they could make country life more viable economically and socially. "Wiring the bush," rolling out digital services to the rural population, constitutes a persistently unfulfilled promise of recent Australian politics. It sits awkwardly with the ongoing privatization of the telecommunication universal service provider, Telstra Corporation. The almost daily discussions of these issues in Australian mass media at the time figured little in day-to-day work around RAMOSS. However, a mediated version of the country/city divide surfaced in a pervasive anxiety among the Forge management and RAMOSS project leaders that the contract for RAMOSS could be canceled prematurely.

RAMOSS feeds into the enormous and large-scale percolation of communications across the so-called digital divide by promising to reconfigure an aging but valuable analog telephone service into a centrally monitored and managed digital network. For the software developers at Forge, the technical problem of how to manage this move between analog and digital looms largest. Much of their imagining, planning and anxiety focuses on that unspecified zone where RAMOSS encounters POTS (Plain Old Telephone Service). RAMOSS follows approaches pursued in South Africa, India and other places where existing infrastructure cannot be profitably re-cabled. It capitalizes on existing analog telephone infrastructure by retrofitting it digitally. The technique of "multiplexing" or switching between different signals rapidly on the same line allows RAMOSS to apparently channel many communications down cables that used to accept only one communication at a time. Multiplexing increases the capacity of the existing infrastructure—at the price of new complications in network configuration and management.

How are boundaries crossed?

RAMOSS' locality was organized by two related divisions: between city and country, and between digital and analog networks. Just as Java faced the problem of moving executable code between different parts of the Internet, RAMOSS faced the problem of moving digital information between different network infrastructures, the Internet and POTS. How does RAMOSS negotiate them? How does code move across technical, geographical, political and legal/property boundaries? Like the strategies of virtualization discussed in the previous chapter, RAMOSS seeks to bridge a geographically distributed divide (in this case, the analog/digital divide) by distributing computational hardware throughout existing (rural telephone) networks. If RAMOSS goes ahead, new remote unit cards (RU cards) will be installed in thousands of roadside pits, junction boxes and rural exchanges. These cards perform the one-to-many work of multiplexing.

However, as mentioned, multiplexing brings management overheads. The equipment that multiplexes multiple conversations along one telephone line itself entails distributing computational processes to many nodes in the telephone infrastructure. Because each multiplexing RU card carries an onboard computer, a management problem implicit in Greg's earlier description arises: if RAMOSS will "manage these things called systems," it will need, in fact, to manage thousands of them. How can RAMOSS manage potentially tens of thousands of remote computers, each of them with an operating system, all of them emitting alarms and making requests for data? Each connection that runs through one of these cards to a local telephone loop will need to be individually configured, and each card will need regular monitoring and occasional software updates. The scale of the configuration work is staggering, given the difficulties associated with reliably configuring even a single computer.

Designing software to handle such a situation has potentially many dark, unspecified pitfalls. Forge Research is a cautious software producer; for RAMOSS, designers made use of heavily instrumented, closely monitored and procedurally sophisticated software design and production processes, based on a mixture of telecommunication system models and approaches to software engineering. Paul, the managing director of Forge, sketched the problems in terms that drew on population metaphors:

> Object-oriented software is no different to having large populations of individuals. Where you have a few individuals interoperating with each other, you can be reasonably confident that you can keep a handle on what's happening. As soon as you get tens of thousands and millions of objects interoperating with each other, it's impossible to predict all the combinations of what may occur.... So when you're in RAMOSS's case, and you have a large number of end-users sitting on the system, you have a large population of cards, you may have strange combinations of circumstances that we just never contemplated.[6] (Paul, interview with author)

Population is more than an apt metaphor: the software that is RAMOSS would be located within a communications infrastructure sprawling, however sparsely, across a continent, and potentially accommodating a national population of "interoperating" individuals. Flows of digital data depend on linked paths running between the edges of the network and points within it. To make those paths available, RAMOSS must maintain a fairly coherent grasp ("a handle") and representation of tens of thousands of configurable computers; otherwise the network will begin to unravel. How can RAMOSS —and Forge—get a handle on such a diffuse extended locality?

Software between-places

Forge has made distributed computer systems before. Discussions about RAMOSS problems in the meeting room often mentioned an earlier system, ANTOSS, built by Forge several years prior. The experience of building ANTOSS, an operational support system for a different telecommunications network, changed Forge itself as locality. Forge became a kind of "between-place" where diverse telecommunicative realities encountered each other, a place that facilitated imagining movement across boundaries.

One of my early visits to Forge began with a tour through the office suite and the Technology Park facilities. After the café, which was visited daily by the developers, the real tour began—with a trip to the server room. Server rooms are usually the least visited, most inhospitable and restricted zones in organizations, in part because the air conditioning makes it too cold for most people. But in Forge's glass-fronted server room, the back and side walls directly indexed the separation between the two networks, the Internet and POTS. On the back wall to the west, many computers stood in racks, some generic PCs, others unfamiliar, more expensive-looking machines—

including a resplendent purple Sun Enterprise Server. A high-capacity commercial computer designed to run Java software, it would later sit in the control bunker and host some core components of RAMOSS. Barry pointed out several Linux computers along the west wall as well. They were intended to serve as "satellite boxes"; in network terms, that means they would be situated outside the corporate firewall that prevented unwanted network traffic from entering the infrastructure management systems. Finally, near the back wall stood a rack to hold RU cards, the hardware that would eventually go into the far-flung pits of the rural telephone networks. Ranged alongside each other in close proximity, these different computational elements—the enterprise server, the Linux computers, the RU cards—would have to communicate more and more extensively with each other as RAMOSS developed.

On a side wall to the north, the hardware looked very different. Here dozens of plugs, jacks, cables, telephone handsets and small boxes were lined up. From sockets on this wall fanned out a dozen "primary rate" ISDN (integrated services digital network) connections into the national telecommunications infrastructure, as well as many standard telephone connections. The wall afforded a level of access to the national infrastructure that the Forge engineers felt quite privileged to have. Forge regarded that degree of access—the team leader said one day (on the telephone, of course), "We are the highest primary rate users in the country"[7]—as crucial to RAMOSS and to the constitution of a locality where things moves differently, sometimes crossing previously impervious boundaries. In the server room, Forge turned itself into a miniature version of the national telephone infrastructure, or at least of some salient facets of it.

The Internet and POTS stood apart from each other within this densely equipped and computationally patterned place, just as they did nationally. In order to open up new movements within that infrastructure, and to afford the geographical/technical boundary crossing which the RAMOSS project imagines for rural Australia, the separate elements would have to be interlaced with each other. The enterprise server must listen and talk to the RU cards, passing through the Linux boxes and the ISDN connections. A telephone handset adjacent to the north wall must be able to call a nearby telephone handset via the RU cards lining the west wall, cards themselves administered through ISDN connections running out of Linux computers—computers networked with the enterprise server. These walls, in short, must move closer or be folded into each other, gradually interlaced through a lightweight fabric of code and protocols. Only then, if that interlacing held in this especially pliable place of dense connectivity, would RAMOSS migrate to another place of dense connectivity, the control bunker in metropolitan Sydney, or perhaps later, Forge hoped, to networks in some other country.

The constitution of locality in software is peculiar. Forge as a locality occupies a "between-place" with respect to the national telephone infrastructure. The "between-place" is made with a view to crossing boundaries and divides: it is neither inside nor outside. Its points and levels of access to that infrastructure permit it to interconnect new paths within the infrastructure. It can elaborate new routes, new loops and new detours from one part of the infrastructure to another. It can introduce new modes of movement through the infrastructure, for instance, by moving chunks of operational code from the enterprise server across the ISDN networks through the satellite boxes into the RU cards. It is located within a gap, an unrealized potential of a telephone infrastructure with respect to the Internet. While it sounds straightforward, the interlacing of the two walls of the server room is anything but. The work done at Forge over several years entailed painstaking attention to the minute attributes of the elements loosely stacked in the server room. The work of software and telecommunication engineers, web developers, project managers, system administrators and technicians brought those walls into contact by coding a tissue of partially imagined and partially materialized connections.

Mobilizations: Process in software

The server room is not the only ground on which Forge imagines RAMOSS. In principle, Forge software developers and telecommunications engineers wanted to read and write code that would permit controlled, predictable and scaleable movement between the walls of the server room. Their many drawings, diagrams, models, and discussions of code, objects, classes, methods, variables, "config files" and so on sought to marshal those movements along certain lines. Latour (1996) argues, "The engineer substitutes for the signs he writes the things that he has mobilized; he attaches them to each so they'll hold up; then he withdraws a little, delegating to another self, in the form of a chip, a sensor, or an automatic device, the task of watching over the connection. And this delegating allows him to withdraw even further—as if there were an object" (81). In this case, however, the mobilized "things" move in different ways or in different dimensions, depending on what kind of imagining they flow from. Two major trajectories are important: first, ideas of work process loom large in system-building, and second, collective imaginings of movement flow into Forge in the form of topical code constructs, system models, platforms, and communication protocols. They pattern the design of RAMOSS.

"Process talk" constituted a strongly valorized way of imagining or projecting RAMOSS as if it were already a system sitting in the server room. Early in my study, Barry, the engineering director, arranged a session in the meeting room. On an electronic whiteboard (whose persistent beeping sounds couldn't be silenced, even by the engineering director himself, due to an obstinate onboard computer), he drew diagrams of telecommunication infrastructure to help explain what RAMOSS would do. The description of RAMOSS as a system was involved and emphasized the unknowns of scaleability and configurability mentioned by the managing director, Paul. Next, logging onto a nearby computer and starting a data projector hanging from the ceiling, Barry began a kind of protracted lecture about "Forge process." The diagrams projected onto the wall during the session resembled flowcharts. Boxes and areas expanded at the click of the mouse, revealing the phases and steps in specifying, designing, modeling, implementing and testing the system. The process was "culled out," as Barry mentioned, from the rational unified process (RUP), a mid-1990s software design methodology that seeks to provide comprehensive methods, software tools, books, and courses for designing and developing object-oriented software (IBM 2004b). Moving back and forth between the projector screen and keyboard, he detailed how RAMOSS had moved through various phases and would soon enter others.

Why deliver a description of Forge process to a non-engineer, an observer? We could regard this talk about "Forge process" as part of a parasitic "quality management" discourse, a symptom of Forge's localized microvision of modernity. Latour (1996) suggests a different view:

> People who study technological projects take too little interest in the official doctrines dealing with the actual management of the projects. This metalanguage appears parasitical. Yet it plays the same essential role that strategic doctrines play in the conduct of wars. In the course of a battle or a project, ideas about the way to handle battles or innovations play a performative role.... Writing a project's history also means writing the history of the ambient theories about project management. (113)

"Forge process" was heavily infused with ambient theories of project management. Later, showing me a book about the capability maturity model (CMM) (Dymond 1995), Barry said that Forge was not seeking full CMM accreditation because that was only suitable for large organizations like IBM, but that were trying to conform to the model at a high level.

The social organization of engineering work as a project has been described in sociological studies as "a prominent way in which engineering work is socially organised so as to confront the sorts of contingencies that face software engineering ... such as the threatened curtailment because of, for example, drastic slippage, or such as the pressures to abandon good practice" (Button and Sharrock 1996, 372). The Forge process, with its complicated itinerary of stages and phases, certainly attempted to counter these kinds of exigencies. But the fact that the engineering director wanted to convince an outside observer of the importance of process poses a different question. It is as if the formal process of developing RAMOSS meant something more than a practical social organization of work. Amid the complications of the Forge design methodology, and all the different kinds of diagrams, syntax, software tools and how-to texts that clustered around it, it seemed RAMOSS could only be concretely represented it in terms of this process. The phases, steps and stages for implementing RAMOSS were an important way in which people at Forge projected what RAMOSS would be. Reinforcing this point, Barry mentioned more than once that the first task for trainee software engineers, "the young lads" recruited from nearby universities, was "to spend a month on process." People working on RAMOSS were carefully inducted into Forge process. New software developers, eager to begin cutting code when they arrived, instead started by learning about Forge process, and as they took on the modeling skills and practiced documentation, they became part of that process.

The "collaborative craftwork" (Suchman and Trigg 1992, 173) of producing the documents, specifications, architectures and class diagrams required by Forge process did not move RAMOSS effortlessly or evenly. Process showed uneven traction among members of the team who possessed different levels of experience and different levels of willingness to adhere to process. Barry's asides about the "young lads" highlight how the software developers needed coaching to move things like texts, diagrams and code in the right ways. At base, Forge process meant reading and writing many documents, some of them in carefully formatted and numbered text, some diagrammatic, some including code and some not. Often large, these documents took shape laboriously. During a meeting, the team leader might ask someone to sketch on the whiteboard how a particular problem could be approached. Typically, the whiteboard diagram would then be modified in the light of suggestions, questions, objections and sometimes long-running struggles over expertise and architectural style. Later, a developer would take some parts of the diagram—the outcome of several hours' discussion around the meeting table about topics such as which objects would manage other objects—and translate it using Rational Rose, a software tool that supports object-oriented modeling using diagrams (Boggs and Boggs 1999; White 1994; Quatrani 1998; IBM 2004b). Nearly all traces of the fairly complex negotiations over how the system should work on a very specific point would disappear, replaced by a formal abstract diagram of boxes, arrows and labels.

The proliferation of formalisms produced large "documentation trees." The documentation tree for RAMOSS was vast. Thousands of files had been hierarchically organized, many generated automatically by software tools such as Javadoc, a program that extracts HTML-formatted code documentation directly from comments programmers have put in the Java source code. People refined and transformed documents using whiteboard markers, foolscap pads, diagram editors, text editors and databases. They exchanged version information and tips on how to manipulate the software tools applied to the documents. Calls for help rang out: "Using flowcharter in Worm, where are the tools?" ("Using the flow-charting extensions to Microsoft Word, how does one display a toolbar?")

Some documents possessed a key significance in Forge process. The statement of requirements (SOR) document, for instance, underwent intensive reading and writing; at least four people worked on versions of the large SOR document for RAMOSS over a period for months. The highly templated structure of this document was laid down in advance, and various components of the document were stored in a database from which the document was dynamically generated whenever it needed to be circulated in an official version. Indeed, prior to circulation, the SOR was made uneditable so that no unauthorized or accidental changes could be introduced by different reader-writers. Frequently, developers debated the status of documents, querying whether they could still be changed. Different kinds of formalisms—legal, modeling, syntactic, diagrammatic—applied to these documents. Forge process mentioned some of them explicitly. "Computational modeling," an important phase in system design, derives from twin telecommunications industry standards: RMODP, the reference model for open distributed processing (ISO/ITU-T 1998) and TINA, telecommunications infrastructure networking architecture (TINA 1999). Drawing more directly on RUP (rational unified process), the unified modeling language (UML) guided the production of "class diagrams," the object-oriented software models of low-level components of RAMOSS, and "sequence diagrams," diagrams showing the planned order of events meant to occur when the system ran.

While the developers gradually wrote and rewrote RAMOSS as a program, a somewhat static description of a projected thing in the world, the program ultimately becomes a system only by becoming a process or processes. We could say that the RAMOSS software precipitated as a side effect of process. In his orientation presentation to Penny O'Hara and me, Barry spoke of systems and process together. These abstract terms are deeply integrated. Systems exist as and consist of processes: a system unfurls temporally as process. Yet the ultimate event, when a program fully transubstantiates into a system, may not arrive for a long time—may not ever arrive. The contract for full development of RAMOSS might not be signed. In the meantime, RAMOSS as a system hovers between something loosely called "Forge process" (a set of representations and ways of working with representations) and the more fragmented processes that run on various developers' workstations and on the Sun enterprise server when components of the system are coded up and tested.

Forge process regulates the production of a set of specific written projections that visualize what the system will be. RAMOSS as a system increasingly embodies processes that, in terms of the topography of the server room, put the walls in touch with each other. But in the meantime, the between-place of Forge, system-as-projection and system-as-process circle around each other, interacting and exchanging attributes. Even after release, when the system runs in the control bunker and lives amid the networks, a final and full coincidence between projection and process would be an ideal whose realization is ever-deferred. It exists somewhere between the relatively visible projections and descriptions embodied in documents and jostling technical fragments—software tools, implementations of different communication protocols, network cards, virtual machine implementations, and executable/readable code on developers' computers. Process seeks to compact those fragments together and increasingly restrict their movements —to establish a static central subject position. The team, to the extent that it collectively embodies the effects of the imperatives issuing from process, is meant to identify with, if not occupy, that position.

RAMOSS imagined remotely

Forge and the RAMOSS project constitute a fold or wrinkle on the

Australian telecommunication technoscape; they tentatively remap, via a distributed information network, certain paths and neighborhoods of Australia's telecommunication infrastructure, connecting them more directly to the Internet. Forge Research, a kind of between-place that enfolds portions of the infrastructure within its server room, brings two surfaces, one computational, the other telephonic, into intermittent, flickering contact. RAMOSS, as it was developed, began to emit signals across boundaries: city/country, analog/digital, public/corporate. It reconfigures an existing infrastructure, the copper wire rural telephone networks. At the same time, a genre of writing called "the system," projected in a complex formal process and maintained by many informal maneuvers, focuses on generating documents and moving formalisms across different supports: whiteboard, pad, screen, database and code repository. Between these two facets—a between-place full of potential connections and process, and a system-oriented way of working—relations are both made and unmade by practices of imagining.

The importance of imagining in this context appears in another element of the infrastructure at Forge. On the walk back from the café where the developers go each afternoon, we often passed the large, humming bulk of what a large sign labelled as "Australia's first commercial fuel cell." This impressive technical installation, emblazoned with a corporate advertisement of Australia's desires to be at the cutting-edge of alternative energy innovation and spouting a plume of steam, supplied some of the electricity for Forge's own computers. The engineers often joked about the fuel cell causing problems at Forge Research: computer monitors failed unpredictably because the fuel cell introduced "harmonics" on the Technology Park's power grid. In fact, a legal wrangle developed around the fuel cell at the time of RAMOSS's development, and a compensation claim against the fuel cell's owners was in the offing. Ironically, the makers of RAMOSS, a remote operational management system, were unable to change the running of the fuel cell because it was managed by a computer somewhere in Ohio. Remote management—the function of RAMOSS—distorts locality in interesting ways. Even something as elementary as the main power supply at Forge can refer elsewhere, to a set of rhythms and patterns emanating from the control center in Ohio.

Just as the strange harmonics introduced by the fuel cell on the local electricity grid made computer monitors at Forge hum slightly off-key, outside resonances inflected and modulated the network of relations between people and things working on RAMOSS at Forge. These resonances induced imaginings, where imagining is understood as an awareness of "our own bodies together with those of others" (Gatens and Lloyd 1999, 27). An important dimension of the encounter between individuals and infrastucture is revealed through the collective imagining that crosshatches RAMOSS. This encounter is energized by many different ideas of what a system might do, how it might come together, and how it could be constructed.

With mass media and migration in mind, Arjun Appadurai (1996) wrote that "ordinary people have begun to deploy their imaginations in the practice of their everyday lives. This fact is exemplified in the mutual contextualizing of motion and mediation" (5). Quotidian imagining materialized prosaically in the developers' suite. Modular workstations faced the walls, and mugs, stuffed toys, books, baseball caps, assorted pamphlets and books littered the bookshelves above each workstation. These artifacts flagged the imagining of other relations running through RAMOSS. Books with titles like *Java Enterprise in a Nutshell* (Flanagan 1999) came from the crowded computer sections of bookshops. Online, developers regularly visited favorite websites including Slashdot, "News for Nerds" (http://www.slashdot.org), JavaWorld (http://www.javaworld.com) and various documentation sites (above all, Sun Microsystems 2005b). Just like the "gimme" souvenir mugs, toys, pens and caps, which constitute seductive minor mediations of the products they promote (ORACLE databases, Orbix2000, the JavaOne annual conference), the websites and books constantly consulted by the developers attest to something important about the fabric of RAMOSS as system. RAMOSS includes or cites many other systems, conventions and artifacts. The development of RAMOSS cited and cross-referenced code, design patterns, software libraries, software components, protocols, virtual machines and reference models. Almost nothing in RAMOSS started from scratch.

Forge process envisaged a clear road running past milestones of models, documents and text, provisionally ending in a program—the binary code— delivered to an ultimate destination, a machine-centered control room. Yet as the RAMOSS team advanced through the process, folding together the telephonic and computational surfaces of the server-room walls, their collective work introduced many switchback turns and layers of "indirection." These layers make the system seem very difficult to understand, even unnecessarily complicated. For instance, Greg was often working on implementing the screens that technicians in the bunker would see. These screens, the user interface of RAMOSS, were conceived as webpages viewed through Internet Explorer. When I asked why he used XML instead of the more usual HTML, Greg said, "It will have more loops, but be more flexible." At that time, XML (extensible markup language) had been attracting a lot of attention as a potential successor to HTML. Covers of computer magazines and periodicals, dozens of websites, and a large number of specification and how-to articles had heavily promoted XML. Many of them focused on the idea of flexible onscreen layout: different devices or applications could display the same XML code in completely different ways. Standard HTML, by contrast, specifies layout on a screen once and for all. Wanting to keep the link between what is displayed and how it is displayed flexible, RAMOSS developers were using XML so that data could be laid out onscreen differently without changing any underlying code.

Thus developers inscribe internal boundaries in the system that derived less from technical, operational or geographical problems than from a vision of flexibility and configurability attached to imported protocols, models and architectures. These imported models, architectures and protocols, moreover, are subject to fashion, are evaluated as "cool" or "uncool," and can therefore be seen as bearers of contemporary collective imaginings of flexible, configurable and intercommunicating code processes from outside the process—from the standards committees of bodies such as the World Wide Web Consortium (W3C 2004), from the Object Management Group's definition of the common object request broker architecture (OMG 2004) or from Sun Microsystems' latest addition to Java (Sun Microsystems 2003b). These imported protocols and standards arrive via electronic journal and periodical articles and thick computer books published by O'Reilly or Addison-Wesley. In addition, imported standards and protocols flow in and out via software modules used as prefabricated components of the system.

By virtue of imagining indirection and detour in the name of configurability, nothing about RAMOSS stands alone. Bowker and Star (1999) figure the interwoven texture of contemporary infrastructures as an "inner space": "In the past 100 years, people in all lines of work have jointly constructed an incredible, interlocking set of categories, standards, and means for interoperating infrastructural technologies. We hardly know what we have built. No one is in control of infrastructure; no one has the power centrally to change it…. Infrastructure is now the great inner space" (319). In a vital sense, the protocols, models, code patterns and standards in RAMOSS crystallize an inner space inhabited by software developers. The list of the many different technical standards and protocols being cited, implemented, or customized in RAMOSS kept growing during its development, ranging from XML, CORBA, SNMP, MIB, SSL, IDL, to TCP/IP, to name a few. Many of these standards and protocols were threaded into other standards and protocols. Day-to-day work on RAMOSS as I observed it often consisted of grafting together different protocols and arranging and adjusting standards, classifications and naming schemes so that they could hold together. The standards exist as mixed entities, part convention and part physical form: "All classification and standardisation schemes are a mixture of physical entities, such as paper forms, plugs, or software instructions encoded in silicon, and conventional arrangements such as speed and rhythm, dimension, and how specifications are implemented" (Bowker and Star 1999, 39). As this section shows, books, tutorials, websites, user-groups, software tools, institutions and communities with complicated histories twine around the standards.

Flexibility and mobility as collective imagining

The mixed entities threaded through RAMOSS incorporate an awareness of bodies in relation, including the bodies of programmers as workers who have particular knowledges, skills and interests. RAMOSS must span the different computer platforms and operating systems lining the server-room wall (Sun, Microsoft NT, and Linux, each thoroughly saturated with different standards and protocols) without falling apart. In contemporary software culture, such boundaries produce kinks and folds in software architecture. They absorb much reading, writing, design, talk, coding and testing time. The Forge team, on the basis of their previous experience building distributed software, hoped that by embodying appropriate protocols and standards, RAMOSS would vault across the boundaries between computer platform and operating system in two respects. Firstly, by coding in Java, the team gave RAMOSS a running start on jumping between hardware platforms: Paul, the managing director, mentioned that "the last technical direction I kicked Forge in, in association with the other guys was, the agreement to work solely in Java. Or to do the bulk of our development in Java." Secondly, by coding certain external features of the system to the CORBA (common object request broker architecture) standard, RAMOSS would be able to interface with software systems not written in Java, such as the many other network management systems that the telecommunications company was already running.

Major consequences flow from CORBA's presence in RAMOSS. It promises very desirable architectural flexibility and plasticity for RAMOSS. Charlie described the flexibility of RAMOSS in the following terms:

> As a system, it resides on, the main process resides on one machine, but it doesn't have to. At this stage, it resides on one machine and these, what we call satellite boxes exist in outlying exchanges, or they could be co-located wherever. And they

are the ones that actually form the connections to the networks elements that they manage. I guess you would say that it is centralised from that perspective, but it's still a distributed system. It could be distributed more if they wish to.... I mean the satellite boxes are being forced on us to a certain extent by their firewall architecture, and the need for the isolation between ISDN connections to the outlying exchanges, to be isolated from their corporate data network. But it's still not a bad architecture because it gives us diversity in some aspects of these systems. But it would not be necessary if they didn't have that. We could put everything back in the main box, and do it all from there. And they still could do that. So, if someone else wanted a similar network management system, we could put it all on one box.[8]

The idea that RAMOSS might be distributed in different configurations, or running on different networks, ran strongly through software development at Forge. The team's use of models such as RMODP and CORBA flowed from an imagining of systems that can change their topology and move easily into different contexts. A vision of RAMOSS being decontextualized animated much of the design and configuration work. Implementing such imagined flexibility, however, is hard. CORBA necessitated intricate configuration work to prepare for architectural permutations. Building with collectively accepted and well-known protocols and architectures such as CORBA meant the team could import software modules or subsystems to do some of the work of the system. But each imported module brings its own configuration problems. The team grafted the hardware and software elements onto each other using a combination of software tools, books, websites, telephone help lines and downloaded documents, and drew on their individual and collective experience. Still, when configuring products that Forge purchased as ready-made components, the team experienced configuration work as risky.

The imagining of flexibility and reconfigurability imposes new boundaries, seams and discontinuities into RAMOSS. Flexibility and reconfigurability as concepts bear little reference to the technogeographical milieu of rural telephone infrastructures, but much to the imagined movement of the system into different places. Responding to the question of "What is RAMOSS?" Charlie provided an architectural plan:

Well there are components called distributed processing components, and they form a distributed processing environment. Now at the base of that you've got such things as the ORB, CORBA, but above that you meet such things as cluster managers where you're clustering these computational elements together ... You have to have something to manage the clusters, which is what we call a node manager. You need to have things called traders for finding what resources and services, you need notification services which allow you to forward events between different processes. They are all distributed processes which help to make the environment work.[9]

In saying, "You need to have these things called traders," Charlie refines Greg's claim that "the whole idea is to manage these things called systems." However, managing things called systems entails traders imported from the CORBA specification, in which market metaphors of "brokerage," "trading," "services," "leases" and "transactions" are central to the figuring of flexibility and reconfigurability. These imports affect the texture of RAMOSS, refigures it as "an environment" rather than a unified system. The incorporation of different models, standards and protocols means that the system gradually takes on an open yet highly interlocked texture of different metaphors or tropes, many of which bring associations quite remote from telephone networks and rural network access. RAMOSS teems with figures such as "managers," "services," "events," "traders," "transactions" and "brokers." Elements of the design, such as the division of the system into different software services (broker, trader, notification, management), import different imaginings of relations between bodies into the system.

So, for instance, a "BusinessManager" component in RAMOSS that manages user requests for information concerning the status of a particular RU card in a pit somewhere would at another level of the design need to be coded in a way that complied with CORBA. Following the CORBA architecture, a detailed design must be specified for the BusinessManager in a "declaration language" called IDL, the interface definition language (OMG 2004). IDL provides a way of describing different types of objects and how they interact with each other over networks. But in CORBA terms, there are only really clients and servers. In the CORBA view, the BusinessManager object may well appear as a client. Within the same system, what is a manager from one perspective is a client from another. Even if the core system of RAMOSS ends up running on a single machine in a telecommunications bunker, its design contains many internal boundaries and interfaces (between components, between services, between clients and servers) that could potentially open and spread out over a greater distance.

Reading the specifications of the CORBA standard (OMG 2004b) would hardly keep most people awake at night, but software developers find them very intriguing. Against a background of configuration difficulties, frustrations with moving code between different machines, or connecting different computing and communication platforms, CORBA promises enhanced mobility or flexibility, even at the cost of an involuted schematic imagining of elements in the system. Watching software developers at work reveals how the code they write is modulated from afar by a certain vision of flexibility or reconfigurability figured via social or communicative conventions such as request, transaction or notification.

Flexibility, extensibility, mobility and the capacity to "scale up" code objects exert powerful attractions on the cultures of software development, even as they bring layers of complication. The Forge team, for instance, purchased a software product called IONA OrbixWeb (IonaTechnologies 2004) to use as a central component in their molding of RAMOSS to CORBA. A system compliant with CORBA needs to have an ORB (object request broker) accessible to each process in the system: the ORB handles communication between parts of the system and reduces the need for integration or customization of parts by translating requests or responses. However, making sure that local and remote machines can find and communicate with the ORB can be complicated. Even apart from all the design work needed to implant CORBA in RAMOSS, just starting IONA OrbixWeb reliably on different computers proved difficult. After several hours of increasingly frustrating work, Bryan, one of the more experienced members of the team, grabbed Tux, a stuffed penguin, from the top of his computer monitor, punched it a few times and put it back. Tux, a semiofficial icon for the Linux operating system, became the target of Bryan's frustration because he could not configure and run Orbix on a Linux machine. The team wanted to use Linux machines as the satellite boxes (computers outside the corporate firewall), because Linux machines are perceived to be more secure, reliable and cheaper than commercial products (see chapter 4). OrbixWeb, however, was developed primarily to run under commercial operating systems such as Windows NT or Solaris. On the other hand, OrbixWeb is written in Java, and the main promise of Java is, of course, "Write once, run anywhere"—so it should run on any other operating system that supports Java (including Linux), at least in principle. The heavy pile of IONA manuals stacked on Bryan's desk was unhelpful since they all assumed Windows or Solaris machines would be used. Several days later, Bryan managed to initialize the ORB after modifying Orbix's standard configuration scripts. Sometimes, however, Orbix still did not start reliably, and errors or "exceptions" streamed down the screen. After many calls to a help line, a consultant from IONA arrived at Forge to help stabilize the configuration and make starting Orbix reliable.

The formation of relations in software

Individuals and groups meet infrastructure in strange ways during software development. The Orbix episode illustrates the fairly prosaic point that obstacles thwarted the Forge process. Plans, tricks, "workarounds" and "clean cuts" failed, and expertise was brought in from the outside. But it also shows something more significant: the detailed technical knowledge and configuration experience that developers gain as they build RAMOSS or any other software is magnetized by larger-scale imagining of mobility embedded in the protocols, models and standards they want to use, and developers are prepared to pay quite a high cost for their commitment to the figures of flexibility and mobility. Collective imaginings present in the models, protocols and standards that pattern contemporary software figure movement across some gaps and boundaries. In imagining, something happens to obstacles: they disappear. But imagining also entails awareness of corporeal transitions and changes that might occur. Software development is embodied as definite, highly focused orientations to code, machines, programs, diagrams, software tools and most intensely, other programmers, as the next chapter will discuss. In infrastructural software development, imagining circulates in particular ways. Conventional "things" make connections between disparate "things" such as telephone lines and telephone exchanges. Certain protocols, specifications and standards (Java, Linux, CORBA) mesmerize software developers because they promise no obstacles in connecting or transporting things in a given domain. Although obstacles and difficulties do arise, figures of imagined flexibility, free movement and open communication pervade software and modulate software from a distance. The encounter between individuals and infrastructures is mediated by cross-cutting collectives. Making or changing infrastructure entails a complicated, even turbulent confluence of mobility and imagined mobility.

In *Aramis*, Latour (1996) wrote about alternatives to "putting things in their context": "What this requires is not to 'replace projects in their context,' as the foolish expression goes, but to study the way the project is contextualized or decontextualized" (133). This chapter has investigated some of the contextualizing and decontextualizing processes that energize RAMOSS. In the RAMOSS project, contextualization and decontextualization occurred at the same time, not alternating or opposed to each other. The server room at Forge expresses a topological problem: how can the team remap the rural telephone infrastructure so that telephone exchange and information network coalesce? The mapping slips constantly, not because of any lack of expertise on the team's part, but because RAMOSS occupies a between-place. The Forge process projects the ideal of a system as the output of series of stages, following in order and gradually merging into an integrated system. Yet the cross-cutting imaginings of mobility and reconfigurability—embodied in programming languages such as Java, platforms such as Linux, and in standards, protocols and specifications such as Corba (themselves embedded in software, tools, documents and websites)—constantly suggest new connecting pathways, open new perspectives and introduce new interfaces and obstacles.

Through the attraction they exert on the team and their pervasive material presence in the fabric of everyday life at Forge, these imaginings both enable and trouble the smooth translation across boundaries: between systems, between surfaces of inscription, between different kinds of infrastructure, between Forge and its client's corporate strategies and maneuvers. They induce detours, torsions and convoluted trajectories that take RAMOSS further afield. The configuration work done by the team multiplies, resulting in multilayered and distributed designs, with all the attendant complexities of documentation, diagramming and implementation. The processes of contextualizing and decontextualizing create a finely patterned composition in the technoscape. Latour says, "It is in the detours that we recognize a technological act; It is in the detours that we recognize a technological act; ... And it is in the number of detours that we recognize a project's degree of complexity" (1996, 215). A key point of this chapter is that detours might simultaneously contextualize and decontextualize software.

Code understood as a collective imagining seems a long way from code as a program of instructions for a machine to execute. However, practices of imagining are not purely mental operations; in no way does imagining reduce to a detached, abstract fantasy. It constitutes collective relational realities. Software attaches different localities to each other because it diffuses relations between them. The composite texture of software is reliant on unfinished exchanges between code and coders. Imagining generates relations over time, a sort of unfinished business, in which "delay or lag between transactions" (Gell 1998, 81) results in binding social force. Like Java, RAMOSS cannot fully exist as program or process, but constantly oscillates between them. The neighborhood of relations associated with software is characterized, as we have seen, by a composite texture. It is by nature incomplete.

Chapter 7

Extreme programming: Code as prototype for software

Contemporary labor has introjected into itself many characteristics which originally marked the experience of politics. Poiesis has taken on numerous aspects of praxis.

Virno, P. *A grammar of the multitude: for an analysis of contemporary forms of life,* 2004, 50

Because it deals with information, software has been regarded by programmers and by cultural theorists and social scientists as the epitome of abstract or immaterial work. It takes the form of analytical and symbolical tasks, which break down into creative and intelligent manipulation on one hand and routine symbolic work on the other (Hardt and Negri 2000, 293). Algorithms are typically regarded as the way in which creative-intelligent manipulation becomes routine symbolic manipulation. One practical version of the abstract tendencies in software production, as we've seen in chapter 5, appears in Java's concern with virtualization. Another version is uneasily implicit in the Linux kernel's unstable relation to commodity hardware and commercial software platforms (chapter 4).

It might seem that programmers, who work at shaping flows of information, want to make their work "indifferent to its particular form" (Marx 1973, 297) or to the specificity of different situations. But the experience of programming seems to be somewhat different. Ellen Ullman (1997) expresses it this way: "You write some code, and suddenly there are dark, unspecified areas. All the pages of careful documents, and still, between the sentences, something is missing" (21). Rather than becoming mechanical or predictable, over the course of time the flows of information managed by software become more dynamic, complex and unstable. Increasingly, programmers interact with worlds that are not abstract, mechanical, formalized, or in any simple sense, globalized (see chapter 4 on the tension between commodity hardware computing platforms and traits of the Unix philosophy).

From the standpoint of a political economy of software, this is a curious inversion. Rather than dealing with increasing abstraction, programming is constantly beset by conflicts between different processes of abstraction. Analyses of new media and information cultures that predicate abstraction as a key process (Wark 2004; Hardt and Negri 2000) need to address this apparent contradiction between abstraction and specificity in software. This chapter addresses some ways in which programming work resists its own abstraction through an ethnographic case study of a popular software development methodology called "extreme programming" (Auer and Miller 2002; Beck 2000; Jeffries 2004; Succi 2002; Wake 2001). Amid the growth of "extreme" sports[1] such as "aggressive" inline skating, snow-boarding, "vert" biking, "extreme bouldering" and base jumping, why would computer programming and software development need to become "extreme"? Extreme sport, like extreme programming, relies on minimal technical backup and technical equipment. Extreme bouldering, for instance, involves climbing large rocks with minimal assistance from ropes, carabiners, harnesses, pitons and cleats. Extreme sports heighten exposure to specific forms of physical danger. However, it could be argued that even in this exposure, extreme sports seek a special form of protection, a special place or time lifted out from a world that seems to gloss over differences, that generalizes, abstracts, globalizes and above all, seems to constantly throw up unwanted changes.

When, as in extreme programming or XP (not to be confused with the many other XP products such as Windows XP or the Athlon XP CPU chip that appeared around the same time), software development allies itself to extreme sports, when it strips down to a bare minimum of equipment, the hope is that programming could be disentangled from an overly gadget-enhanced, system-managed experience. It seeks to shed the encumbrance of unwanted abstractions, discourses and practices that trammel coding work. "XP aims to replace modern and late-modern methodologies," as Noble and Biddle (2002, 10) suggest. Like many other cultural processes (media, art, design, architecture, management, politics, science), programming has sought over the last decades to reinvent itself without, or in resistance to, some of its own modernist baggage. But in the name of what does XP does this? XP, as we will see, asserts the agency of programmers engaged in the act of coding. In order to do this, it has to generate viable representations of what coding is. The effort to sustain the primacy of programming in software production triggers new permutations in the agential relations associated with code. Code agency still pivots on the double-faceted mode of code's existence as both expression and process. But in XP, the act of coding or programming itself becomes a prototype, an entity that the code-as-index is held to represent (as discussed in chapter one, in Gell's sense; see Gell 1998, 25–27) for the work of software development more generally. Certain aspects of coding work, such as writing, compiling and running code, are singled out as prototypical coding activities to which all software production should be attached. This is a tactical abstraction of certain coding practices in resistance to formalizing abstractions associated with software engineering and project management. It attempts to position coding itself as the most significant activity in software development in order to challenge certain relations of production associated with other forms of software engineering (for instance, the processes used in developing RAMOSS described in chapter 6). Making code and coding into a prototype for software production seems very recursive, but in terms of the contestations of agency associated with software, the primacy of coding can be seen as asserting the identity of programmers as the originators of software.

Unwanted equipment

How does extreme programming reduce technical equipment to a minimum? How do a group of software developers change their work practices in light of extreme programming, and what work do they do to make XP into a software-development process? For those answers we must explore what actually happens in an XP project, ranging from seating arrangements, the timetabling of programming, the techniques of integrating different components of contemporary software systems, the conversations and arguments over how code executes, and the material culture of a software development project. Observations of these seemingly mundane matters are relevant to a more global question about the contemporary production of software in risk-averse post-dotcom crash network cultures: How do software developers, software engineers and project managers cope with a new economy increasingly imagined in terms of human and code mobility (Kelly 1998)?

Since the mid-1960s, software engineering methods have sought to instrument the process of software development and to batten down against a stormy outside world. Software industries have developed many general methodologies, systems and organizational practices in attempts to render the production of software manageable and predictable (Sommerville 2000). In their account of why highly formalized or structured systems of collaboration fail, the sociologists Susan Leigh Star and Karen Ruhleder argue that the obstacle to generalized systems of collaboration usually resides in local practices:

> Experience with groupware suggests that highly structured applications for collaboration will fail to become integrated into local work practices.... Rather, experimentation over time results in the emergence of a complex constellation of locally-tailored applications and repositories, combined with pockets of local knowledge and expertise. They begin to interweave themselves with elements of the formal infrastructure to create a unique and evolving hybrid. This evolution is facilitated by those elements of the formal structure which support the redefinition of local roles and the emergence of communities of practice around the intersection of specific technologies and types of problems. (Star and Ruhleder 1996, 132)

The hybridization of local knowledge and infrastructure described by Star and Ruhleder is redoubled in XP. Just as Java cites other programming languages, XP resists other software production methodologies by citing programming itself as core activity. Importantly, XP promotes selected elements of local practice into production processes, as if programmers have learnt a lesson on how to construct constellations of interwoven elements as local-global hybridizations.

Extreme programming began to make a name for itself in 2000. XP conferences, websites, how-to books and articles, list-groups and user-groups established themselves and expanded rapidly (see Jeffries 2004). Most articles and books either provide a formal, somewhat doctrinal account of XP as a software development process, or closely reflect the personal experience of participants or proponents (e.g., Beck 2000; Wake 2001). All these approaches understandably reflect the interests of people in doing XP (or sometimes resisting it). Few detailed ethnographic studies of software development address how software production is caught up in wider contestations of agency (but see Ó'Riain 2000; Button and Sharrock 1996; Aneesh 2005). An ethnographic study of XP would not try to explain what XP would ideally look like, nor would it judge whether XP really lives up to the claims. Rather, ethnographic observation should help us understand an encounter between a programmer-centric software-production discourse and a group of actual programmers. The aim of such an investigation is not to develop general models of ordinary activity, but to examine the hybridization between densely embodied local practices and abstract, infrastructural or formal elements. For a long time, ethnography meant observing how people interacted with other in situ, and how they ordered things to maintain their place. But more recently it has come to mean, as Marcus (1995) argues, "locating the detectable system-awareness in the everyday consciousness and actions of subjects' lives" (111). This bifocal emphasis on relations between people and things in a given locality (cards, computers, documents, software, tables, memo boards, books, telephones, pens, papers), and "system awareness" means seeing people and software as connected by a "logic of association" (Marcus 1995, 105) that connects different sites. Looking at people or things (computers, software, furniture, books, networks, etc.) separately from "system-awareness" would mean abstracting from important parts of the process that develops and configures software.[2]

When my study started in mid-2001, a software development project was well underway at Knowledge Management Systems (KMS), a software production house in Manchester Science Park, which is situated near the universities east of Manchester's city center in northwest England. A small, somewhat fluctuating team of software developers, testers and managers (six to twelve people) were working on a knowledge management system called Deskartes Universal. The name of the system hints at both a valuation of knowledge (the philosopher Descartes sought clear and distinct knowledge of the world), globalization (hence "Universal") and office work ("Desk").[3] Described in basic terms, KMS's Deskartes system offers organizations access to knowledge embedded in their documents. It organizes documents within a heavily keyworded, cross-referenced repository that can process and "learn" from natural language search queries. The system captures "expert" replies to common queries. Once deposited in Universal, knowledge becomes accessible through natural-language queries ("What is …") typed into forms in a web browser. Proprietary neural network algorithms developed by researchers at the nearby Manchester University form the basis of Universal. Universal brings up relevant information more directly than most standard search engines and "improves" its search based on feedback from human operators. As a software product, Universal was targeted to call centers, help desks or wherever in organizations the same questions are asked repeatedly in endlessly slightly different variations.

When the cards are down: XP as a game of software development

From the standpoint of the programmers at KMS, the important attributes of this system for their work were its reliance on Java and JavaScript/HTML as programming/scripting languages, its use of a distributed component-based architecture (enterprise JavaBeans running on an application server) and its reliance on standard web-browser software as a user interface. These features situate Deskartes Universal as a typical Internet-based commercial software application of the late 1990s or of early 2000. Such features of the software development environment impinge fairly strongly on the day-to-day work of the development team.

When I arrived in June 2001, programming on Universal was moving over to a version of the XP process. In one of our early conversations, Dave, leader of the developer team, framed the move by talking about code quality in a previous version of Universal that had been outsourced to a software development team in India. The results were regarded, rightly or wrongly, as so poor that a new, local KMS team had to begin again almost from scratch. A long printout of some of the "worst" code from the outsourced project has been stuck to the wall in the developers' area. The extensive UML diagrams (unified modeling language: see Fowler and Scott 1997) sent by KMS to the Indian development team had been more or less ignored, according to Dave. These diagrams, consisting of many boxes, arrows and labels, were themselves the product of different software design methodology, popular in the late 1990s, the Rational Rose process (now owned by IBM). Although the KMS developers still occasionally drew UML diagrams, the diagrams were generally sketched on a whiteboard instead of onscreen, and only served as a temporary help in working through some current problem, rather than providing a map of the overall system. Driven by the interest and enthusiasm of two senior developers (Dave and Roger), and eased by the relatively small team size, many of the ways in which KMS' developers worked, the software and hardware tools they used, and the kind of system they were writing, reflected XP's influence.

On a typical day in the developers' area of KMS, most of the developers could be found seated facing inward around tables pushed together to form one large rectangle in the main part of the room. Computer monitors, laptops, PalmPilots, telephones, Coke bottles, snack food, network cables and the odd book (Dilbert cartoons, or computer books such as Fowler and Beck 1999) lay scattered over the tables. In a departure from images of headphone-wearing late-night programmers, developers rolled their chairs alongside each other so that two people could look at one screen as they "pair-programmed" (discussed later). Occasionally a developer would say, "Flag's up," stand and go to the end of the table to use a computer identified with a scrawled paper notice as "Build Machine." Sometimes a developer would go to a board covered with blue, orange and pink cardboard cards and add or take down cards. On occasion a developer might sit outside this large communal table at a separate workstation. Against a back wall, large bookcases held several hundred computer books, manuals and periodicals. In one corner of the room near the entrance, Kirsty, the project manager, worked in a glass-walled office. Just outside the entrance to the developers' area, the software testers have a work area. Also near the entrance, a small meeting room almost filled by a large table, chairs and a whiteboard was used for developers' "stand-up meetings" or longer planning meetings.

Some of these features—the snack food, the mobile phones and handhelds, the thick semipopular computer how-to books—are common to software development teams. Yet the environment at KMS was patterned to ensure that software systems were developed in certain ways and not others: the build machine at the end of the rectangular table, the memo board with colored cards, the chairs rolled together and the arrangement of the tables into a central island signify a somewhat unusual mode of organization of software development.

"Programming itself" (with just a few small things added)

More than one copy of the books by Kent Beck (2000), a key figure in extreme programming, lay on the developers' tables, and they had been read, at least in part, by various members of the team; Dave pointed them out and recommended them to visitors. Beck proposes that the best way of understanding XP lies in the metaphor of programming. In a slightly paradoxical statement, he writes:

XP uses the metaphor of programming for its activities—that is, everything you do looks in some way like programming: Programming in XP is like programming with a few small things added, like automated testing. However, like all the rest of XP, XP development is deceptively simple. All the pieces are simple enough to explain, but executing them is hard. (Beck 2000, 97)

There are two issues here. First, how can software projects be reorganized by taking programming itself as a metaphor for software development? Second, why would software developers want to use programming as a metaphor? Beck's statement hints that software projects have had trouble in the past with activities that did not "look like" programming. For instance, structured software design methods "normally involves producing graphical system models and results in large amounts of documentation" (Sommerville 2000, 58), which then has to be maintained by someone. Design documentation, as ethnographies of engineering have shown, creates trouble for engineering projects in general because it does not look like software development:

[W]ithin the particular work-a-day world of engineers efforts are made to upgrade the production of documentation in order to ensure that it is built into the engineer's work. Upgrading the work is a general device that is used to ensure that 'dirty work' gets done and within software engineering there are a number of such upgrading devices that are used in this respect. (Button and Sharrock 1996, 382)

Making "use cases" (as in the rational unified process) or drawing class diagrams (using unified modeling language) might not look much like programming to programmers used to writing lines of program code, compiling them, running them and then writing more code. When Beck says that "XP uses the metaphor of programming for its activities," the iterative cycle of writing, compiling and running code is extended as metaphor for the whole of software development. Arguably, programmers embody that practice of cycling through coding, compiling and running code at a fairly basic level. Their competence, craft skills and even identity as programmers hinges on that process. XP extrapolates the "close to the machine" practice of programming to a more explicit software development process.

Formal software development methodologies tend to situate coding at one point on a multistepped waterfall or a multilooped spiral process. During more conventional processes, the successive phases of risk analysis, development of a statement of requirements, prototyping, simulations, development plans, requirement validation and so on remain discrete and precede the final steps of coding, unit testing and acceptance testing (Sommerville 2000, 54). Nearly all software design methods allow shuttling back and forth to revise earlier design decisions and adjust specifications in light of changed circumstances. The spiral model makes these revisions and adjustments explicit. Yet overall development of the system heads towards a single endpoint marked at the outset. Steering all work toward that endpoint becomes the most important goal of methodologies, and a lot of noncoding work goes into producing plans, models and progress reports. The production of software has for decades been seen as resistant to industrial or Fordist techniques (e.g., Brooks 1995; see Aneesh 2001). The very term "software developer" conveys a certain open-endedness that software development methodologies attempt to close off. XP is "extreme" in that it abandons this linear process and withdraws into coding work. Although it is an "agile" methodology, in XP, every part of the designing and building of the system is constantly looping back on itself. Looping or iterating, a fundamental formal structure of most programming languages, becomes in XP a rhetorical tactic used to refigure all software development as something akin to coding. It seeks to shield coding from being overtaken by the dangers that Ellen Ullman refers to when she laments the "dark, unspecified areas."

Cardboard as programming tool

How does the metaphor of programming play out in practice? As one example, rather than gathering requirements (the formal statements of what a system will do, to which the software developers are usually contractually bound) at the beginning of a project, an XP project passes through many requirements-gathering cycles. Incremental gathering of requirements occurs throughout the life of the project. Without any final goal, development takes on an open-ended character. It may end up quite different than originally anticipated—as Deskartes Universal eventually did—without the project having necessarily failed.

The brightly colored cardboard cards scattered on tables and pinned to the memo board at KMS visibly derived from the XP method. To understand how software development can "look like" programming, as Beck promises, the movements of these cards provide a key example. KMS's color-coded cards—orange for "stories," blue for "tasks" and pink for "defects"—were also implicitly coded for hierarchy and work processes. An orange story card would, in principle, have been written by a customer, a system user; a blue task card would have been written by a developer; and a defect card either by a system tester or user. Usually the different kinds of cards were kept apart. Over the 3–4 weeks of each development cycle, cards were filled out, shuffled, dealt out, handed in, "spawned" (as in, "Let's spawn a card for that"), displayed, swapped, counted, stored, taken back, written on and put away. They circulated constantly through different members of the team, were visible in different places, and were used for different purposes.

Essentially, the cards were very simple forms with no more than ten lines of text in the main description field. Often, a card held just one line (e.g., "load security level frame for current result") as well as a date, a story, task or defect number, and space for brief details about completion times and dates. The simplicity and limited capacity of these cards to carry information give pause in this context. Why resort to something as archaic as index cards? They seem a fairly trivial tool—old-fashioned, clumsy, inflexible—compared to the sophisticated project-management, scheduling and software-design tools available to software developers. However, the color-coded cards are an explicit part of XP. In discarding those sophisticated software-based tools for an archaic graphic medium like index cards, in replacing "requirements engineering" with "gathering stories," XP scales software development back—and shields it from management scrutiny. As earlier chapters have suggested, whenever code or programming becomes an object of attention as such, agency is contested. Here, the contest was played out between different doctrines for the control of software production. These cards literally moved control of the project away from the eyes and hands of managers.

How did the cards move around? What propelled them from meeting table to memo board, from memo board to developer table, from developer table back to memo board, from memo board to tracker's desk and so on? The slow movement of the cards is significant. Cards were strewn on tables singly and in packs; they were pinned to the memo board in rows and sometimes in envelopes. People walked to the memo board, put cards on and took them off. Individual cards were scattered between workstations. On her desk, Kirsty, the "tracker" who kept track of the team's work rate, copied numbers and dates from stacks of cards into a spreadsheet pinned up each week on the memo board as a summary of project progress. The production, distribution and consumption of these cards threaded through much of the work of the Universal team.

Like playing cards, XP cards carried different values at KMS. Like most card games also, the cards were shuffled and dealt in rounds (see discussion below of the release, iteration and task loops). They circulated through different hands: customer, developer, tracker and tester. The colors immediately differentiated work. Putting an orange story card on the table in the meeting room, for example, indicated something relatively portentous because a story card usually involved substantial subsidiary tasks and a lot of developer time. Moreover, because they moved across boundaries between the development team and the outside world, XP story cards called for careful evaluation.

Calculating time: "Ideal Graham days"

It would be onerous to document all the ways in which cards moved around. However, their movement has a few salient features. Importantly, cards did not move automatically between developers' desks, meeting room tables, memo board and managers' desks. There was no online or automated handling of these documents. Rather, talking triggered, accompanied and steered the movement of cards. Questions, comments, argument, instructions and directions surrounded the production, movement and reading of cards.

Unlike playing cards, whose value is fixed by the rules of the game, the value of a story was subject to much negotiation at KMS. A "points estimated" field in the bottom corner of the card reflected (in a very condensed form) a whole series of judgments, evaluation, estimations and guesses performed by the software developers during a planning meeting. The weight of a story card—its worth—was worked out by the developers through a complex set of negotiations carried out in team meetings. The stories had been written by Dave, the team leader, in collaboration with Mike, the XP "customer" or notional user of Universal. At KMS, story cards were read to developers during planning meetings. Afterward, the tasks composing the story needed to be worked out. For instance, at the start of a planning meeting, Dave would write the stories for discussion on the whiteboard. After several hours of fairly intense discussion, the points-estimated field in the lower right-hand corner of the card could be filled in with a numerical result like 4.0G, which summed up long analysis about how to implement the story as a set of tasks and how long it would take in "ideal Graham days" (a measurement based on the estimated amount of work that one developer, Graham, could do in a day). Developers would then break the story card down into stacks of blue task cards.

A story underwent translation onto blue task cards through spoken interactions between different members of the team. The following conversation explores, fairly tentatively, how this translation could occur and what work it would involve. The coach (another term that links XP to extreme sports), stood near the whiteboard and pointed to a line of writing:

> DAVE: This is the nasty controversial one. [Laughter.] All right, the detailed selection tags that we've got from there [pointing at another story on the whiteboard]. Now what we kind of figured is that tags will be some fairly ordinary tags from the JSP page [Java Server Pages, a part of the web-server infrastructure used to construct the web-browser interface to Universal], we'll probably have some scripts that trigger things going on. So, you're probably going to be doing a bit of reuse in both cases. And this reuse might actually now be direct reuse with the exception that this tag [pointing at a list on the board] you don't want to prepopulate.
>
> ADAM: Sorry, I missed something. Umm, the reuse of tags thing is going to actually be quite small, isn't it?
>
> DAVE: Yeah.
>
> ADAM: It's the JSP page that may well have to be working out how it works again?
>
> DAVE: Well, you should be able to make the code easily using any code that's lying around.
>
> ADAM: A quarter for each one then.

The last line of the transcript seems abrupt and unrelated, but that was where the whole exchange (and many others like it) was heading. "A quarter for each one" means 0.25G, or a quarter of an ideal day's work for each task. So the exchange between Dave and Adam arrived at a numerical score for the amount of work involved, which could now be written on the top right-hand corner of a blue card. Adam, in fact, immediately reached across the table and began writing on some blue cards. At the same time, all the other developers in the meeting heard how this particular piece of work could be carried out. References and reminders of code already written for previous tasks form an important component of the exchange. The conversation brought new cards into circulation, and at the same time, the future circulation of those cards in the group was foreshadowed. A trajectory for the card was established and an allocation of time (as represented in the score) agreed upon so that later, when a developer took that task card off the memo board, her work would be scaffolded by the talk that surrounded the card's creation: the consequences of taking on that task had been anticipated and collectively estimated.

The cards marked the outcome of flexible dialogical interactions in planning meetings or conversations around the workstations concerning the production of code. Talk precipitated point estimations, new task cards and brief notes. At the same time, the collective composed of developers and cards was somewhat restructured; their relations to each and to Universal were differentiated and the material environment took on a slightly different texture through the advent of new task cards. The cards circulated thereafter as tokens of that structuring of group and system achieved in the meeting. Problems, unanticipated difficulties and implications emerged later, but they were partly framed by a collective cognition already developed in the group. Talk surrounded the creation of cards, and cards often gave rise to much more talk, especially around the developers' work table. Developers wrote cards, collected them, handed them round and swapped them. But a lot of work was attached to cards. In particular, coming into possession of a task card usually meant working on that task for anywhere between a few hours and a day and a half translating the brief written description on the card into some code.

Nested loops and relations with others

In 2001, the Deskartes Universal faced problems familiar to many software projects at the time. Frequent staffing changes, downsizing of some parts of the company, corporate mergers with other software-development companies, shifts in management direction, local aftershocks of the dotcom crash earlier in the year, and technical problems in configuring a distributed system, as well as supporting previous releases, were all affecting the project. In 2002, KMS went out of business, although Deskartes Universal was bought by another company and its development continued there. As mentioned above, the whole focus of mainstream software engineering methods rests on making programming work predictable and ordering work processes so that their timing and outcomes can be steered and measured. A mixture of different technical, social and organizational events tend to resist steering and thwart predictions. XP, with its motto of "embrace change," wants to treat such problems as normal rather than exceptional.

How does XP make instability and unpredictability the norm? Like most software engineering processes, XP divides work into phases or stages. Like the spiral model of software design, XP's stages run in loops. As the very term "loop" indicates, XP works by configuring all software development work as programming, even if that work does not have much to do with programming. Although programming is what programmers know best, in

XP they are also asked to relate to software development in another way: their work process is metaphorically treated as programming, as setting up and running loops over time. Each level of nested loop takes into account different kinds of unpredictability, runs over different time frames and makes use of different ways of organizing communication within the developer team. A "release" cycle will run between two and six months and involves writing stories; an "iteration" will involve programming some stories and last one to four weeks; a "task" will take a few days; and writing "unit tests" (discussed below) and code in pairs will take a few hours.

XP promises to put the system into service in the "real world" right away, in its first release loop. Beck (2000) writes: "The ideal XP project goes through a short initial development phase, followed by years of simultaneous production support and refinement" (131). Normally, clients run acceptance tests at the end of development projects to check that the software matches their original specification or requirements. In XP, those acceptance tests are run at the end of the first release, rather than the end of a project, and this first release will occur a few months into the project, not years later. The question of who would write the acceptance tests for Universal and when they should be written was a vexing question for KMS. In theory, the customer (a role officially defined by XP doctrine) should write them, but at KMS, the customer did not know enough about XP to do that, with the result that in one meeting, Dave, the coach, came in with a stack of printed pages he referred as "the first acceptance tests we have ever had." Professional Services, the part of KMS that would have to actually support Universal at customer sites, had complained that there were no manuals or documents. Rather than write those manuals, the development team was itself going to begin writing acceptance tests, from which Professional Services could infer what the system should do.

The "iterations" at KMS were marked by meetings at which plans were made and difficulties and problems raised. These included meetings planning the next release or the next iteration or addressing day-to-day problems. Most of the time, developers at their workstations were working within that lowest-level loop and marking their iterations by adding and removing cards from the memo boards. Task cards on the board would be taken by developers and when completed, put into a "ready to be tested" envelope for the testing team. Periodically, Kirsty, the project manager and XP tracker (again, an officially defined role; see Beck 2000, 144), collected all the completed cards and copied the completion dates and other details into the spreadsheet she used to calculate the overall "project velocity." These calculations were used to estimate the amount of work that the team could do in the next iteration of the release. A printout of the spreadsheet itself was usually pinned to the memo board.

Exiting the loop

Loops in the XP process flow from the rhetorical figure of programming as an activity that constantly cycles between writing, compiling and running code. But loops run when a program executes. As previous chapters have argued, the interactions between code as something written and read, and code as something executed are unstable, or even metastable. In XP, the locus of agency associated with code shifts again. Programmers themselves adopt and espouse, willingly, a form of agency founded on programming as a special activity (see Graham 2004). If programmers collectively turn their work into a form of embodied program based on loops executed over weeks and months, how is execution linked to production of software? How does the KMS team maintain the regularity of loops?

The other guiding metaphor for XP, driving, is as Beck (2000) says, "the paradigm for XP": "software development is like steering, not like getting the car pointed straight down the road. Our job as programmers is to give the customer a steering wheel and give them feedback about exactly where we are on the road" (28). In principle, the practices that organize work within loops include the planning game discussed above, frequent releases of the software, an aversion to overly complex software designs or architectures, tight limits on working time, and unusual approaches to coding work such as pair programming, collective code ownership, continuous integration and writing tests for the software before the software itself (Beck 2000, 54). Via these practices, the programming team turns itself into a car, presumably an expensive one, driven by the "customer" or client. These practices are the "few small things added" in Beck's characterization of XP as basically programming with a few things added (and hence, an extreme activity). According to the overarching metaphor, a loop continues only when test conditions are met. But how does a development team know when those conditions have been met or that it is headed in the right direction?

The programmers' environment has been modified to afford quick recognition of whether a task has been completed successfully. For instance, at the lowest-level loop, source code created or modified during the course of a task (the smallest chunk of work done by a programming pair) can only be committed into the team's source code repository when all the unit tests (small fragments of code that problem the main source code to see if it behaves as expected) for that code and the rest of the application run cleanly. In XP, a number of crucial relations in the production of code converge on unit tests. Firstly, the unit tests for a given task are written before the code; completion of the task is conditional on passing these tests. Secondly, to the extent that they accept responsibility for checking that all previous unit tests work before adding new code to the shared source-code repository, the programmers collectively "own" all the source code for the software. The use of a source-code repository such as concurrent versions systems (CVS, also used by many open-source projects; see GNU 2004) stands at the core of XP since it allows constant and untrammeled sharing and modification of code. Other software-development environments impose stricter controls over who can change code and when they can change it (e.g., IBM's Visual Age relies on notions of hierarchical privileges, code ownership and publication to control code editing). In XP, programmers premise their work on correctly written and functioning unit tests. Unit tests counterbalance free access to code. Developers commit code to the repository only on the condition that all existing unit tests have been passed. Writing and running code in the form of unit tests allows melding of changes to the shared code of the system itself to become a frequent and relatively uneventful process. The unit tests exist as Java code shared via the CVS. Without a way to meld changes to code, group ownership of source code and scripts would become unworkable. Conversely, without commonly shared code, the idea of writing unit tests that must run fully before declaring any task finished would be meaningless.

Before starting a task, programmers retrieve the last version of the code from CVS. When they retrieve code from the common CVS repository, developers can presume that it will pass all existing unit tests, but as a first step, they often run all the existing tests to make sure. At KMS, work on their own task (as written on a blue task card) began by developing new unit tests and then new code that passes those tests. Finally, if all went well, the tests and the code were put back into the code repository.

KMS used a simple software tool, JUnit, developed by Kent Beck, to automatically run the tests. In JUnit, a solid green line shows a completely successful set of tests. A red line means some test has failed. The KMS developers followed the rule of never putting program code into the CVS repository (maintained on a dedicated computer, the "Build Machine," at the end of the developers' table) without having first obtained the green light from JUnit. While seeing that green line would not guarantee that they had completed their own task as required (since they may not have written adequate unit tests for their own code), it did allow them to gauge whether the changed code had "broken" any existing tests.

The JUnit test software shows something else important. Software developers nearly always work on a localized part of a project. At KMS, developers usually worked on different parts of the system in isolation from the system as a whole. Such is the complexity of contemporary multitier web-based systems, that only the occasional semiautomated work of building a full release of Universal could be said to involve the whole system. Yet work on one part of Universal nearly always impinged on other parts of the system. Rather than just testing their own code, developers typically ran all the tests written to date to ensure that hidden conflicts between changes and other parts of the system became visible as early as possible. Running all the tests before committing code constituted an important feature of daily, even hourly, work. It meant that system integration problems that might otherwise have appeared late in development appeared early and often. The practice of testing merges in this example with continuous integration, so that production becomes something more like continuous modulation. As Latour (1996) writes, "By accumulating little solidities, little durabilities, little resistances, the project ends up gradually becoming somewhat more real" (45–46).

Programming talks code into existence

Testing works against the unexpected side effects of ongoing code changes. The green or red line on JUnit quickly shows if existing tests have been broken by someone's newly added code. But running JUnit assumes code has come into existence, or that coding work has occurred. "At the end of the day, there has to be a program. So, I nominate coding as the one activity we know we can't do without," writes Kent Beck (2000, 44). XP plays down images of heroic late-night coding sessions by taciturn headphone-cocooned programmers buzzing along on Jolt cola. It replaces that figure with pair programming.

For programmers, pair programming seems to be the most startling feature of XP. It forces them to forfeit coding autonomy. At KMS, almost all work on Universal was being done in pairs, but not always willingly. Occasionally, a team member would work away from the group, but usually not on coding (the two members of the team doing acceptance tests, the tests that determine whether the system does what it was meant to do, almost always worked alone). The computing hardware installed in the developers' area reflected KMS's shift to pair programming. Development work was done on laptops docked to an external monitor and network, which lent a somewhat temporary, provisional feel to that space compared to the heavily organized space at other workplaces (such as the server room at Forge Research). Yet it conformed to XP's grand injunction to work with a minimum of technology. Various programming styles had to be accommodated in the pairing of programmers. Although some programmers paired more frequently than others, mixing and swapping of partners occurred. Sometimes laptops moved around between pairs. Some developers kept a closer hold on a particular development machine than others: Paul, for instance, installed a complete Linux development environment on a machine, including the substantial Enterprise JavaBeans application server and web-server components needed to run Universal (that machine became consistently his own.)

These changes in the workplace setup generated a great amount of talk about code and coding. Usually programming and software development are seen as solitary and cerebral rather than oral. During a typical pair-programming session at KMS, Roger and Pete, a relatively new member of the team, paired to deal with a "defect" task. They took the card labeled "Template.java defect" from the memo board where a tester, Mark, had pinned it and moved to a machine. Roger took the keyboard and ran the unit tests using JUnit:

ROGER: Right, let's just see how far we go with this and then go back.

PETE: So there's no specific place for running the system?

[A green line comes up on JUnit.]

ROGER: Ah, there we go.... This is the version that should have everything substituted into it.

PETE: Right, so is that the form of the tag that the template [uses]?

ROGER: Yeah. [Taking a piece of scrap paper and writing on it] What happens is that you have a template file with most JSP pages, and in that file it has all the variable bits delimited by underscores. So that by the time it gets rendered into HTML, all the underscore something or rather underscore should have been converted into something real. [...] The way they substitute URL is ... [looks for another piece of paper] here it is. Now, this is all right, this is a ready drawn piece of paper. Before ... right, so you have a template, you do [writing] "t = new Template." And you give it a string full of ordinary text, with things delimited by markers that are going to be substituted. That creates your template. You then do a whole load of sets. [...] You then do String results = t.value. t.value() which is the method we've changed, is the thing that actually substitutes all the "underscore thingy-ma-jigs underscore" into actual values.

Right, that's not a problem at all if you do it the way we used to do it, which is that you go through the hashtable of things that you're going to substitute. Because when you do one of these, it basically puts it in a hashtable. The way we used to do it is that you'd go through the hashtable looking for "underscore name underscore." When you found it, you do a global ... Sorry, when you found it, you'd go to the hashtable, iterate over all the keys, for each of the keys, you'd go and look in here and do a global search and replace on "underscore name underscore" for Vladimir. With me?

PETE: No.

ROGER: [Laughs.]

This interaction continued as Roger explained to Pete the underpinnings of the defect they'd taken responsibility for. This pair-programming dialogue unfolds as a kind of lesson. Roger and Pete sat at the computer, but they did not actually write code for the program. Roger wrote fragments of code on a piece of paper as he explained a part of Universal's workings, but no working code came from that. It was only written so that Pete could understand how code would need to be written to deal with the defect.

Understandings of the system design, how it works and how it can be made to work differently, were often circulated and contested between pairs. Without an articulation of how the system works, programmers cannot code as a pair. By this simple measure, XP attaches talking and intersubjective communication to programming. At KMS, talk attempted to generate a shared understanding of what had happened or should happen in some part of Universal. This was not always very straightforward. In the following snippet, a programming pair (Daniel and Roger) tried to comprehend some anomalous database behavior, while Dave stood nearby:

DANIEL: So you think it's throwing an exception and the "finally" [a particular line in the program code] is not executing for some reason.

DAVE: "Finally" always executes.

ROGER: Even when JBuilder—
DANIEL: JUnit?

ROGER: JUnit is ...

DAVE: What?

ROGER: is polling the …

DAVE: Yeah, "finally" always executes.

DANIEL: I don't think JUnit has some magical control over this.

DAVE: No.

DANIEL: Yeah, it's just a classloader. When it invokes a method, it probably just does it in a "try" and a "catch." And if you don't throw it up, you don't ever see it, right?

ROGER: Doesn't it give you a bit more of a [performance]?

DANIEL: I don't think it's going back to the old database for whatever reason.

ROGER: Well, it must be.

DANIEL: After the second run.

ROGER: It must be something we've done.

DANIEL: [doubtfully] Oooh.

ROGER: It must be!

DANIEL: Go ahead, try it.

DAVE: Do you want a stand-up?

Several interesting strands of pair programming as a practice intersect in this example. Roger and Daniel were discussing why a particular set of unit tests failed. In XP, success with unit tests implies completion of a programming task. In this exchange, Roger and Daniel struggled to determine whether the cause of the test failures lay in the database or in the way JUnit, itself a piece of Java software, ran the tests. Daniel argued that JUnit hadn't done anything "magical" or hidden from their understanding of the situation, while Roger maintained that JUnit had done something they didn't understand. A few lines into the exchange, the discussion dropped into a more theoretical inquiry into how the Java Virtual Machine executed code. At this point, Dave, an experienced developer, entered the exchange and forthrightly asserted that a certain Java code construct could only work in one way: "'Finally' always executes." This allowed Daniel to reinforce his own interpretation of JUnit's behavior, in particular to emphasize the point that JUnit could not be responsible for their current problem. In response, Roger moved to a slightly different and less specific position, suggesting that the problem must "be something we've done." Daniel rejected this move and in turn suggested that they no longer talk about it but actually try it out in practice. Dave, for his part, moved in the opposite direction, invoking the collective intellect of the Deskartes programming team. Switching roles into XP "coach" mode, he asked, "Do you want a stand-up [meeting]?" In other words, he proposed escalating the problem into an impromptu but more formal general discussion among the whole development team. As it turned out, Roger and Daniel did not want that. They resolved the problem by running some code.

In each of these exchanges, little or no code was written. Yet in miniature, each incident stages a contestation around where agency lies in the production of software. Small knots, kinks or hitches that snag the execution of code loops in the XP process are not just problems to be ironed out. They indicate points where different materializations of agency are at stake, where who does what is decided.

Timing between development and production

As well as installing gauges such as JUnit to check that looping conditions have been met and scaffolding coding with conversation, XP also removes some important thresholds and stages on which other software-development processes fixate. System integration, an important step in most software-development processes, does not figure as a discrete step in XP. The acute uncertainty felt by software-development teams on the day they first put all the components and subsystems together disappears. "Will the system hang together?" doesn't loom large because the continuous integration entailed in writing and running unit tests has pre-empted that question.

It would be incorrect to assume that continuous integration worked effortlessly or that XP cleanly produced software where other methods fell short. Many small incidents at KMS show the difficulties in translating principles into practice, as in the following episode.

SANJAY: What was the issue then with Eric?

ROGER: Just saw something that surprised us when we updated our files.

SANJAY: Local copy?

ROGER: Yes. We've got a builder script, and Eric changed the way that it works so that it actually changes the date of the files. It actually touches the files.

SANJAY: And that meant that you weren't sure whether you had the latest version?

ROGER: Well, it meant we weren't sure whether we should check them in or whether we should leave them alone.

This incident concerns what happens to time during continuous system integration. Roger and Daniel had made some changes to the code, run the tests, seen JUnit go green and were ready to place their work in the shared CVS repository. They went to the CVS machine at the end of the developers' shared table. Just as they were poised to commit their changes, they noticed the CVS program was marking some files with red icons. They had expected to see all white icons, which would have reassured Roger and Daniel that the files were all current and that nothing else needed to be done. As with JUnit, the CVS program served as a sort of gauge, this time on the state of the repository. Red icons meant the files had been modified but not committed or finally checked in by someone else. If Sanjay and Daniel had committed their work at this point, they might have overwritten someone else's work. Instead, a conversation ensued in which Roger asked Eric to help him interpret the anomaly. It turned out that due to recent changes in the scripts that automatically build Deskartes, certain classes of files (those "touched" by the "builder script") looked as if they had been changed when in fact they hadn't.

Continuous system integration includes complicated temporal coordination between members of the development team and shared spontaneous articulation of contingent interpretations of the current state of code development. In this case, red icons on certain build files in the CVS repository henceforth only meant that a build script had been run; in the past they had signaled the need for action, but in the future they could be safely ignored. Two points emerge from this incident. Firstly, the proximity of developers around a shared table does not arise just from shared values of communication or feedback. Without the possibility of quickly constructing verbal agreement on what those icons meant, Roger and Daniel's work would have been on hold. They could not have committed their changes to the code repository without risking overwriting someone else's work. Secondly, removing a major stumbling block such as the conventional system-integration phase means redistributing all the configuration work needed to integrate the system throughout the duration of the project. Instead of "big bang" integration, XP promotes "steady state" expansion of the system.

Work sometimes falls outside the planned XP loops when execution of the loops is interrupted or fails. At KMS, iterations were not always fully complete before company priorities changed. One morning, three developers were suddenly asked to build a different version (the "Corp X. branch") of Universal as a demonstration installation for two potential clients. This configuration task was not scheduled on any of the task cards that normally described work to be done on the project.

Kirsty, the project manager, had asked them to have the demonstration ready by lunchtime. By just after 10 a.m., the main table was abuzz with normal banter, but the three developers seated along one side of the table (Adam, Paul and Sanjay) were troubled by the failure of the database-configuration scripts to work. They needed to run those scripts to create tables in the relational database, the part of Deskartes Universal that stores all knowledge managed by the system. Adam asked the whole team about it.

ADAM: [shouting] Eh, can I just get your attention for a moment.

[Some talk continues.]

ADAM: And Eric as well.... [All talk stops.] We're running the Corp X. branch at the moment. So it's the older version. And we're having problems with the database stuff. It's, it's not right. Can anyone think of the reasons why if we get the latest database creation scripts, all the schema and other stuff, if anything has changed that could cause any issues?

ROGER: [from the other side of the table] Yes.

ADAM: It has?

ROGER: There's all the security stuff that's gone in there. [Describes "Entity Beans" columns.]

ADAM: No, no. If you're adding columns, it's okay, it's only trying to use columns that exist. But it's whether things have changed ...

ROGER: I'm not sure if that's completely true. I don't understand. You shouldn't be having a problem anyway....

DAVE: Is the problem still just the problem table?

ADAM: No, we're having a rollback exception in EJBException in insertTriggerOnCommunityTable.

DAVE: InsertTriggerOnCommunityTable?

ROGER: Did you run the whole thing? I thought you were just going to cut out the bit with the rollback table.

ADAM: No, we just ran the whole thing.

ROGER: Right, you needed just the problem table.

ERIC: I've run the whole scripts last week.

ROGER: The new scripts?

ERIC: No, for the Corp X.

DAVE: But Roger said his script's on the main branch.

ADAM: Oh. Right.

ERIC: I don't understand why you were on the new branch.

ADAM: No, it doesn't matter.

At this point, Adam swung back to the computer, started up the CVS program and retrieved the database scripts from the Corp X. branch. Everyone else returned to their own work and conversations. What happened in this episode? How did Adam, Dave and Sanjay come to use the (apparently) wrong database script? What does this kind of episode say about the linear execution of nested loops outlined in the XP how-to manuals?

The status of configuration work, a topic that has been of substantial interest to sociologists and anthropologists of technology, remains uncertain in XP. The three developers in this case happened to be working on configuring a slightly different version of the system. This work is more or less invisible in the XP process in several respects. Weeks earlier, trying to get this same branch working with an upgraded version of a piece of commercial software (the BEA WebLogic application server), Roger had put his face in his hands and said somewhat despairingly, "We're in setup hell." In other words, ad-hoc configuration work has no official status in XP. Although there may be information configuration gurus in an XP team (Eric, for instance, knew a lot about setting and configuring the proprietary application server on which Universal relies), none of the loops, tests or dialogical patterns that XP promotes explicitly address configuration. Like a harmful "goto" statement, configuration work can produce tangles.

Configuration work or "setup hell" incessantly troubles software systems, as well as many other technical practices (Suchman 1987). In this episode it interrupted the nested loops of the XP software-development process for a few hours.

Setting up a demonstration installation of the system consumes a lot of energy and forces a jump outside the nested loops of task, iteration and release. If we regard configuration work not as some unlucky contingency that befalls code from the outside, but as part of the normal course of events, what does this episode show? In some respects, XP attempts to sidestep configuration work by maintaining a common source code, a full and automated set of unit tests, and, less clearly, a set of configuration information (such as database scripts) consistent with the source code. Like the syntax of a programming language, these formal aspects of XP software development still emphasize production as a single process. However, while the common source code and fully running unit tests eliminate some configuration problems, other configuration work remains disruptive and unruly.

The problem of the doppelgänger: Simultaneous versions

On the morning in question, the work of the three developers lay on a different branch than the work of the main team (the term "branch" refers to the way different versions of the source code are stored by CVS, the code repository software). The Corp X. branch was a different version of the system being developed at the same time as the main branch. Work priorities had unexpectedly been switched onto the new branch by an outside interruption: a customer for the Universal system had been promised a demonstration by midday—almost as if to prove the agility of the software team. The system configuration problems arose when the team stepped outside the planned XP loops. Whereas XP predicates the release of a quick succession of versions, it does not envisage simultaneous execution of different loops.

How does XP handle a request for different versions of the same system at the same time? After an hour struggling to get the system up and running, Adam asked Dave for help.

ADAM: Dave?

DAVE: Hello.

ADAM: Is there any chance in getting everything working last week for us on this machine that either you or Eric (who isn't here at the moment) …

KIRSTY: [project manager, standing behind the developers] Eric's there.

ADAM: … could have updated anything on our machine, the Java source on our machine, about that Urgency [a feature of Universal that allows queries to be prioritized as urgent] or the notification?

DAVE: No. Ah, we didn't actually have anything to do with what you were doing the whole week.

ADAM: There's going to come a point, right, where, well, we've not even applied it yet. We've got differences on our machine, different to the Corp X. branch in CVS. And we've not made those changes.

DAVE: On the Java code?

ADAM: On the Java code. And we've not made those changes.

DAVE: [to Eric] Did you change any code on Adam's machine?

ERIC: Did I change any code on his machine?

ADAM: Last week, when you were getting stuff working, about Urgency.

DAVE: He couldn't have done it on Friday because he was at Corp X.

ADAM: On any day.

ERIC: I wouldn't have done anything on your machine anyway.

ADAM: It's not, I'm not pointing a finger or anything. [BR] was doing stuff directly on my machine. He might have changed the Java code.

ERIC: I wouldn't change it. Well, no, it wasn't me.

[Pause.]

ADAM: [to Dave and Eric, who are sitting nearby]: I mean, worst-case scenario is it all works and we commit what I've got on my machine into that branch of [Corp. X]

DAVE: But the whole question remains of how it got changed.

ADAM: Well, more, why and what else has been changed that we don't know about that we're going to commit into CVS.

DAVE: Did you do a commit Friday?

ADAM: I've not done a commit or anything with the Java stuff. The Java stuff has worked fine.

A bit later, after the developers trawled through more Java files on their machine, the episode continued.

ADAM: We've just done a diff [a change listing differences between source code documents] between what's on my machine and what's on the Corp X. branch, and there's differences.

KIRSTY: Well, they should be exactly the same.

ADAM: I've only seen a difference on the Query EDA.

ERIC: I, I recut that. [Pause.] I changed the Query entity and committed that on Thursday. I made changes to get it to work with the Corp X. branch.

DAVE: That's it!

ADAM: Right, cool. So we're just reading CVS wrong. Which is beautiful. It makes perfect sense. All we've got to do then … in fact, we can just do "get latest."

In this second scene, again resolved by a changed interpretation of the code repository, more people were drawn into the incident. Rather than three developers (already one more than the usual programming pair found in XP), five or six people were involved, including the project manager, the team leader and other developers. The XP setup of the workspace, with nearly all the developers seated around one large oblong table, staged and accelerated resolution. Once again talk, triggered by an obstacle, elicited recollections and alternative interpretations of the configuration of the development setup (CVS), which eventually allowed a configuration problem to be resolved.

The upshot

Several striking features of software production and the contemporary codescape emerge from extreme programming. Firstly, the potential significance of handwritten index cards in XP should not be underestimated. At KMS, the cards were simple but effective contrivances for specifying and keeping track of work done on code by different people at the same time, acting as lightweight, mobile yet local tags that indexed shared understandings of what Universal would do. They knitted together a very disparate set of work processes and orchestrated the temporally complicated work of developing distributed software systems. Without the cards, the nested-loop structure through which work was organized at KMS could not have been maintained. Taking, swapping, signing-off on and putting back cards—these acts made visible markers of work available to everyone. They allowed visual, almost immediate appraisal of collective work progress.

It is as if software development itself has withdrawn into earlier computational mechanisms like Hollerith tabulators or punch-card machines. The emphatically limited circulation of the cards, that fact that they could not easily be copied or handled away from the hands of the programmers, effectively co-located the production of software into a single room. This channeled the tendency of code to move about into selected circuits. XP insists strongly on the value of co-location, even as it works on software that might be itself highly distributed. The artifices used to coordinate the work of software development—unit tests, card games, code repository—directly address the problems of bulwarking coding against an unstable background of economic and organizational change. Something as simple as a set of cards in conjunction with a small piece of software like JUnit can be used to synthesize forms of practice that inhabit organizational life differently.

The metaphor of programming grafts onto software-development processes because it links software development to familiar, embodied practices of programming. While XP is spoken about in terms of performance, and progress is measured in terms of "velocity," XP reduces exposure to many outside influences, especially the management techniques present in other formal software-development processes. This has consequences for how programming and coding work are understood more generally. In an analysis of how artificial intelligence (AI) researchers used whiteboards, Suchman and Trigg (1992) suggested that

> like any product of skilled practice, the formalism inscribed on the board leaves behind the logic of its own production and use, seen here as collaborative craftwork of hands, eyes, and signs. But analyses of situated practice ... point to the contingencies of practical action on which logic-in-use, including the production and use of scenarios and formalisms, inevitably and in every instance relies. (173)

Suchman and Trigg wanted to counteract abstract models of mental operation predominant in AI research with the concrete, localized and embodied practices of AI researchers. Through their analysis of craftwork in the production of AI models, they sought to render visible the dark matter of AI research, especially as it transpires in the course of conversations and whiteboard writing. From a different direction, XP does something similar for software development. Rather than leaving "behind the logic of its own production and use," XP effectively turns the coordinated craftwork of hands, eyes, keys, screen and signs into the basis of a situated practice that resists formalism.

As an extreme activity, XP pares back software-development projects to programming plus "a few small things." The few small things include card games, talk, unit testing, code sharing and pair programming. In some ways, XP formalizes what would otherwise have remained relatively invisible, informal and negotiable. There's something ironic in using the metaphor of "extreme" for a style of programming that makes intersubjective communication the central activity of production. Like extreme sports, software development and many other collaborative activities do face relatively unstable and risky environments, but XP explicitly tackles the risk in software development by not armoring itself with heavy formalisms. Through its nested loops, it puts flexible organization of time at center stage. As the "setup-hell" episode illustrates, engineering projects, including software-development projects, do not deal solely or even principally with physical or technical risks. Much more than technical risk, the projection of dialogue, argument, agreement and evaluation onto software production through the lens of programming moves communication into the heart of making.

Chapter 8

Conclusion

However, beneath the fabricating and universal writing of technology, opaque and stubborn places remain. The revolutions of history, economic mutations, demographic mixtures lie in layers within it, and remain there, hidden in customs, rites and spatial practices.

de Certeau, *The Practice of Everyday Life*, 1984, 20

What can be learned from studying software? The introduction (chapter 1) to this book suggested that making an ontology of software would could heighten sensitivities to one contemporary site of mutability, contingency and necessity. It argued that software is a symptomatic present-day object that leads a complicated, circulatory existence. Software is a neighborhood of relations whose contours trace contemporary production, communication and consumption. Code is a multivalent index of the relations running among different classes of entity: originators, prototypes and recipients. These classes might include people, situations, organizations, places, devices, habits and practices. In code and coding, relations are assembled, dismantled, bundled and dispersed within and across contexts. Such relations are inextricable from agential effects, from some asymmetry between doing and being done to. Indeed, agency is nothing without those relations.

Many of the situations I've discussed center on very ordinary software (RAMOSS, Java code, Deskartes Universal, Perl poetry, the quicksort algorithm). Here is some Java code that belongs to the ordinary software, OpenOffice 1.1 (OpenOffice 2004), of which I am a user:

```
protected   XMultiComponentFactory   getRemoteServiceManager(String   unoUrl)
throws              java.lang.Exception {
if (xRemoteContext == null) {
      // First step: create local component context, get local servicemanager
      // ask it to create a UnoUrlResolver object with an XUnoUrlResolver n
      // interface
           XComponentContext xLocalContext =

           com.sun.star.comp.helper.Bootstrap.createInitialComponentContext(null);
           XMultiComponentFactory xLocalServiceManager =

           xLocalContext.getServiceManager();
           Object urlResolver = xLocalServiceManager.createInstanceWithContext(
                 "com.sun.star.bridge.UnoUrlResolver", xLocalContext );
           // query XUnoUrlResolver interface from urlResolver object
           XUnoUrlResolver xUnoUrlResolver = (XUnoUrlResolver)
                                                   UnoRuntime.queryInterface(
                       XUnoUrlResolver.class, urlResolver);
           // Second step: use xUrlResolver interface to import the remote
           // ServiceManager,
           // retrieve its property DefaultContext and get the remote servicemanager
           Object initialObject = xUnoUrlResolver.resolve(unoUrl);
           XPropertySet xPropertySet = (XPropertySet)UnoRuntime.queryInterface(
           XPropertySet.class, initialObject);
           Object context = xPropertySet.getPropertyValue("DefaultContext");
           xRemoteContext = (XComponentContext)UnoRuntime.queryInterface(
                       XComponentContext.class, context);
      }
  return xRemoteContext.getServiceManager();


}
```

How, in light of the argument that code is intimately patched into agency, could this be read? It is readable, and with less difficulty than might appear at first glance. For instance, any line beginning with // is a comment meant to be read by a programmer, and many lines contain curly brackets that mark out different subsections. Mostly, however, such writing would not be read, or only by a few people. Code, woven into the background of transactions, habits and perceptions, does not often become visible, except in breakdowns, failures and at certain other moments. Nonetheless, software does become visibly important and perhaps singular in those situations. This book has examined, from several perspectives, that transition from ordinary invisibility to visible importance.

Agency, materiality and sociality in software

According to Patrick Mahoney, the meaning of the term "software," which dates from the late 1950s, gradually became narrower around 1960. What had included the procedures and practices associated with coding shrunk to code itself (Mahoney 2002, 27). My attempt to say what software is runs in the wrong direction, as if it had a counterhistorical bent: instead of becoming more precise, it becomes broader. Code keeps turning into coding, and the biography of software keeps mingling with the lives of programmers. This is not a bad thing in some ways, and it means that we can read the code shown above with reference to a composite field of relations that refuse to be corralled or classified according to essential properties and attributes. Three primary facets of the composition of software can be found in the code fragment above: agency, materiality and sociality. These three concepts, widely discussed in much recent social and cultural theory, come into question in and through software. Put simply, these three general concepts from contemporary social theory are: (1) agency, the concept of who does what; (2) materiality, or what counts as the basic stuff that exists; and (3) sociality, the concept of how we belong together, how attachments form and collective social life coheres. Agency, materiality and sociality are high-level theoretical abstractions that cross social and cultural debates over the politics, work, technology, production and consumption of the Internet and communications. Software, it should be emphasized, only represents one way to revisit these concepts, albeit one that yields interesting results.

Challenges to conventional notions of agency emerged in social theory over the last few decades. In general, challenges were motivated by the desire to understand why social and cultural changes are hard to predict or control. Agency seemed not to be where it should: it didn't change enough, people lacked agency. The conceptual target of these theories has been understandings of agency based on mental states such as intention. Intentions as the origin of social actions have been replaced by understandings of actions emerging from networks of relations between bodies and things (Clark 1997; Latour 2004; Law and Hassard 1999). Occasionally, an intention does something, but that is an exceptional event. How does a relational view of agency in software emerge from examination of the construction, design, circulation and operation of code?

In its apparition as new media, software has been represented and understood through different attributes and properties such as hypertextuality, virtuality, interactivity and digitality (see Lister et al. 2003, introductory chapter; Manovich 2001). It has been associated with processes of identity formation, new modes of production, commodification and consumption (in the digital economy), and sometimes as a reinvented public sphere (Rheingold 1994). These conceptualizations of software carry with them notions of agency, either in relation to what software does as a technology or what people do with software as they make or use it. In this situation, where software is sometimes a force and sometimes a tool, what place does code have? What does it do?

The scenario from *Swordfish* (Sena 2001), in which the gifted hacker Stan goes to work on a cryptographic system, illustrated the relative opacity of software as a cultural object (chapter 1). Some of the more awkward lines of code in my selection above (for instance, the first line: "protected XMultiComponentFactory getRemoteServiceManager(String unoUrl) throws java.lang.Exception {") exemplify this opacity. As a material, code has this opacity because it links different actions in intricate patterns. In the first line, ideas of making ("Factory"), things ("Component"), quantities ("Multi"), distances ("Remote"), availability ("Service"), retrieval ("getServiceManager"), control ("Manager"), writing ("String"), network media (the Internet, in "unoURL") and unforeseen contingency ("throws ... Exception") cluster densely. The multiplicity of relations assembled in code triggers an unpredictable dynamism that intricately alters our sense of matter or stuff. In a recent address to the Association of Computing Machinery Special Interest Group Graphics (SIGGRAPH), science-fiction author Bruce Sterling said:

> Listen to this: ProE, FormZ, Catia, Rhino, Solidworks. Wifi, bluetooth, WiMax. Radio frequency ID chips. Global and local positioning systems. Digital inventory systems. Cradle-to-cradle production methods. Design for disassembly. Social software, customer relations management. Open source manufacturing.

> These jigsaw pieces are snapping together. They create a picture, the picture of a new and different kind of physicality. It's a new relationship between humans and objects. (Sterling, 2004)

The "new and different kind of physicality" has been emerging for a while now. Its dynamics are strongly marked in the way software or code is produced, circulated and consumed. These terms, and the framework of analysis from which they originate, start to break down in software.

Any physicality or materiality is also sociality. Although software structures and manages information for retrieval, transactions, communication and control, it also deals intensively with sensation and perception (see also the notion of "blips" in Fuller 2003). In commonsense understandings, sensation and perception, let alone materiality, are not intrinsically political or social: they are just givens, the stuff of experience and of the world. Much recent social theory has questioned this understanding of materiality. What counts as matter, and the outlines of what we touch, see and hear, are now regarded as a social-historical zone of contestation (Crary 1999). Perceptions of materiality and the materialities of perception figure centrally in relation to software. Just as it can be seen as a contestation of agency, of who does what, software can also be seen as a rematerialization of existing media (books, comics, films, catalogues, notebooks, calendars, newspapers, magazines and albums). It affects existing habits of looking, reading, touching and hearing (Bolter and Grusin 1999).

While these shifts are difficult to read directly from code (some practices of contemporary coding do offer extremely interesting pointers), it is possible to see how code shifts sociality, or the nature of collective belonging together, to the forefront. Sociality is a theoretical term for the relations that make social formations and groups. Like other media, software makes sociality possible. But sociality, like materiality, is not given once and for all. A "principle of uncertainty" (the term comes from quantum mechanics and Heisenberg's uncertainty principle) applies to social life: "it's a principle of uncertainty about what the collective is made of, or will be made of," write Callon, Barry and Slater (2002, 288). Sociality is mutable relationality, constantly challenged, mobilized and transformed. Collective is not given, but contested and subject to reinvention.

From this general perspective, a primary object of software design and programming work is sociality itself, and how sociality can be transformed, redistributed or deployed. As software expanded since the mid-1990s (particularly through the Internet and the web), one relation that surfaced concerned who could access what information under what conditions. The general promise of the Internet is access to all forms of information, anywhere, anytime. The lines

```
Object urlResolver =
xLocalServiceManager.createInstanceWithContext("com.sun.star.bridge.UnoUrlRes
olver", xLocalContext );
```

indicate some of the complications of access, and, in particular, how access is accompanied by many measures seeking to regulate flows of information. In these lines, a URL is treated as a point of access to a remote service manager, a body of code that will provide or offer certain coordinating functions. Within this line, a namespace is embedded (in the form of "com.sun.star.bridge") to provide a way for the code to find a remote service manager. If software is central to the construction of increasingly complex barriers, thresholds and gateways on the web, code and coding can begin to provide a different perspective on the topology of that space. Differential access could be used to generate economic, political and social value, as is well known.

Perhaps more importantly, we can see within code how communication itself becomes a productive force. The political theorist Paulo Virno (2004) writes, "When 'subjective' cooperation becomes the primary productive force, labor activities display a marked linguistic-communicative quality, they entail the presence of the others. The monological feature of labor dies away: the relationship with others is a driving, basic element, not something accessory" (63). Code written in Java or other programming languages (such as Perl, Javascript, Python, PHP, Lisp, and C++) was the primary means of constructing differential access to information and communication during the 1990s, but coding also permitted a wide variety of social relations to be "introjected" (Virno 2004) into the web as a primary site of information access. Scanning the lines of the code sample above, the prevalence of terms such as "manager," "service," "resolver," "helper," "context," "query," "interface," "remote" and "local" suggests just how basic cooperation has become to the very fabric of software. Code dissolves and crystallizes the presence of others.

Ordinary and singular coding

Everything that happens is an event. Notwithstanding this general eventhood of things and situations, some events are singular or important, while others are ordinary. Events have different consistencies or textures that are often hard to discriminate. None of the perspectives on software I've developed here are particularly sweeping or large scale. In fact, one of the principal traits of the software ontology in this and other studies such as (Fuller, 2003) has been its tendency to re-focus high-level concerns about processes of abstraction and global networks of information onto mundane experimentation with platforms, protocols, intersubjective relations and project management. It is interesting, however, to treat this tendency for the ontology to collapse on itself as a relevant symptom. Antonio Negri and Michael Hardt (2000) assert, "The anthropological metamorphoses of bodies are established through the common experience of labor and the new technologies that have constitutive effects and ontological implications. Tools have always functioned as human prostheses, integrated into our bodies through our laboring practices as a kind of anthropological mutation both in individual terms and in terms of collective sociality" (217). Foremost among these, coding as contemporary labor practice displays enormous ambiguity.

On the hand, as the scene from *Swordfish* figured it, coding work is highly valued because it is somewhat arcane and otherworldly in its abstraction. Agency is attributed to programmers on the basis that their mental effort is distinctively inventive and not generally available. The agency of programmers as originators is also figured in some of the software art discussed in chapter 2. Correspondingly, the figure of the programmer has altered since the mid-1990s. A comparison between Dennis, the systems programmer in the film *Jurassic Park* (Spielberg 1993), and Stan, the programmer in *Swordfish* (Sena 2001), two films separated by almost ten years and the growth of the Internet, indicates some important differences. Dennis is overweight, self-absorbed and greedy. Stan is fit but poor, and concerned about the pernicious effects of Hollywood on his daughter. Dennis eats junk food; Stan knows tai chi, wine and cigars. The work of programming is also figured differently. Dennis's system is complex and full of bugs, as if he represents mass-market software-industry applications, overburdened with features and effects; Stan's work is elegant and simple, as if it represents the programming of distributed web services, minimal in complexity yet highly effective.

On the other hand, as chapters 4, 5 and 7 argued, the agency of programmers as originators is managed, contested and even itself commodified in various ways as the work of programming becomes more widely relevant. Neither film scenario says much about the nature of programming work as a social process of cooperation. In Hollywood's image of programming, software is produced by individuals. But as my examination of software development has shown, the organization of programming work is actually a social-cognitive process replete with power relations and economic value. Programming work is constituted and accompanied by its own style of organizing coding. The development of the Linux kernel was characterized by a distributed, concentric circulation of code spiraling outwards and gradually becoming less adaptable as it fell behind the expanding perimeter of files that represent the latest kernel version. The mobility of the Linux kernel, ported to many platforms and found in many distributions, was predicated on the Unix philosophy and expressed in its architectural features (file and processes) and work ethos (a system for "programmer convenience"). In contrast to the distributed space and time of the Linux kernel, the Java Virtual Machine and Java programming language mobilized the ideals of cross-platform mobility in the promise of virtuality: "Write once, run anywhere." This promise linked coding as something programmers and software developers do to code as an executing process. Taken further, software-development methodologies such as extreme programming seize on this relation between coding as work and code as executing process and turn cutting code itself into the execution of a program carried out by programmers. Highly recursive, extreme programming treats "the program" as both the object and model of work.

Program as ideal repetition

Is it a problem that what started as an account of software (based on methodical attention to the status of a single material, code) ends up mostly investigating coding practices? Software is sometimes understood as a program. The very term for someone who makes software, "programmer," embodies this notion. The perception of coding as a programming relies on an idea of software as program. The program is a highly problematic figuration of software for several reasons. Rendering software production predictable has been an important goal of software engineering (see chapters 6–7). Firstly, as we have seen, programming work itself cannot be disentangled from ideas of what software should do and how it should behave. Secondly, what is often regarded as the distillation of the formal essence of software, the algorithm, hides unexpected complexities and inconsistencies (see chapter 3). Rather than the abstract relations and operations on sets of entities envisaged by theoretical computer science, actual algorithms display a composite or mosaic texture that concatenates different regions and neighborhoods of relations. It is hard to argue with the belief that algorithms embody highly refined, often formalized repetitions. However, from another angle algorithms are heterogeneous materials that handle repetition in interestingly variable ways (for instance, taking into account the time and space of computational resources). Furthermore, the repetition and circulation of algorithms themselves, the way in which their style of operating is imitated, is highly unstable. In the code sample from OpenOffice shown above, the sequence of steps—creating a local context, getting a local service manager, using the local service manager to create a URL resolver, then asking the URL resolver to get a remote service manager from a URL—reflects a software architecture patterned according to the Internet and a large corporation, even though the software in question, a word processor, seems to have little to do with the Internet or corporations per se.

The presence of an Internet-style architecture gives pause for thought. If the program epitomizes predictable, mechanical repetition of operations, it also represents what cannot be fully predicted: it might allow new forms of identity, sociality, materiality, communication, politics, production or consumption to emerge. The precondition of any attribution of agency in the neighborhood of software hinges on what exceeds mechanical, law-like or regular behavior. Predictable events tend to lack agential effects. However, software harbors surprising kinks, tricks and folds that are rarely brought to light. These surprises are not solely attributable to system complication. At several points in the preceding discussion, a creative abstraction or hack in software was explored. The work called *forkbomb.pl* (chapter 2) draws on and twists the Unix process of abstraction back against itself. While forkbombs in general are frowned on by system administrators, this artwork turns a trait of Unix operating systems and the Perl programming language into an occasion to explore interactivity and operating systems. Algorithms are distinguished from brute-force computation by the sometimes counterintuitive reorderings of the space and time of operations they embody. A dynamic programming-based algorithm (chapter 3) reverses the commonsense approach of solving only the specific problem at hand, instead solving every possible variation of the problem. Similarly, the virtuality of Java (chapter 5) is suspended between a software system (the Java Virtual Machine) and a programming language (Java) that in principle match perfectly, but in practice are slightly mismatched. Actual coding often takes into account the material singularities of the JVM, and new versions of the JVM take into account the code that will typically be run on it. More generally, code as expression and code as action never coincide fully. In terms of the software ontology explored here, code, the material that lies at the core of software, is unstable because it is both expression and action, neither of which are materially nor socially stable. In saying something, code also does something, but never exactly what it says, despite all its intricate formality.

Does code do what it says?
Force and form in code

For an ontology of software, all of the examples studied in this book represent transcontextual mutations: that is, they complicate any simple attribution or withdrawal of agency to programmers or recipients ("users") of software. This situation has wider implications since it suggests the value of directing attention to the lives of actors and practical arrangements that underpin larger-scale processes of abstraction (commodification, globalization, communication, mobilities and so on).

Because they increasingly embody hidden states or folds, algorithms construct "microworlds" (Thrift 2004a, 584) from concatenations, collections and paths they bring into mosaic conjunction. These microworlds possess qualities that texture the experience of force, movement, feeling and duration. Some of these qualities are indexed in coding practices. The contrasting treatments of code found in telecommunications software, operating-system software, in Java programming, software art, or in bioinformatics' algorithms suggest that software does different things because of the relations threading through it as code. As we've seen in chapter 4, in the Linux kernel, the architecture of the object is reflected in the proliferation of files produced by programmers pointing to different commodity hardware devices. Linux architecture also congregates around the abstractions of "file" and "process" cloned from Unix. The way in which the Linux kernel is produced and continually changes cannot be separated from its structure as a coding project. The performance of Linux as a contemporary operating system cannot be detached from the circulation of Linux kernel code through code repositories and software distributions. The same software may appear in different contexts, preserving form as it circulates, but the force of the action associated with the software does not come from form alone. In the case of Linux, the social relations between programmers—grounded in reading and writing code—coalesce with the social force of Linux as an alternative to mass-market software industry products. Performance of code cannot be separated in this instance from a description of that performance lodged in the code itself. This inseparability between coding as form and code as force is not unique to software, but heightened by the clustered social relations it attracts.

As a form, code supports many idealizations, such as Java's write-once, run-anywhere claim (chapter 5). Extreme programming's ideal of doing nothing that does not look like programming is another such idealization (chapter 7). Code itself as a material is organized by many forms of idealization borrowed from mathematics, logistics and information sciences. It is hard to argue against the practical idealization underpinning the language Lisp that every computable problem can be expressed as a recursive function; hard, too, to object to the idealization underlying a language such as Java that the world can be represented as a set of objects sending messages to each other. In this respect, every programming language is already an ontology.

But code's ideality is perpetually undercut by contestations of coding work that come both from programmers themselves and from the far-from-ideal situations to which software is exposed. In writing systems that interact with existing infrastructures, software developers find themselves between two divergent realities. In the case of Forge (chapter 6), one reality relates to a technoeconomic and geographical milieu of telecommunications infrastructure, and the other to contemporary models of computational processes and architectures. The process of writing a system means moving back and forth between the two, but this movement itself is modulated by other signals coming from afar: current discourses on managing software development, contemporary styles and patterns of software architecture, and broader, diffuse expectations tied to the digital economy. In the case study of extreme programming (chapter 7), this between-place of software development is also contested. In XP, system architecture and coding style are no longer the primary concerns; rather, relations between programmers themselves become the primary preoccupation of coding work. The consolidation of relations between programmers forms a defensive perimeter against the management of software development from the outside. The very elaboration of extreme programming as a process based around the notion of "the program" suggests the nonideal conditions under which code exists today.

Software discourses

Whenever software becomes widely visible, a discourse concerning code and coding is attached to it. Sometimes this is very minimal, as in the programmers' comment lines scattered through the code. By virtue of shifting attributions of agency, different actors figure in these discourses, which themselves circulate more or less widely: in code itself, in technical forums, academic and research publications, industry events and mass media. Often, the producers of software put themselves at the center of these discourses (Knuth 1968; Himanen 2001; Graham 2004; Raymond 2001) as the originators of software. In some code-like artworks, the programmer appears as originator. However, in the shifting permutations of agency associated with code, the originator can just as well be subject to the action of the prototype, as we have seen. The Linux kernel in its very name combines originators: a programmer (Linus Torvalds) and a prototype (Unix). The ongoing production of Linux relies on coupling prototype and originators. The singularity of Linux as a contemporary object in information cultures cannot be detached from the circulation of representations of the value of its originators.

However, sometimes what becomes discursively salient is not the prototype or originators but some aspect of the code itself. In my discussion of Java (chapter 5), the capacity of code to move across platforms was central. This capacity, although only partially and provisionally effective, amounts to a different attribution of agency. No longer is an existing operating system providing an authorizing context (as Unix does for Linux), but code as something written and code as something executed are moved into a different, more proximate relation, magnetized by the network. The agency of originators shifts and expands to cross platforms, but at the cost of close identification with a proprietary, corporate-controlled product (Java). Coding as practice becomes identified with a brand.

All software-development processes adopt prototypes: models, situations, hardware or persons that elaborate a more or less explicit representation of something that code stands in for. Nonetheless, these prototypes, as implied in the mixture of types found in the OpenOffice code sample, are often hybrid entities. The elaboration of a prototype for the RAMOSS system (chapter 6) drew on a general model of process that steered development. In extreme programming, "story" becomes a prototype that acts on and steers software development, a prototype that often displays complex agential relations to recipients and to code itself. On the one hand, XP produces a prototype that directs the action of programmers, but this prototype is itself subject to the action of recipients (users, customers, clients, etc.).

Across all permutations of agency, the growth of software discourse in documents, books, magazines, online articles and discussion attests to instabilities in the neighborhood of relations associated with software. The extended judicial consideration of whether code is expression or function found in the deCSS case (chapter 2) highlights the contestations of agency attached to software. At different scales, and with widely varying visibility, code attracts discursive elaboration only to the extent that some contestation of agency is associated with it. Sometimes these contestations play out in the immediate vicinity of programmers themselves, but on many occasions they run beyond, extending to the peripheries of mass-media attention or state regulation.

Convolutions and involutions of agency

Michel de Certeau (1984) wrote of the opaque and sedimented places that lie "beneath the fabricating and universal writing of technology" (201). De Certeau was referring to the everyday practices and inscriptions that remained invisible and irreducible to the homogenizing, strategic gaze of technological discourses. Where does software stand in relation to this universal writing of technology, and in relation to the general tendency toward abstraction (in commodification, globalization, communication and movement) that social and cultural theory often attributes to contemporary social formations? One implication of the software ontology we have been discussing is that the "writing of technology" is by no means universal; the opaque and stubborn places do not lie simply beneath technology, but are wrapped around and in it. Viewed as an ensemble of relations, software is particularly susceptible to the incorporation of heterogeneous places (see, for instance, the discussion of algorithms as mosaic concatenations of relational frames in chapter 3). No particular symbolism, socioeconomic order, territorial unity or politics absolutely dominates in software. This is not to say that software displays no geopolitical differences (Brazil is known for free and open-source software; Russia, hackers and crackers; Northern Europe, participatory design; the West Coast of the United States, venture-capital funded innovation; India, commercial implementations).

Although it is very hard to ignore the dominant figure of the individual user that accompanies much popular software, even the identity and capacities of the user are contested figures in software, perhaps just as much as the consumer is in advertising. Notwithstanding the ideologies of control and freedom associated with the user interactivity, the contrast between various examples discussed in this book suggests that two broadly different patterns of agential relations occur in software. The first of these turns agential relations inward. The anthropologist Clifford Geertz used the term "involution" to describe the increasingly elaborate cultural production that occurs in certain socioeconomic conditions (Geertz 1994). The production of the Linux kernel relies on increasingly elaborate forms of code circulation that distribute agency in time and space. Authorizing conventions drawn from a history of operating systems running back several decades encounter an ongoing proliferation of commodity computing hardware. The organization of the body of kernel code reflects this encounter. Similarly, although it plays out quite differently, the organization of programming in XP strongly patterns code according to a set of relations modeled on programming or coding and then applied to programmers themselves. One of the effects of involution of agency in code is that software takes on increasingly self-referential aspects. Software generates discourse because involution tends toward self-identity. In certain respects, software discourse is about nothing more than software development.

The other principal patterning of agential relations could be termed "convolution" because it takes existing relations and combines them into a composite relation that blurs or echoes the starting relations. The RAMOSS system organizes relations between diverse elements of an infrastructure and a process-driven vision of distributed information architecture. Such a system is a convolution of agency because it combines different fields of action. In a highly compressed yet simple fashion, *forkbomb.pl* also draws attention to the character of contemporary programming languages and their relation to platforms. These relations are not purely formal or conventional. They have material consequences. The texture, lability and ductility of software allow external forms and forces to fold into software. Over time, code objects take on a pleated, eroded character. Composite forms of agency are not unique to software. Many processes and practices incorporate ensembles of relations that complicate who says or does what. The specificity of software, if it exists, consists in the convolutional production of these relations in a material with particular properties and practices associated with code.

A general dynamics of software?

Does the abundance of involutions and convolutions in software mean that it offers new possibilities for change, for circumventions and subductions of existing orderings of life, labor and language? Many trajectories run through programming work. Ellen Ullman (1997) writes, "I may be wrong, but I have this idea we programmers are the world's canaries" (146). Altered conditions of work are deeply implicated in software production. In a significant and relevant sense, software could be seen as the epitome of work under the conditions of "new capitalism" (Sennett 1998) or as "immaterial labour" (Hardt and Negri 2000, 293). Paramount here are notions of flexibility, speed, just-in-time production and teamwork, some of which previous chapters have shown at work. However, an important result emerges from reading code and examining coding as a process. Coding and code are not simply produced and then sent out into the world. Code and its circulation, production and consumption are deeply entwined in software. Analysis of code as the material of software cannot be detached from analysis of coding as making software.

The concept of agency that threads throughout this book has a generic quality: it refers to those occasions when something does something to something. But this generic character is not just an artifact of analytical approach to software framed in terms of abstract prototypes, originators, recipients and code indexes. It can be attributed to software itself, to its processing of materiality and sociality. The kinks, folds, tricks or slippages that imbue software with a specific texture are also styles of relation, ways of connecting and concatenating actions and events in commonplace or generic ways. While they are not totally new in themselves, these relations are concentrated in software. Where does that come from? In their well-known account of contemporary communication, Hardt and Negri (2000) argue:

> Communication not only expresses but also organizes the movement of globalization. It organizes the movement by multiplying and structuring interconnections through networks. It expresses the movement and controls the sense and direction of the imaginary that runs throughout these communicative connections; in other words, the imaginary is guided and channelled within the communicative machine. What the theories of power of modernity were forced to consider transcendent, that is, external to productive and social relations, is here formed inside, immanent to the productive and social relations. Mediation is absorbed within the productive machine. The political synthesis of social space is fixed in the space of communications. This is why communications industries have assumed such a central position. They not only organize production on a new scale and impose a new structure adequate to global space, but also make its justification immanent. (33)

There is much to elaborate in this quote, but the part that is particularly relevant to software concerns the "immanence" of social space within the "productive machine." Many of the occasions when software becomes visible concern this absorption of mediation and communication into the contemporary systems of production; software accepts constant experimentation with imagined connections. The "imaginary" to which Negri and Hardt refer has broad similarities to Appadurai's understanding of "imagination" when he suggests that "imagination in the postelectronic world plays a newly significant role" (1996, 5). Software provides material to think through and link up social spaces with their "immanent justification." The introjection of communicative relations in extreme programming, the formative role of process in software engineering, and the commodification of coding itself as a productive activity can all be seen as transporting a social space into the "networks" of software.

Nevertheless, this flattening of distinctions between production and consumption, between technology and culture, between abstract and concrete is not completed effortlessly, consistently or even fully. New structures "adequate to global space" and organizations of "production on a new scale" are unstable. The absorption of mediation is uneven, partial—and contested.

Notes

Chapter 1

1. A Dictionary of Computing, *Oxford Reference Online*, s.v. "software," http://www.oxfordreference.com/views/ENTRY.html? subview=Main&entry=t11.e817 (accessed 20 September 2004).
2. Ibid, italics in original.
3. "A grammar in which the left-hand side of each production is a single nonterminal, that is, in which productions have the form V ? w (that is, "rewrite V as w"), where w is a string of terminals and/or nonterminals. These productions apply irrespective of the context of A." See A Dictionary of Computing, *Oxford Reference Online*, s. v. "context-free grammar" (by Valerie Illingsworth), http://www. oxfordreference.com/views/ENTRY.html?subview=Main&entry=t11.e10 29 (accessed 12 January 2005).
4. These concepts may be expressed as a formal standard or in a database of concepts (for example, OpenCyc, an "upper ontology for all of human consensus reality" CyCorp. "OpenCyc.org formalized common knowledge" http://www.opencyc.org (accessed 2 August 2004).
5. The parallel between art and code is not foreign to programmers. Graham (2004) has suggested that "hackers and painters" have a lot in common (18). There is a long literature in computer science, programming and software engineering that links software to art forms such as music, architecture, poetry and prose, as well as painting (Knuth 1968, 1992). For programmers, the question of what programming language to use is highly complex. In newsgroups, online and print publications, and countless café, bar, workplace and conference discussions, the merits of different programming languages and styles are hotly debated. In these discussions, many different issues are at stake, but aesthetic value is

certainly one of them.

6. If programmers are invisible—if they become fashionable, celebrities, pariahs or criminals—if software production is moved to India or China —how would any of those possibilities effect changes in what software does? Changes in software production signify changes in what software is. As we will see in chapter 4, changes in production have to be understood in conjunction with changes in consumption. Some models of culture treat production and consumption as separable phases of cultural process, but software production raises questions about that separation. This is partly because the tools needed to produce software are widely available for use on PCs. Although backyard silicon-chip fabrication is still difficult, a sophisticated piece of software can be created at home (although more likely will not be done there anymore).

Chapter 2

1. For an examination of the prospects of doing research into "software cultures," see Fuller (2003).
2. See Paul (2003) for a survey of new media artworks.
3. What complicates any attempt to simply "unearth" software is that code has become a site of collective imagining in the guise of "opening" or "baring." In 1996, the anthropologist Arjun Appadurai described how imagining, especially collective imagining (as distinct from individual fantasy) had become a staging ground for action (7). Movements of people and things are accompanied by imaginings of those movements.
4. Later chapters do some of this work using the notion of "commonplaces" of ordinary language developed in Virno (2004).
5. Universal City Studios, Inc. et al. v. Shawn C. Reimerdes et al. 2000, 326.
6. For contemporary examples of software art, see Software Art Repository (2004).
7. "Everyday life" has come to assume great importance in media, communication and cultural studies and sociology as a way of deflecting attention away from high-profile cultural events and figures to the percolating melange of communication practices associated with new media (Poster 2004).

Chapter 3

1. For analysis of a different algorithmic in terms of this contestation of agency, see Mackenzie, Adrian. (2006) "Convolution and alogrithmic repetition: a cultural study of the Viterbi algorithm." In *Network Time*, edited by R. Hassan and R. Purser. Palo Alto: Stanford University Press.

2. An important issue for discussion concerns the nexus between bioinformatics' algorithmics and the enterprise-wide grafting of property relations into sequence data. The interface between bioinformatic processing of sequence data and the political economy of biotechnology is complex. The last part of the chapter discusses some ways in which sequence and other biological information undergoes ordering and integration within bioinformatic systems. That integration reinforces the need to think of bodies and property relations together in an "enterprise" context.

3. Both the protein-folding and sequence-alignment problems pose vexing computational difficulties. Enormous computational obstacles hinder any direct mapping between protein-sequence data and protein shape or biochemical function. During the few hundred milliseconds that it takes a strand of amino acids to fold up into a minimal energy configuration, an astronomical number of energetic interactions between different parts of the strand take place. Predicting computationally how an amino acid sequence will fold means finding a way to model the combined effects of all those interactions. IBM responded to the tidal wave of sequence data by announcing a bioinformatics supercomputer, Blue Gene, a heavy piece of computing hardware dedicated to working out how proteins fold (IBM 2004a).Responding to the same difficulty of marshaling sufficient processor power, distributed computing projects such as *Folding@Home* (available as a Google toolbar; see Folding@Home 2003) and United Devices' THINK personal computer screensavers (see United Devices 2004) invite individuals to donate their computers' spare processing power to large-scale scientific projects. In the case of THINK, a "rational drug design" project, researchers were looking for molecules that can bind to certain "active sites" on a protein. They want to "dock" other molecules into the active sites and find out how well that docking "binds" or neutralizes active sites on the protein. In its distribution of work processes across a semipublic network of computers, the peer-to-peer screensaver software THINK shows pharmaceutical research tapping at an infrastructural level into the "free" resources of a

computing public constituted since the mid-1990s by the Internet. (Similar strategies have been pursued by peer-to-peer file-sharing systems such as BitTorrent and by Trojan-horse viruses that convert infected PCs into email spam servers.) The computational burden of targeting drug candidates was shifted onto thousands of privately owned computers. The program farmed out protein structure problems to desktop computers through the Internet. "Members"—over half a million by mid-October 2001, on almost a million PCs (Patrizio 2001)—who download and run the THINK software on their desktop machines belong to a membership program complete with "WebMiles" reward points. Like the *SETI@HOME* project (SETI@HOME 2002), which forged the idea of publicly distributing heavy computational work to an interested lay public's home and office computers, the THINK cancer research project uses spare processor time on PCs. In this case, rather than looking for meaningful patterns in cosmic radio signals, the THINK devices look for possible anticancer drug candidates. The website explains:

> The research centers on proteins that have been determined to be a possible target for cancer therapy. Through a process called "virtual screening", special analysis software will identify molecules that interact with these proteins, and will determine which of the molecular candidates has a high likelihood of being developed into a drug. The process is similar to finding the right key to open a special lock—by looking at millions upon millions of molecular keys (United Devices, 2004).

While the THINK software displays a graphic explaining its function to users, the algorithmic process of testing candidates to see whether they can dock with the target protein goes on invisibly. Only the real "users" of THINK software in Oxford or at United Devices access the output of the processing. The screen displays a count of hits, but lay users cannot see what the hits are. (Controls on the THINK software consist basically of an on/off switch.) The relatively anonymous membership has no claim or control over the research. Their mental or intellectual effort has been deliberately figured out of the software, and their computers' execution of the "virtual screening" processes largely disappears into a calculative background. As during the 1990s, when much of the design, construction and maintenance of the web was figured as "free labour" (Terranova 2004), being a member of United Devices THINK means donating computer cycles.

4. The thoroughly rehearsed understandings of biological life as an

information-communication system developed during the last century (Canguilhem, Jacob, Monod, Dawkins, Haraway, Oyama, Kay, and others) form the background here. I rely also on the general conceptual framework of biosociality described in Rabinow (1992).

5. For FASTA sequence-comparison programs, see Lipman and Pearson (1985); Pearson and Lipman 1988). For BLAST (Basic Local Alignment Search Tool), see Altschul et al. 1990.

6. NetGenics. 2001. DiscoveryCenter. http://www.netgenics.com/ng/ discovery.html (accessed 21 October 2001).

Chapter 4

1. Wikipedia, s.v. "kernel (computer science)," http://en.wikipedia.org /wiki/Kernel_%28computer science%29 (accessed 7 November 2004).

2. Free software, as promoted by the Free Software Foundation (GNU 1996), is supported by a liberal civil-rights discourse of free speech. Open-source software, with much closer links to corporate and industry groups, is a pragmatic approach to software development based on access to source code and the right to distribute and circulate the source code (Open Source Initiative 2003). On the evolution of this distinction, see Coleman and Hill (2004).

3. Sony has given software developers access to the "proprietary Emotion Engine." On the one hand, games platforms are centered on the production and manipulation of affect through visual, audio and tactile events. In game play, certain kinds of labor "in the bodily mode" heavily interact with audiovisual (and tactile) information objects. Some of the most dense and complicated interfaces to information systems are found in gaming. On the other hand, as the fine print on the PlayStation Linux site reveals, Sony is not giving any programmatic access to the DVD or CD drives. Understandably, they are trying to prevent PlayStation from becoming a DVD copying device, something that would undermine Sony's broader audiovisual entertainment business.

4. Unix's influence is broad: Microsoft's Windows NT/2000/XP developers spent much time reviewing and borrowing ideas from it.

5. As of mid-2005, a Unix company, SCO, has threatened massive legal action against all commercial uses of Linux. SCO's argument is that Linux contains hidden Unix code and therefore constitutes an infringement of intellectual property rights vested in the current owners

of the original Unix licenses, SCO. See Jones, Pamela. "Groklaw." http://groklaw.net/ (accessed 12 June 2005).

Chapter 5

1. *Oxford Dictionary of Computing*, s.v. "Virtual Machine," http://www.oxfordreference.com/views/ENTRY.html?subview=Main&entry=t11.005712 (accessed 14 June 2003). According to the *Oxford Dictionary of Computing*, the virtual machine concept originated in Cambridge, Massachusetts in the late 1960s as an extension of the virtual memory system of the Manchester Atlas computer.
2. Like so many other projects, Green never came to market. Commercial agreements between Sun, set-top box manufacturers such as Mitsubishi and media companies such as Time-Warner fell through.
3. As of mid-2005, the Java Desktop was being sold as a standalone product by Sun Microsystems. It combines a Linux distribution with a Java-based user interface (Sun Microsystems 2005e).
4. Thor Olavsrud, "Sun Wins Injunction against Microsoft in Java Case," Internetnews.com, 24 December 2002. http://www.internetnews.com/ent-news/article.php/1561231 (accessed 12 June 2003).
5. Such as JavaJam, offered by Geek Cruises, http://www.geekcruises.com (accessed 23 June 2003).
6. Quoted in Paul Krill, "Sun's McNealy Cites Java Successes," Infoworld 12 November, http://www.infoworld.com/article/03/06/13/HNmcnealyjavaone_1.html (accessed 12 December 2004).
7. See debates posted on the newsgroup comp.lang.java.programmer.

Chapter 6

1. The Object Management Consortium "produces and maintains computer industry specifications for interoperable enterprise applications" (OMG 2004).
2. A good description of distributed software development is provided by Sean Ó'Riain (2000). Ó'Riain's account of Irish and American software developers convincingly describes the kinds of localities, temporal patterns and disruptions associated with a globally distributed workplace. He focuses almost exclusively on people in movement. Bearing in mind

social studies of technology's interest in accounting for people and things together, without assuming an a priori ontological divide between them, Ó'Riain asks, what can be said about technologies themselves? Where do they stand in relation to the "collective social fact" of imagined movement?

3. Greg G., interview with author on 12 November 2000, at Forge Research, Redfern, Australia. All names of interviewees have been changed.

4. Reflexively, it also points to what ethnographers struggling to order materials face as they try to understand how a fragile locality materializes (see Newman 1998 on this point).

5. The term "technoscape" follows from Appadurai's (1996) notion of ethnoscape. Ethnoscape melds multifarious vectors—tourism, migration, education, asylum-seeking, business travel—with diverse collective imaginations of movement circulating in various media (film, the Internet, print). The notion of ethnoscape suggests a complex topography crosshatched by movements of people. Importantly, those movements enter into "mutual contextualisations" (Appadurai 1996, 5) with stories and imaginings of movement. Appadurai's specific historical claim, one I think can be usefully developed in relation to infrastructural things such as RAMOSS, addresses the expansion and proliferation of these interactions between movements of people and the imaginings of movement: "What I wish to suggest is that there has been a shift in recent decades, building on technological changes over the past century or so, in which the imagination has become a collective, social fact. This development, in turn, is the basis of the plurality of imagined worlds" (1996, 5). People experience themselves as "between-places," in Appadurai's terms, because of this entwining of collective imagining and movement. References to elsewhere permeate the everyday production of locality because collective imaginings have taken on a hitherto unregistered momentum. Appadurai also proposed the notion of technoscape to complement the ethnoscape. Technoscape is "the global configuration, … ever fluid, of technology and the fact that technology, both high and low, both mechanical and informational, now moves at high speeds across various kinds of previously impervious boundaries" (Appadurai 1996, 34). Some aspects of this definition resemble globalizing accounts in problematic ways. Talk of fluidity, and technology moving at high speeds sounds like it might be glossing the production of locality and movement too quickly. With its connotations of effortless movement and fluidity, images and stories of technological speed still magnetize the notion of technoscape. The ethnoscape's

mixture of movement and images of movement disappears, supplanted by pure movement. Borrowing from the richer notion of ethnoscape, we could ask whether the technoscape displays the same kind of mutual contextualizing between movement and imaginings of movement as the ethnoscape. Rather than affirming the speed and power of technical systems to move across boundaries, we might be able to say how the effects of speed and power flow from that interaction.

6. Paul D., interview with author on 16 November 2000, at Forge Research, Redfern, Australia.

7. Chris B., observed during field visit September 2000, at Forge Research, Redfern, Australia.

8. Charlie M., interview with author on 23 November 2000, at Australian Technology Park Cafe, Redfern, Australia.

9. Charlie M., interview with author on 23 November 2000, at Australian Technology Park Cafe, Redfern, Australia.

Chapter 7

1. For instance, UK cinemas in 2001 showed an advertisement for Saab cars in which a golfer tees off over the edge of an ice crevasse, a skier slaloms down what looks like a rock face, a high-diver dives into a frozen pool, and so on. The car itself, the ad implied (not without irony), also copes with difficult conditions. A second advertisement, usually shown a few minutes after the first, made the irony explicit when it claimed that the frightened, freezing golfer lost several hundred golf balls during the shooting of the ad.

2. Understanding the differences between ethnography and other observational methods means going into fairly heavy-duty conceptual arguments about science, method and knowledge. Importantly, ethnography differs from survey and quantitative methods in that it tries to analyze one or a few localities in depth. It does not seek to generalize by looking for regularities across a large number of different cases. These arguments have been developed in detail in many places, including Lynch (1993).

3. The fieldwork for the study involved visiting KMS two to three times a week for three months, watching programming, sitting in on team meetings and reading code-repository logs, code and design documents.

References

2600. 2002. DVD lawsuit archive. http://www.2600.com/dvd/docs/ (accessed 12 September 2004).

Abbate, J. 2000. *Inventing the Internet*. Cambridge, MA: MIT Press.

Abelson, H., A. W. Appel, D. Boneh, and E. W. Felten. 2000. Cryptographers' amicus curiae brief. http://www.2600.com/dvd/docs/2001/0126-speech.html (accessed 14 December 2004).

Agnula. 2004. The Agnula project. http://www.agnula.org (accessed 12 December 2004).

Altschul, S. F., W. Gish, W. Miller, E. W. Meyers, and D. J. Lipman. 1990. Basic local alignment search tool. *Journal of Molecular Biology* 215, no. 3: 403–10.

Anderson, C. 2004. The new face of the silicon age. *Wired*, February. http://www.wired.com/wired/archive/12.02/india.html?pg=6 (accessed 12 January 2005).

Aneesh, A. 2001. Skill saturation: Rationalization and post-industrial work. *Theory and Society* 30, no. 3: 363–96.

———. 2005. *Virtual migration: The programming of globalization*. Durham, London: Duke University Press.

Apache Software Foundation. 2005. The Apache Jakarta tomcat project. http://jakarta.apache.org/tomcat/ (accessed 14 March 2005).

Appadurai, A. 1996. *Modernity at large: Cultural dimensions of globalization*. Minneapolis: University of Minnesota Press.

Arnold, K. and J. Gosling 1998. *The Java programming language*. Reading, MA: Addison-Wesley.

ArsElectronica. 1999. Golden Nica for Linux/Linus Torvalds (Finland) "LINUX". http://www.aec.at/en/archives/prix_archive/prix_projekt.asp?iProjectID=2183&iCategoryID=2548 (accessed 12 August 2005).

Auer, K., and R. Miller. 2002. *Extreme programming applied: Playing to win*. XP Series. Boston: Addison-Wesley.

Azeem, A. 1995. Internet: Net retains its capacity to surprise. *Guardian*, 28 December.

Baudrillard, J. 1994. *Simulacra and simulation*: The body, in theory. Trans. S. F. Glaser. Ann Arbor: University of Michigan Press.

Baumgärtel, T. 1997. "We love your computer": The aesthetics of crashing browsers. Interview with jodi. *Telepolis*, 6 October, http://www.heise.de/tp/english/special/ku/6187/1.html (accessed 18 November 2003).

Beck, K. 2000. *Extreme programming eXplained: Embrace change*. Reading, MA: Addison-Wesley.

Berry, J. 2003. Bare code: Net art and the free software movement. *Monocular Times*, n.d. http://www.monoculartimes.co.uk/vatangardening/barecode_2.shtml (accessed 10 October 2004).

Bezroukov, N. 1999. Open source software development as a special type of academic research. *First Monday* 4, no. 10 http://www.firstmonday.org/issues/issue4_10/bezroukov /index.html (accessed 12 December 2004)

Boggs, W., and M. Boggs. 1999. *Mastering UML with Rational Rose*. San Francisco: Sybex.

Bolter, J. D., and R.Grusin. 1999. *Remediation: Understanding new media*. Cambridge, MA: MIT Press.

Borland Corporation Inc. 2005. JBuilder: The leading development solution for Java. http://www.borland.com/jbuilder/ (accessed 9 March 2005).

Bourne, S. R. 1987. *The UNIX system V environment*. International Computer Science Series. Wokingham, MA: Addison-Wesley.

Bowker, G. C. 1994. Information mythology: The world of/as information. In *Information acumen: The understanding and use of knowledge in modern business*, ed. L. Bud-Frierman, 233–45, London: Routledge.

Bowker, G. C., and S. L. Star. 1999. *Sorting things out: Classification and its consequences*. Cambridge, MA: MIT Press.

Brin, S., and L. Page. 2002. The anatomy of a large-scale hyptertextual search engine. Paper read at Southern Cross University, Lismore, Australia.

Brooks, F. P. 1968. *The mythical man-month: Essays on software engineering*. Anniversary ed. Reading, MA: Addison-Wesley, 1995.

Butler, J. 1997. *Excitable speech: A politics of the performative*. London: Routledge.

Button, G., and W. Sharrock. 1996. Project work: The organisation of collaborative design and development in software engineering. *Computer Supported Cooperative Work* 5: 369–86.

Cadenhead, R. 2004. *Sams teach yourself Java 2 in 21 days*. Indianapolis, IN: Sams.

Callon, M. 1987. Society in the making: The study of technology as a tool for sociological analysis. In *The social construction of technological systems: New directions in the sociology and history of technology*, ed. W. E. Bijker and T. P. Hughes, 83–103. Cambridge, MA: MIT Press.

Callon, M., A. Barry, and D. Slater. 2002. Technology, politics and the market: An interview with Michel Callon. *Economy and Society* 31, no. 2: 285–306.

Campbell-Kelly, M. 2003. *From airline reservations to Sonic the Hedgehog: A history of the software industry*. Cambridge, MA: MIT Press.

Castells, M. 2000. *The rise of the network society*. Oxford: Blackwell Publishers.

———. 2001. *The Internet galaxy: Reflections on Internet, business, and society*. Oxford: Oxford University Press.

Chan, P. 1999. *The Java developer's almanac*. Reading, MA: Addison-Wesley.

Clark, A. 1997. *Being there: Putting brain, body, and world together again*. Cambridge, MA: MIT Press.

Claverie, J.-M., and C. Notredame. 2003. *Bioinformatics for dummies*. New York: Wiley.

Coleman, B., and M. Hill. 2004. How free became open and everything else under the sun. *M/C: A Journal of Media and Culture* 7. http://www.mediaculture.org.au/0406/ 02_Coleman-Hill.html (accessed 14 January 2005).

Couldry, N. 2000. *Inside culture: Reimagining the method of cultural studies*. London: Sage.

Cox, G., A. McLean, and A. Ward. 2002. The aesthetics of generative code. http://www.generative.net/papers/aesthetics/index.html (accessed 12 July 2005).

Crary, J. 1999. *Suspensions of perception: Attention, spectacle, and modern culture*. Cambridge, MA: MIT Press.

De Certeau, M. 1984. *The practice of everyday life*. Berkeley: University of California Press.

Delanda, M. 2002. *Intensive science and virtual philosophy*. London: Continuum.

Derrida, J. 1982. *Margins of philosophy*. Brighton, UK: Harvester Press.

Distrowatch. 2002. Linux distributions. http://www.distro.org (accessed 12 December 2002).

Dymond, K. M. 1995. *A guide to the CMM: Understanding the capability maturity model for software*. Annapolis, MD: Process Inc.

Edwards, P. N. 1996. *The closed world: Computers and the politics of discourse in the Cold War*. Cambridge, MA: MIT Press.

Farnady, K. 1996. Biotech dream job: Geeks and genes. *Wired*, 19 December 1996. http://www.wired.com/news/business/0,1367,1061,00.html (accessed 12 March 2003).

Feenberg, A. 1995. *Alternative modernity: The technical turn in philosophy and social theory*. Berkeley: University of California Press.

Fish, S. E. 1980. *Is there a text in this class? The authority of interpretive communities*. Cambridge, MA: Harvard University Press.

Flanagan, D. 1999. *Java enterprise in a nutshell: A desktop quick reference*. Sebastopol, CA: O'Reilly.

———. 2002. *Java in a nutshell: A desktop quick reference*. 4th ed. Sebastopol, CA: O'Reilly.

Folding@Home. 2003. Your computer's idle time is too precious to waste. Google. http://toolbar.google.com/dc/offerdc.html (accessed 7 November 2004).

Foucault, M. 1991. *The history of sexuality*. Trans. R. Hurley. London: Penguin.

Foucault, M., and P. Rabinow. 1984. *The Foucault reader*. Harmondsworth, UK: Penguin, 1986.

Fowler, M., and K. Beck. 1999. *Refactoring: Improving the design of existing code*. Object Technology Series. Reading, MA: Addison-Wesley.

Fowler, M., and K. Scott. 1997. *UML distilled: Applying the standard object modeling language*. Object Technology Series. Reading, MA: Addison-Wesley / Longman.

Freeman, E., S. Hupfer, and K. Arnold. 1999. *JavaSpaces: Principles, patterns, and practice*. Reading, MA: Addison-Wesley.

Friedman, G. 2003. To err is creative in net art. *Wired*, 12 May. http://www.wired.com/news/culture/0,1284,58736,00.html (accessed 12 December 2004).

Fuller, M. 2003. *Behind the blip: Essays on the culture of software*. New York: Autonomedia.

Galloway, A. R. 2004. *Protocol: How control exists after decentralization*. Leonardo Series. Cambridge, MA: MIT Press.

Gatens, M., and G. Lloyd. 1999. *Collective imaginings: Spinoza, past and present*. London: Routledge.

Geertz, C. 1994. *Agricultural involution: The process of ecological change in Indonesia*. Berkeley: University of California Press for the Association of Asian Studies.

Gelbart, W. M. 1998. Databases in genomic research science. *Science* 282: 659–61.

Gell, A. 1998. *Art and agency: An anthropological theory*. Oxford: Clarendon Press.

Gibas, C., and P. Jambeck. 2001. *Developing bioinformatics computer skills*. Beijing: O'Reilly.

Gilbert, W. 1992. A vision of the Holy Grail. In *The code of codes: Scientific and social issues in the Human Genome Project*, ed. D. J. Kevles and L. E. Hood, 98–111. Cambridge, MA: Harvard University Press.

GNU. 1996. GNU operating system. Free Software Foundation. http://www.gnu.org/ (accessed 23 October 2003).

————. 2004. CVS (concurrent versions system). http://www.gnu.org/software/cvs/ (accessed 21 July 2005).

Gosling, J. 1995. Java: An overview. http://java.about.com/cs/technologies/a/-javawhitepaper.htm (accessed 22 June 2003).

Gosling, J., B. Joy, and G. Steele. 1996. *Java language specification*. Reading, MA: Addison-Wesley.

Graham, P. 2004. *Hackers and painters: Big ideas from the computer age*. Sebastopol, CA: O'Reilly.

Graham, S. 2004. Beyond the "dazzling light": From dreams of transcendence to the "remediation" of urban life: A research manifesto. *New Media & Society* 6, no. 1: 16–25.

Graham, S., and Marvin, S. 2001. *Splintering urbanism: networked infrastructures, technological mobilities and the urban condition*. London: Routledge.

Grosz, E. 1999. Thinking the new: Of futures yet unthought. In *Becomings: Explorations in time, memory and futures*, Ithaca, NY: Cornell University Press, 15–28.

Gruber, T. R. 1993. A translation approach to portable ontologies. *Knowledge Acquisition* 5, no. 2: 199–220.

Haraway, D. 1997. *Modest-witness@second-millennium.femaleman-meets-oncomouse: feminism and technoscience*. New York: Routledge.

Hardt, M., and A. Negri. 2000. *Empire*. Cambridge, MA: Harvard University Press.

Heidegger, M., and W. Lovitt. 1977. *The question concerning technology, and other essays*. New York: Harper and Row.

Heim, M. 1993. *The metaphysics of virtual reality*. New York: Oxford University Press.

Helmreich, S. 2000. *Silicon second nature: Culturing artificial life in a digital world*. Updated ed. Berkeley: University of California Press.

Himanen, P. 2001. *The hacker ethic and the spirit of the information age*. London: Secker & Warburg.

Hoare, C. A. R. 1961. "Partition: Algorithm 63," "Quicksort: Algorithm 64," and "Find: Algorithm 65." *Communications of the Association of Computing Machinery* 4: 321–22.

Hood, Leroy. Under biology's ood, Q & A with Leroy Hood. 1 September 2001. Available: http://www.technologyreview.com 12 June 2004.

Howard, K. 2000. The bioinformatics gold rush. *Scientific American*, July.

Husserl, E., and J. B. Brough. 1991. *On the phenomenology of the consciousness of internal time* (1893–1917). Trans. J. B. Brough. Dordrecht, Netherlands: Kluwer Academic Publishers.

Hutchins, E. 1995. *Cognition in the wild*. Cambridge, MA: MIT Press.

IBM. 2004a. IBM Blue Gene/L tops list as world's fastest supercomputer: Commercial Blue Gene system now available. http://www.research.ibm.com/bluegene/ (accessed 8 November 2004).

————. 2004b. Rational software. http://www-306.ibm.com/software/rational/ (accessed 12 November 2004).

————. 2005. WebSphere software: The leading software for on demand business. http://www-306.ibm.com/software/info1/websphere/index.jsp?tab=eclipse/index (accessed 14 March 2005).

Institute for Systems Biology. 2001. http://www.systemsbiology.org (accessed 21 October 2001).

IOCC. 2004. International obfuscated c contest winning entries. http://ioccc.org/years.html (accessed 15 October 2004).

IonaTechnologies. 2004. Orbix. http://www.iona.com/products/orbix.htm (accessed 2004 [cited 17 November 2004].

ISO/ITU-T (International Standards Organisation/International Telecommunications Union). 1998. Information technology: Open distributed processing; Reference model: Overview. http://isotc.iso.ch/livelink/livelink/fetch/2000/2489/Ittf_Home/PubliclyAvailableStandards .htm (accessed 10 Dec 2004).

JavaOne. 2003. JavaOne conference. Moscone Center, San Francisco, CA, 9–13 June 2003. http://javaone.medialiveinternational.com/sf2004/index.html (accessed 26 June 2003).

JavaWorld. 2003. Developer tool guide. http://www.javaworld.com/javaworld/tools-/jw-tools-ide.html (accessed 25 June 2003).

————. 2005 For the week of March 5. http://www.javaworld.com/ (accessed 8 March 2005).

Jeffries, Ronald E. 2004. XProgramming.com. An extreme programming resource. http://www.xprogramming.com/index.htm (accessed 12 November 2004).

jodi. 1997 (Paesmans, D., and J. Heemskerk) %Statistic | HQX. http://wwwwwwww.jodi.org/100cc/hqx/i900.html (accessed 8 December 2004).

————. 1999. %Location | http://wwwwwwww.jodi.org. http://wwwwwwww.jodi.org (accessed 12 December 2004).

————. 2002. SOD.1%. http://sod.jodi.org/ (accessed 8 December 2004).

————. 2003. INSTALL.EXE. New York: Eyebeam Gallery.

Jones, N. C., and P. Pevzner. 2004. *An introduction to bioinformatics algorithms: Computational molecular biology.* Cambridge, MA: MIT Press.

Karre, A. 2003. A do-it-yourself framework for grid computing: Learn to build your own grid computing application using open source tools. *JavaWorld*, April 2003 http://www.javaworld.com/javaworld/jw-04-2003/jw-0425-grid.html (accessed 25 June 2003).

Kay, L. E. 2000. *Who wrote the book of life? A history of the genetic code.* Writing science. Stanford, CA: Stanford University Press.

Keller, E. F. 2000. *The century of the gene.* Cambridge, MA: Harvard University Press.

Kelly, K. 1998. *New rules for the new economy: Ten radical strategies for a connected world.* New York: Viking.

Kember, S. 2003. *Cyberfeminism and artificial life.* London: Routledge.

Kernel. 1994. Linux Kernel 0.11. http://www.kernel.org/pub/linux/kernel/Historic/old-versions/ (accessed 12 December 2004).

Kernel. 2002. Linux kernel 2.4.28. ftp.kernel.org (accessed 12 December 2004).

Kernighan, B. W., and D. M. Ritchie. 1978. *The C programming language.* Englewood Cliffs, NJ: Prentice-Hall.

Kittler, F. 1997. There is no software. In *Literature media information systems*, ed. J. Johnston, 147–55. London: G&B Arts International.

Knorr-Cetina, K., and U. Bruegger. 2000. The market as an object of attachment: Exploring postsocial relations in financial markets. *Canadian Journal of Sociology* 25, no. 2: 141–68.

Knuth, D. E. 1968. *The art of computer programming.* Reading, MA: Addison-Wesley.

————. 1992. Literate programming. *Lecture notes, no. 27.* Stanford, CA: Center for the Study of Language and Information.

Krill, P. 2003. Sun's McNealy cites Java successes. *InfoWorld*, 13 June. http://www.infoworld.com/article/03/06/13/HNmcnealyjavaone_1.html (accessed 12 December 2004).

Lander, E. S. 1996. The new genomics: Global views of biology. *Science* 274: 536–39.

Lash, S. 2002. *Critique of information*. London: Sage.

Latour, B. 1987. *Science in action: How to follow scientists and engineers through society*. Cambridge, MA: Harvard University Press.

———. 1993. *We have never been modern*. New York: Harvester Wheatsheaf.

———. 1996. *Aramis, or the love of technology*. Trans. C. Porter. Cambridge, MA: Harvard University Press.

———. 1999. *Pandora's hope: Essays on the reality of science studies*. Cambridge, MA: Harvard University Press.

———. 2004. How to talk about the body? The normative dimension of science studies. *Body & Society* 10, no. 2: 205–29.

Law, J. 1994. *Organizing modernity*. Oxford: Blackwell.

Law, J., and J. Hassard. 1999. *Actor network theory and after*. Oxford: Blackwell/Sociological Review.

Lee, B., and E. LiPuma. 2002. Cultures of circulation: The imaginations of modernity. *Public Culture* 14, no. 1: 191–213.

Lesk, A. M. 2002. *Introduction to bioinformatics*. Oxford: Oxford University Press.

Lessig, L. 1999. *Code and other laws of cyberspace*. New York: Basic Books.

Lévy, P. 1998. *Becoming virtual: Reality in the digital age*. Trans. R. Bononno. New York: Plenum Press.

Lew, A. 1985. *Computer science, a mathematical introduction*: Prentice-Hall International series in computer science. Englewood Cliffs, NJ: Prentice-Hall International.

Lindholm, T., and F. Yellin. 1996. *Java virtual machine specification*. Reading, MA: Addison-Wesley.

Linux Developers. 2004. Linux kernel. http://www.kernel.org/ (accessed 23 September 2004).

Lipman, D. J., and W. R. Pearson. 1985. Rapid and sensitive protein similarity searches. *Science* 227: 1435–41.

Lister, M., J. Dovey, S. Giddings, I. Grant, and K. Kelly. 2003. *New media: A critical introduction*. London: Routledge.

Lohr, S. 2002. *Goto: Software superheroes from Fortran to the Internet age*. London: Profile Books.

Lunenfeld, P. 2000. *Snap to grid: A user's guide to digital arts, media, and cultures*. Cambridge, MA: MIT.

———. 2005. User: *InfoTechnoDemo*. Cambridge, MA: MIT Press.

Lynch, M. 1993. *Scientific practice and ordinary action: Ethnomethodology and social science*. Cambridge: Cambridge University Press.

Lyotard, J.-F. 1993. *The inhuman: Reflections on time*. Cambridge: Polity Press.

Mackenzie, A. 2003a. Bringing sequences to life: How bioinformatics corporealizes sequence data. *New Genetics and Society* 22, no. 3: 315–32.

———. 2003b. These things called systems: Collective imaginings and infrastructural software. *Social Studies of Science* 33, no. 3: 385–87.

Mackenzie, A., and S. Monk. 2004. From cards to code: How extreme programming re-embodies programming as a collective practice. *Computer Supported Cooperative Work* 13, no. 1: 91–117.

Mahoney, M. S. 2002. Software as science. In *History of computing: Software issues* (International Conference on the History of Computing, ICHC 2000, April 5–7, 2000, Heinz Nixdorf Museums Forum, Paderborn, Germany), ed. U. Hashagen, R. Keil-Slawik and A. L. Norberg, 25–47. Berlin: Springer.

Manovich, L. 1996. The labor of perception. In *Clicking in: Hot links to a digital culture*, ed. L. Hershman-Leeson, 183–193. Seattle, WA: Bay Press.

———. 2001. *The language of new media.* Cambridge, MA: MIT Press.

Marcus, G. E. 1995. Ethnography in/of the world system: The emergence of multi-sited ethnography. *Annual Review of Anthropology* 24: 95–117.

Marx, K. 1973. *Grundrisse. Foundations of the critique of political economy.* Trans. M. Nicolaus. New York: Random House.

Massumi, B. 2002. *Parables for the virtual.* Durham, NC: Duke University Press.

McLean, A. 2002. forkbomb.pl. http://www.runme.org/project/+forkbomb/ (accessed 12 May 2004).

McLuhan, M. 1994. *Understanding media: The extensions of man.* Cambridge, MA: MIT Press.

Miller, D., and D. Slater. 2000. *The Internet: An ethnographic approach.* Oxford: Berg.

Mitcham, C. 1994. *Thinking through technology: The path between engineering and philosophy.* Chicago: University of Chicago Press.

Mitchell, W. J. 2003. *Me++: The cyborg self and the networked city.* Cambridge, MA: MIT Press.

Moody, G. 2001. *Rebel code: The inside story of Linux and the open source revolution.* Cambridge, MA: Perseus.

NCBI. 2004. National Center for Biotechnology Information. GenBank. http://www.ncbi.nlm.nih.gov/Genbank/index.html (accessed 12 December 2004).

Needleman, S. B., and C. D. Wunsch. 1970. A general method applicable to the search for similarities in the amino acid sequence of two proteins. *Journal of Molecular Biology* 48: 443–53.

Neff, G., and D. Stark. 2004. Permanently beta: Responsive organization in the Internet era. In *The Internet and American life*, ed. P. E. N. Howard and S. Jones, 173–188. Thousand Oaks, CA: Sage.

Newman, S. E. 1998. Here, there, and nowhere at all: Distribution, negotiation and virtuality in postmodern ethnography and engineering. *Knowledge and Society* 11: 235–67.

Noble, J., and R. Biddle. 2002. Notes on postmodern programming. In *Technical Report CS-TR-02/9.* Wellington, New Zealand: Victoria University School of Mathematical and Computing Science.

Ó Riain, S. 2000. Working for a living: Irish software developers in the global workplace. In *Global ethnography: Forces, connections, and imaginations in a postmodern world*, ed. M. Burawoy, 198–220. Berkeley: University of California Press.

OMG. 2004a. Object Management Group. http://www.omg.org/ (accessed 14 May 2004).

———. 2004b. CORBA basics. http://www.omg.org/gettingstarted/corbafaq.htm#WhatIsIt (accessed 12 November 2004).

OpenOffice. 2004. OpenOffice source code. http://www.openoffice.org/ (accessed 12 January 2005).

Open Source Initiative. 2003. The open source definition. http://www.opensource.org/docs/definition.php (accessed 23 October 2003).

Oracle Corporation. 1999. Unbreakable performance. *Economist* (December 1999).

O'Reilly, T. 2000. You must read this book: Lessig's code. Oreilly.weblog, 15 May 2000. http://www.oreillynet.com/pub/wlg/4173 (accessed 15 January 2004).

Patrizio, A. 2001. Devices unite to find drugs. *Wired*, 21 September 2001.

http://www.wired.com/news/medtech/0,1367,47013,00.html (accessed 20 May 2004).

Paul, C. 2003. *Digital art*. London: Thames & Hudson.

Pearson W. R., and D. J. Lipman. 1988. Improved tools for biological sequence comparison. *Proceedings of the National Academy of Sciences* 85, no. 8: 2444–48.

Permungkah. 2002. "Great quote!" use Perl; 13 February. http://use.perl.org/comments.pl?cid=4434&sid=3218 (accessed 15 January 2003)

Philipkoski, K. 2001. Getting the genome letter-perfect. *Wired*, 19 June 2001. http://www.wired.com/news/medtech/0,1286,44623,00.html (accessed 18 November 2004).

Pink, D. H. 2004. The new face of the silicon age: How India became the capital of the computing revolution. *Wired* 12, no. 4. http://www.wired.com/wired/archive/12.02 /india_pr.html (accessed 12 March 2005).

PNNL (Pacific Northwest National Laboratory). 2005. Systems biology at PNNL 2005. http://www.sysbio.org/ (accessed 12 January 2005).

Poster, M. 2004. Consumption and digital commodities in the everyday. *Cultural Studies* 18, nos. 2–3: 409–23.

Quatrani, T. 1998. *Visual modeling with Rational Rose and UML*. Object Technology Series. Reading, MA: Addison-Wesley.

Rabinow, P. 1992. Artificiality and enlightenment: From sociobiology to biosociality. In *Incorporations*, ed. J. Crary and S. Kwinter, 234–252. New York: Zone.

———. 2003. *Anthropos today: Reflections on modern equipment*. Princeton, NJ: Princeton University Press.

Radioqualia. 2002. RadioFreeLinux. http://radioqualia.va.com.au/freeradiolinux (accessed 2 December 2002).

Raymond, E. 1996. *The new hacker's dictionary*. Cambridge, MA: MIT Press.

———. 2001. *The cathedral and the bazaar: Musings on Linux and open source by an accidental revolutionary*. Rev. ed. Beijing: O'Reilly.

Redhat Corporation. 2004. Redhat: The open source leader. http://www.redhat.com (accessed 24 September 2004).

Rheinberger, H.-J. 1997. *Toward a history of epistemic things: Synthesizing proteins in the test tube*. Stanford, CA: Stanford University Press.

Rheingold, H. 1994. *The virtual community: Finding connection in a computerized world*. New York: Secker & Warburg.

Ritchie, D. M., and K. Thompson. 1974. The UNIX time-sharing system. *Communications of the Association for Computing Machinery* 17, no. 7: 365–75.

Rodowick, D. N. 2001. *Reading the figural, or, Philosophy after the new media*. Durham, NC: Duke University Press.

Rowe, G. W. 1997. *An introduction to data structures and algorithms with Java*. London: Prentice-Hall.

Salus, P. H. 1995. *A quarter century of UNIX*. Reading, MA: Addison-Wesley.

Sands, J. 1998. JFC: An in-depth look at Sun's successor to AWT: Swing into great UI development. *JavaWorld*, (January 1998). http://www.javaworld.com/-javaworld/jw-01-1998/jw-01-jfc.html (accessed 12 June 2003).

Schoen, S. 2000. How to decrypt a DVD: In haiku form. Gallery of deCSS de-scrambles, 28 January. http://www-2.cs.cmu.edu/~dst/DeCSS/Gallery/decss-haiku.txt (accessed 12 March 2005).

Sena, D. 2001. *Swordfish*. Los Angeles, CA : Warner Brothers Pictures.

Sennett, R. 1998. *The corrosion of character: The personal consequences of work in the new capitalism*. New York: Norton.

SETI@home. 2002. The search for extraterrestrial intelligence at home. http://setiathome.ssl.berkeley.edu/ (accessed 6 November 2004).

Setubal, J. C., and J. Meidanis. 1997. *Introduction to computational molecular biology*. Boston: PWS Publishers.

Shah, R. 2002. The penguinista's PDA. *Linux World*. 22 June (accessed 4 August 2005).

Shields, R. 2003. *The Virtual*. London: Routledge.

Smith, T. F. 1990. The history of the genetic sequence databases. *Genomics* 6, no. 4: 701–07.

Smith, T. F., and M. S. Waterman. 1981. Identification of common molecular subsequences. *Journal of Molecular Biology* 147: 195–97.

SN Systems. 2002. PlayStation2. http://www.snsys.com/PlayStation2/ProDG.htm (accessed 2 December 2002).

Software Art Repository. 2004. Say it with software art! http://www.runme.org/ (accessed 3 October 2004).

Sommerville, I. 2000. *Software engineering*. 6th ed. International Computer Science Series. Harlow, England: Addison-Wesley.

Spielberg, S. 1993. *Jurassic Park*. Los Angeles, CA : Universal Studios and Amblin Entertainment, Inc.

Star, S. L., and K. Ruhleder. Steps toward an Ecology of Infrastructure: Design and Access for Large Information Spaces. *Information Systems Research* 7.1 (1996): 111–34.

Sterling, B. 2000. *Distraction*. London: Millennium.

————. 2004. When blobjects rule the earth. Paper presented at ACM SIGGRAPH (Special Interest Group Graphics), 10 August, Los Angeles, CA.

Sterne, J. 2003. Bourdieu, technique and technology. *Cultural Studies* 17, nos. 3–4: 367–89.

Stocker, G., and C. Schopf, eds. 2003. *Code, the language of our time* (ArsElectronica 2003). Osterfildern-Ruit, Austria: Hatje Cantz Verlag.

Strathern, M. 1999. *Property, substance and effect: Anthropological essays on persons and things*. Linton, UK: Athlone.

Succi, G. 2002. *EXtreme programming perspectives*. XP series. Boston, MA: Addison-Wesley.

Suchman, L. A. 1987. *Plans and situated actions: The problem of human-machine communication*. Cambridge: Cambridge University Press.

Suchman, L. A., and R. H. Trigg. 1992. Artificial intelligence as craftwork. In *Understanding practice: Perspectives on activity and context*, ed. S. Chaiklin and J. Lave, 144–178. Cambridge: Cambridge University Press.

Sun Microsystems. 2003a. Certification in Java technology. http://suned.sun.com/US/certification/java/index.html (accessed 12 December 2003).

————. 2003b. Overview of the Java 2 platform, enterprise edition. http://java.sun.com/j2ee/overview.html (accessed 12 April 2005).

————. 2005a. Java "get powered" logo quiz. http://www.java.com/en/partners/quiz.jsp (accessed 18 February 2005).

————. 2005b. Java 2 platform standard edition 5.0 API Specification. http://java.sun.com/j2se/1.5.0/docs/api/index.html (accessed 14 March 2005).

————. 2005c. Lesson: Object-oriented programming concepts; The Java tutorial. http://java.sun.com/docs/books/tutorial/java/concepts/ (accessed 12 March 2005).

————. 2005d. Products and technologies: Java technology. http://java.sun.com/ (accessed 14

March 2005).

———. 2005e. Sun Java Desktop System. http://www.sun.com/software/javadesktopsystem/ (accessed 14 March 2005).

Tanenbaum, A. S. 1987. *Operating systems: Design and implementation*. Software Series. Englewood Cliffs, NJ: Prentice-Hall.

Taylor, R. 1999. Red Hat shares surge on debut. *Financial Times* (London), 12 August 1999.

TechCentral. 2003. Beijing to promote Linux. TechCentral.com, 23 June 2003. http://startechcentral.com/tech/story.asp?file=/2003/6/26/technology/26chinlinx&sec=technology (accessed 15 July 2004).

Terranova, T. 2000. Free labor: Producing culture for the digital economy. *Social Text* 63, no. 18: 33–57.

———. 2004. *Network culture: Politics for the information age*. London: Pluto Press.

Thacker, E. 2004. *Biomedia*: Electronic mediations. Vol. 11. Minneapolis: University of Minnesota Press.

Thrift, N. 2004a. Movement-space: The changing domain of thinking resulting from the development of new kinds of spatial awareness. *Economy and Society* 33, no. 4: 582–604.

———. 2004b. Remembering the technological unconscious by foregrounding knowledges of position. *Environment & Planning D: Society & Space* 22, no. 1: 175–191.

TIGR. 2005. The Institute for Genomic Research. http://www.tigr.org/ (accessed 14 January 2005).

TINA. 1999. Telecommunications information network architecture. Tina specifications. http://www.tinac.com/ (accessed 10 December 2004).

Torvalds, L. 1991. Subject: Free minix-like kernel sources for 386-AT. 5 October 1991. comp.os.minix (accessed 24 July 2003).

Touretzky, D. S. 2004. Gallery of CSS descramblers. 10 July 2004. http://www.cs.cmu.edu/~dst/DeCSS/Gallery (accessed 4 October 2004).

Transmediale. 2002. Transmediale 2002 prizes. http://www.transmediale.de/en/-02/pressreleases.php (accessed 15 Jan 2003).

Tuomi, I. 2000. Internet, innovation and open source: Actors in the network. *First Monday* 6, no. 1. http://www.firstmonday.org/issues/issue6_1/tuomi/-index.html#author (accessed 12 November 2004).

Turbolinux. 2002. Turbolinux outsells Microsoft Windows in China. http://www.turbolinux.com/news/pr/federal.html (accessed 25 November 2002).

U. S. Congress. 1998. *Digital Millennium Copyright Act*. http://thomas.loc.gov/cgi-bin/query/z?c105:H.R.2281.ENR: (accessed 11 March 2005).

Ullman, E. 1997. *Close to the machine: Technophilia and its discontents*. San Francisco: City Lights Books.

United Devices. 2004. GRID.ORG Cancer Research Project. http://www.grid.org/projects/cancer/ (accessed 5 December 2004).

Univeral City Studios, Inc., et al., v. Shawn C. Reimerdes, et al. 2000. United States District Court, Southern District of New York. 111 F.Supp.2d 294, 326.

Virilio, P. 2000. *The information bomb*. London: Verso.

Virno, P. 2004. *A grammar of the multitude: For an analysis of contemporary forms of life*. Semiotext(e) foreign agents series. Los Angeles: Semiotext(e).

W3C. 2004. World Wide Web Consortium. Extensible markup language (XML). http://www.w3.org/XML/ (accessed 12 March 2005).

Wake, W. 2001. *Extreme programming explored*. Reading, MA: Addison-Wesley.

Wall, L. 1999. Perl, the first postmodern computer language. Perl.com. http://www.perl.com/lpt/a/1999/03/pm.html (accessed 3 July 2003).

Wark, McKenzie. 2004. *A hacker manifesto*. Cambridge, MA: Harvard University Press.

Wen, H. 2002 Opening up the Playstation 2 with Linux. http://linux.oreillynet.com/pub/a/linux/2002/03/21/linuxps2.html,. (accessed 21 March 2002).

White, I. 1994. *Rational Rose essentials: Using the Booch method*. Redwood City, CA: Benjamin / Cummings.

Winterbottom, A. 2000. If ((light eq dark). *Perl Journal* 5, no. 1: 17.

Wirth, N. 1976. *Algorithms + data structures = programs*. Englewood Cliffs, NJ: Prentice-Hall.

Index

General Editor: Steve Jones

Digital Formations is an essential source for critical, high-quality books on digital technologies and modern life. Volumes in the series break new ground by emphasizing multiple methodological and theoretical approaches to deeply probe the formation and reformation of lived experience as it is refracted through digital interaction. **Digital Formations** pushes forward our understanding of the intersections—and corresponding implications—between the digital technologies and everyday life. The series emphasizes critical studies in the context of emergent and existing digital technologies.

Other recent titles include:

Leslie Shade
  Gender and Community in the Social Construction of the Internet

John T. Waisanen
  Thinking Geometrically

Mia Consalvo & Susanna Paasonen
  Women and Everyday Uses of the Internet

Dennis Waskul
  Self-Games and Body-Play

David Myers
  The Nature of Computer Games

Robert Hassan
  The Chronoscopic Society

M. Johns, S. Chen, & G. Hall
  Online Social Research

C. Kaha Waite
  Mediation and the Communication Matrix

Jenny Sunden
  Material Virtualities

Helen Nissenbaum & Monroe Price
  Academy and the Internet

To order other books in this series please contact our Customer Service Department:
(800) 770-LANG (within the US)
(212) 647-7706 (outside the US)
(212) 647-7707 FAX
To find out more about the series or browse a full list of titles, please visit our website:
WWW.PETERLANGUSA.COM